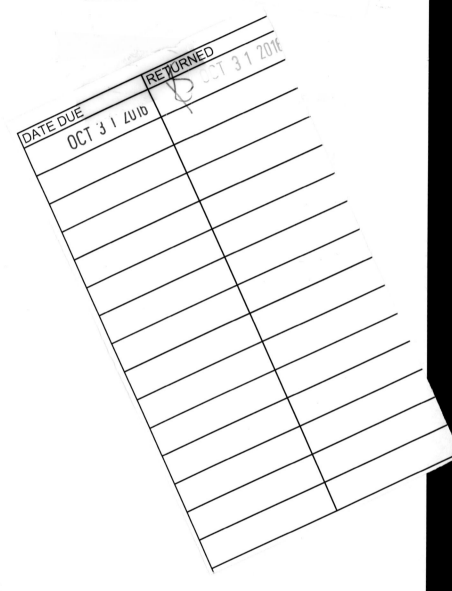

OTHERWISE THAN BEING

OR BEYOND ESSENCE

EMMANUEL LEVINAS

TRANSLATED BY
ALPHONSO LINGIS

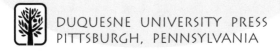

DUQUESNE UNIVERSITY PRESS
PITTSBURGH, PENNSYLVANIA

Library of Congress Cataloging in Publication Data

Lévinas, Emmanuel.
  [Autrement qu'être. English]
  Otherwise than being, or, Beyond essence / Emmanuel Lévinas ;
translated by Alphonso Lingis.
    p. cm.
  Originally published: Dordrecht, Netherlands : M. Nijhoff, 1974,
in series: Martinus Nijhoff philosophy texts.
    Includes index.
    ISBN 0-8207-0299-4 (pbk. : alk. paper)
    1. Ontology. 2. Essence (Philosophy)   I. Title.
  B2430.L483A8313   1998
  111—dc21   98-19597
                                                CIP

    ISBN-13: 978-0-8207-0299-5

Published by

DUQUESNE UNIVERSITY PRESS
600 Forbes Avenue
Pittsburgh, Pennsylvania 15282

First paperback edition printing, 1998
by arrangement with Kluwer Academic Publishers.
Printed in the United States of America.

∞ Printed on acid-free paper.

Seventh printing, February 2008

To the memory of those who were closest
among the six million assassinated by the
National Socialists, and of the millions on
millions of all confessions and all nations,
victims of the same hatred of the other
man, the same anti-semitism.

לזכר נשמת אבי מורי ר' יחיאל בר' אברהם הלוי,
אמי מורתי דבורה בת ר' משה,
אחי דב בר' יחיאל הלוי, ועמינדב בר' יחיאל הלוי
חותני ר' שמואל בר' גרשון הלוי, וחותנתי מלכה בת ר' חיים·

תנצב"ה

Or if a righteous man turn from his righteousness and do what is wrong, and I make that the occasion for bringing about his downfall, he shall die; because you did not warn him, he shall die for his sin, and the righteous deeds which he has done shall not be remembered, but his blood will I require at your hand.

Ezekiel, 3:20

Then he...said to him, "Pass through the city – through Jerusalem – and set a mark upon the foreheads of the men who sigh and cry for all the abominations that are done in the midst of it." And to the others he said in my hearing, "Pass through the city after him, and slay without mercy or pity. Old men, young men and maidens, little children and women – strike them all dead! But touch no one on whom is the mark. And begin at my sanctuary!"

Ezekiel, 9:4-6

The sages have said "Do not read 'begin at my sanctuary,' but 'begin with those that sanctify me,'...as teaches the Talmudic Treatise Sabbath, 55a.

Commentary of Rachi on Ezekiel 9:6

..."That is my place in the sun." That is how the usurpation of the whole world began.

Pascal's *Pensées*, 112

...They have used concupiscence as best as they could for the general good; but it is nothing but a pretense and a false image of charity; for at bottom it is simply a form of hatred.

Pascal's *Pensées*, 404

CONTENTS

FOREWORD

Otherwise than Being or Beyond Essence (1974) is the second of Levinas's two mature philosophical works, after *Totality and Infinity* (1961). It is the last of Levinas's four original philosophical books, including the two shorter schematic volumes, *Time and the Other* (1947) and *Existence and Existents* (1947). Each work elaborates an increasingly rich and comprehensive philosophy of ethical metaphysics, built upon careful phenomenological investigations and Levinas's unique appreciation for the extraordinary impact of moral exigencies, the obligations, responsibilities and call to justice which inform the whole of social life and constitute the very humanity of the human. The sheer originality and range of Levinas's thought demand nothing less than a fundamental reorientation of Western spirit —philosophy, logic, rhetoric, praxis, ontology, science, art, politics, religion — in the light of morality and justice.

A striking continuity links Levinas's writings. At their heart lies the irreducible ethical proximity of one human being to another, morality, and through that encounter a relation to all others, justice. Each successive text branches out, filigrees, presents successively richer, fuller, more nuanced analyses, testifying to the cornucopian genius of Levinas's central ethical vision. Spanning the last two thirds of the twentieth century, this vision unfolds by a process amplification, augmentation, expansion, extension, magnification, intensification, enlargement, as if Levinas's later writings were commentaries on the earlier ones. A sentence becomes a section, which in turns expands into an entire chapter. *Otherwise than Being* and *Totality and Infinity*, especially, are bound to one another, companions, like two tablets, or one.

Both are works of ethical metaphysics, distinguished by different but complementary emphases. The four parts of *Totality and Infinity* deal successively with justice, sensibility, alterity, and eros. Following from and augmenting these, the themes of *Otherwise than Being* are moral sensibility and language. The latter are announced in *Totality and Infinity*, pronounced in *Otherwise than Being*. *Totality and Infinity* is focused on ethical alterity, *Otherwise than Being* on ethical subjectivity.

The primary labor of *Totality and Infinity* is to establish and elaborate the otherness the other person as moral "height and destitution." Transcendence is found in the "face" of the other, the other person's imperative height whose first command is "thou shalt not murder," unsettling, disrupting, inverting the more or less sophisticated economies of immanence, sensibility, labor, knowledge and reason. Only an excessive metaphysical desire, a desire for goodness — obligations, responsibilities, the call to justice — can do justice to the radical otherness of the other person. *Otherwise than Being* elaborates this ethics of alterity like ethics itself, by turning back to the moral sensibility of the subject awakened by the other, to its unique temporal and moral de-phasing, a fissured self, traumatized, held hostage by the other. The moral subject arises in subjection, "despite itself," introjected deeper than its own synthetic activities, suffering an "immemorial past" never contracted in the present, the trace of a diachrony, to the point of obsession, substitution for the other, turning the self inside out, hostage to and for the other, for the other's needs, for the other's life, to be sure, but also for the other's responsibility, even for the other's evil, in an an-archic moral inspiration expiating even for the other's persecution. I am my brother's keeper, all the way. The alterity of the other is no less radical in *Otherwise than Being* than in *Totality and Infinity*, but Levinas's focus is now on the asymmetrical repercussion, the shock, the implosion of that alterity on a subjectivity subject precisely as moral subjection to and for the other.

There is also an intensification, a greater emphasis on language, the "saying of the said." To be sure, again, in *Totality and Infinity* Levinas had already named "the relation with the Other, discourse." There he had already analyzed the ethical dimension of language as expression, relating its disruptive surplus to the economies of logic, reason, representation, thematization, signification and disclosure. The excessive significance of signifying was explicated in terms of teaching, speech, command, judgment, prophecy, apology, saying and "unsaying the said." "Language," Levinas had written, "is perhaps to be defined as the very power to break the continuity of being or of history." *Otherwise than Being* amplifies and nuances these analyses, turning from the infinity of expression to the inexhaustible response of the self as saying.

The title and the content of *Otherwise than Being or Beyond Essence* alert us to the priority Levinas gives to his ongoing contestation of Heideggerian thinking. Otherwise than Heideggerian being; beyond Heideggerian essence. In the aftermath of the failure of modern science to ground itself, to form a seamless totality, a new and future *gigantamachia* has arisen in the twentieth century, and for the foreseeable future: between aesthetics and ethics, the struggle of David and Goliath, Homer and the Bible, oracles and revelation. Levinas is perhaps the one philosopher who has seen farthest, all the way through and beyond Heideggerian *Denken*. The dispute is over the heritage of Husserlian phenomenology. Whereas Heidegger, in *Being and Time*, was led to surpass phenomenology in *ontology* by renewing "the question of being," Levinas, in *Totality and Infinity*, also surpasses phenomenology, but through the sober exigencies of an *ethical* metaphysics.

Edmund Husserl — teacher of both Heidegger and Levinas — had pushed science to new and genuine limits. He had convincingly shown that modern mathematical science would have to expand to return to its original telos: to be a fully justified, verifiable, self-correcting account of the whole. Science could no longer reduce and presuppose but would have to expose all evidences, including the evidences of consciousness *taken on their own terms*. Vast domains of signification hitherto dismissed as unscientific or prescientific, mere perception, mere imagination, mere worldliness, mere duration, etc., reduced to one form or another of illusory subjectivism, would be restored to scientific status by a phenomenology rigorously investigating and uncovering the invariant structures ("essences") constitutive of their meaning. Maurice Merleau-Ponty's *Phenomenology of Perception* (1945), for instance, presented brilliant and novel analyses of perception, not by explaining away perception in terms of causality or a transcendental logic, but by uncovering and describing its inherent sense, its inner coherence. Levinas is quite influenced by this work, transforming and integrating its analyses into his own ethical vision.

Heidegger did the same for time in *Being and Time* (1927). Developing the earlier insights of Bergson into the interpenetrating dimensions of duration and Husserl into "protentional" and "retentional" temporalizing, Heidegger uncovered beneath "clock time" the deeper structures of a synthetic "ecstatic" temporality, essentially linked to and determining the significance of human praxis, knowledge, mortality, worldliness, history, and opening upon the very revelation of being. But undercutting all these forms of ecstatic temporality, and the practical and ontological structures they supported, Levinas discovered an even sharper sense of time's dimensions, its past and future, in the very de-phasing of a moral subjectivity beholden not to being but to the other person. The transcending dimensions of time itself, its core diachrony, would derive from the inter-subjective relation, hence would be ethical, a moral denucleating of self-presence by an "immemorial past never present" and "a future always future" encountered in proximity to the other. Both philosophers inaugurated their radically differing perspectives through careful analyses of time and sensibility: mortal and anxious being in Heidegger, moral and subject responsibility in Levinas.

One of the profound discoveries of *Totality and Infinity* and Levinas's earlier works, whose repercussions are felt and amplified in *Otherwise than Being*, had already been that the sense of sensibility lies deeper than Heidegger had seen in *Being and Time*, where embodiment was described in terms of instrumental praxis, mortal anxiety, and historical engagement in being. The phenomenological analyses of part two of *Totality and Infinity* revealed a more originary layer of sense in sensibility, beginning in the "carefree" contentment of sensing, its self-satisfaction and enjoyment of elemental sensations. The independence of subjectivity would thus lie more deeply embedded in sensibility than the synthesizing temporal ecstasies of praxis, worldliness, or anxiety. Rather, the circuits of subjectivity would begin in the very sensing of sensations. But this also meant that the transcendence of the other would be felt more deeply, in the deepest recesses the flesh, as a suffering for the other, a suffering for the suffering of the other. These intertwined structures of sensibility and ethics undercut the meaning bestowing acts foundational to Husserlian intentionality as well as the freedom Heidegger discovered in the essence of truth.

Ethical exorbitance — the height of the other, the subjection of the self, diachrony deeper than synthesis, otherwise than being, beyond essence — accounts for the peculiar structure of Levinas's writings. In *Totality and Infinity* ethics appears both before (part one) and after (part three) a phenomenological account of sensibility as "separated" being (part two). Morality and justice appear *before* because *ethical priorities* take priority over the a priori syntheses — cognitive or ontological — immanent to sensibility, praxis, knowledge, and history.

They appears *after* because knowledge, which always presents itself as a search for origins, as "first philosophy," finds itself inverted by ethics, which *begins* before *origins*, piercing the ironclad self-presence of first philosophy with a moral "anterior posteriorly." This tracing of diachrony, ethical excess, also structures *Otherwise than Being*. Chapter one, "The Argument," like part one of *Totality and Infinity*, is a beginning prior to origins. The demands of goodness do not wait for the completion of knowledge, though the demand for justice will motivate precisely that quantitative task. Chapters two through five, "The Exposition," renew Levinas's earlier investigations into sensibility, but now building on the whole of *Totality and Infinity*, elucidating in terms of sensibility itself the obsessive trauma of moral exigencies. The final pages, "In Other Words," like the "Conclusions" of *Totality and Infinity*, are neither final nor conclusions; they are reformulations, renewals, a re-saying of the saying of the said — infinite, as ethics.

Otherwise than Being advances Levinas's ethical challenge into the deepest recesses of Heidegger's later "turn" (*Kehre*) to the "end of metaphysics" through "the poetry of thought," the "letting be" (*Gellasenheit*) to "hearken" to the epochal revelatory voice of "appropriation" (*Ereignis*), the "fourfold," language as "the house of being." In *Totality and Infinity* Levinas had already objected: "Speaking, rather than 'letting be,' solicits the Other." In *Otherwise than Being* Levinas deepens this challenge. Before language is a poetic harkening, it is a radical ethical sincerity: saying as "my exposure without reserve to the other" (168), inspiration, witness, prophecy, risk, glory — "proximity and not truth about proximity" (120).

An edifying case: Heidegger's celebrated disciple in France, Jacques Derrida, staked out his own career by borrowing Levinas's notion of the trace of diachrony, an ethical structure. He nonetheless purported to bend it for Heideggerian purposes, forcing its radical alterity and an-archy to serve the end of metaphysics, deconstructed through the questioning of language, the language of questioning, *differance*. Is it any wonder, then, or rather an irony, that Derrida has become — despite himself? — a "Levinasian," not only paying homage to Levinas, but teaching the very ethical teachings of his teacher? Such a case bears witness, one is inclined to think, to the subtlety, force and coherence of Levinas's thought, to the non-ontological (otherwise than being) and extra-linguistic (beyond essence) force of the obligations, responsibilities, and justice called forth by xvi

the transcendence proper to ethics.

Finally, a word about God. Levinas has always "argued" that relationship with God can only "come to the idea" — enter a universal discourse — through ethics. In *Totality and Infinity* he proposed "to call 'religion' the bond that is established between the same and the other without constituting a totality." The focus there was on the absolute transcendence of the other, a transcendence manifest as moral "height and destitution," ethical command, the call to justice. In *Otherwise than Being*, in contrast, where the focus is on language and moral subjectivity, Levinas associates God with justice, and hence with the tasks of knowledge, science, philosophy, with the requirement that morality reach beyond the other who faces to include all others, all humanity, and hence somehow also myself. Levinas is sensitive to the moral and juridical imperfections of our world, such that even an infinite moral response to the one who faces produces injustice for those others not present. To give all to one, is to leave others destitute.

In *Otherwise than Being* Levinas discovers those absent faces troubling the moral self in the very face of the other. Morality, without justice, produces injustice, hence immorality. This structure, the troubling distance in the very face of the other between the one who faces and all others, all humanity, deeper than the "ontological difference" or "differance," is the source of the call to justice, the demand for fairness, measure, quantification, equality, hence the demand for knowledge, science, philosophy, government, the state, order. Justice rectifies *in the name of goodness* the exclusivity of a self infinitely beholden to the other, rectifies the very desire for goodness. Justice detached from morality, indifferent to its own moral motivation, produces tyranny instead. Yet such a rectification cannot be accounted for in the first person singular. The I is infinitely subject to the other. Justice comes to the self not as a right but as a privilege, a "grace" — "thanks to God." "'Thanks to God'," Levinas writes, "I am another for the others" (158). "The passing of God, of whom I can speak only by reference to this aid or this grace, is precisely the reverting of the incomparable subject into a member of society" (158).

Richard A. Cohen
March 15, 1998
Charlotte, North Carolina

TRANSLATOR'S INTRODUCTION

I. REDUCTION TO RESPONSIBLE SUBJECTIVITY

Absolute self-responsibility and not the satisfaction of wants of human nature is, Husserl argued in the *Crisis*, the telos of theoretical culture which is determinative of Western spirituality; phenomenology was founded in order to restore this basis – and this moral grandeur – to the scientific enterprise. The recovery of the meaning of Being – and even the possibility of raising again the question of its meaning – requires, according to Heidegger, authenticity, which is defined by answerability; it is not first an intellectual but an existential resolution, that of setting out to answer for one's very being on one's own. But the inquiries launched by phenomenology and existential philosophy no longer present themselves first as a promotion of responsibility. Phenomenology was inaugurated with the theory of signs Husserl elaborated in the *Logical Investigations*; the theory of meaning led back to constitutive intentions of consciousness. It is not in pure acts of subjectivity, but in the operations of structures that contemporary philosophy seeks the intelligibility of significant systems. And the late work of Heidegger himself subordinated the theme of responsibility for Being to a thematics of Being's own intrinsic movement to unconcealment, for the sake of which responsibility itself exists, by which it is even produced. In Levinas's work responsibility is once again set forth as the determinative structure of subjectivity, and the very form of the supplement of intelligibility philosophy's reductive methods aim to bring to theoretical disciplines.

In Husserl personal subjectivity in the form of a will for self-responsibility is realized in theoretical life. It is the transcendental structure underlying science as a praxis, as a coherent form of discourse, systematized by the will to supply a reason for every fact, and a reason for every reason. In Heidegger authenticity is from the first conceived as the existential structure in which Being is articulated in true logos. In both cases responsibility appears as a prodigy; for Husserl it involves a total suspension of the natural attitude and the leap into an utterly unnatural form of life, devoted to the idea of infinity. In Heidegger it requires an antecedent

xviii

leap beyond what is as a whole, into the abysses of death. The responsibility Levinas aims to exhibit is equally transcendental and bizarre in its
structure, quite inexplicable in mundane or ontic terms – but also inexplicable in transcendental terms, or ontological terms, deduced from the
empirical and expressed as its condition of possibility, or interpreted out of
the ontic and formulated as its realizing "event." The subjectivity structured as responsibility which Levinas means to bring out, although it will
indeed make the theoretical attitude or the ontological articulation possible, has an antecedent and autonomous structure. For before being the
structure by which truth is realized, it is a relationship with the Good,
which is over and beyond Being.

Contracted as a relationship with the Good, responsibility precedes and
makes possible the theoretical will, or the ontological appropriation. It is
first an ethical structure. This book is entirely a labor of articulating the
inevitably strange, nonobjective and non-ontic, but also non-ontological,
terms with which the original form of responsible subjectivity has to be
described. Levinas's attention here is not on the experiences in which an
ethical essence of subjectivity could be intuited, or out of which it could be
deduced. He does not seek this ethical and non-theoretical intention of
subjectivity in special moral experiences, but finds it immediately in the
theoretical intentions, the critical and rational intentions of cognition, and
therefore in language and in philosophical language in particular. For Levinas's project what is difficult is not to locate the place where ethical
responsibility is in force; as soon as one is in philosophy, indeed as soon as
one is in language, one is in that place. But the difficulty is that every
theoretical and ontological intention of philosophy dissimulates the ethical
subjectivity, just by formulating it in its terms, which are those of theoretical and ontological intelligibility. Even the nonrepresentational language
which seeks to articulate the movement of Being itself in the presented or
represented beings dissimulates the subjective movement that before disclosing Being exposes itself to the Good. That the formulation of subjectivity in terms of the objective, or already of the thematizable, or even of
Being, is already this dissimulation is what forces Levinas to speak of a
sphere which is not that of being while not being nonbeing – which is
otherwise than Being.

2. THE FACTS OF RESPONSIBILITY

The critical exigencies of rational discourse, the resolve to think in
response to what Being gives, are movements of responsibility. Every effort
to deduce responsibility, justify or ground it, or even state it in a synthetic

representation, is already an exercise of responsibility. Responsibility is a fact. It is a fact prior to the facts assembled by coherent, that is, responsible, discourse. The theoretical attitude, the ontological logos which articulates Being, owes its energy to this given – or this imposed.

Responsibility is a bond. It is a bond with an imperative order, a command. All subjective movements are under an order; subjectivity is this subjection. This bond does not only determine a being to act, but is constitutive of subjectivity as such, determines it to be.

But – and this is the most distinctive and original feature of Levinas's ethical philosophy – the locus where this imperative is articulated is the other who faces – the face of the other. Facing, which is not turning a surface, but appealing and contesting, is the move by which alterity breaks into the sphere of phenomena. For Levinas responsibility is the response to the imperative addressed in the concrete act of facing. Responsibility is in fact a relationship with the other, in his very alterity. Then a relationship with alterity as such is constitutive of subjectivity.

Responsibility is a form of recognition – acknowledgement of a claim, an order, which is even constitutive of subjectivity – a summons to arise to be and to present oneself. It involves a recognition not of the form but of the force – vocative and imperative and not causal, informative or even indicative force – of the other, of alterity itself. It is realized as a response to the other facing. This recognition is not a cognitive act, that is, an identifying, re-presenting, re-cognizing act. It is effected in expressive acts by which one expresses oneself, expresses one's own being, exposes oneself, to the other. These acts are incarnate acts; indeed exposure is being incarnate, and for Levinas the most basic implication of exteriority in subjectivity is already found in this structure of being an exposedness to another, in the move of responsibility. It is as responsible that one is incarnated. Concretely the acts by which one recognizes the other are acts of exposing, giving, of one's very substance to another. Responsibility is enacted not only in offering one's properties or one's possessions to the other, but in giving one's own substance for the other. The figure of maternity is an authentic figure of responsibility.

How far does responsibility extend? It is already in act. To elucidate responsibility is to bring to light a bond in which one is already held, and where there is still a demand to be answered. Responsibilities increase in the measure that they are taken up. They take form in an unendingly opening horizon, an infinition.

That responsibility has the status of a fact means that it did not originate in an act of subjectivity – in the act of assuming or taking upon oneself. Temporally speaking, that means that responsibility did not originate through an act of presentation or representation. Every representation already misses the originative moment. It does not only have the status of "always already there" when an act originates or begins, but the assembling of oneself and beginning which characterizes the act of consciousness will be shown to be launched from it. In this sense it is "pre-original," prior to all initiatives and their principles, an-archic.

This also means that I am not only answerable for what I initiated in a project or commitment of my will. I am responsible for the situation in which I find myself, and for the existence in which I find myself. To be responsible is always to have to answer for a situation that was in place before I came on the scene. Responsibility is a bond between my present and what came to pass before it. In it is effected a passive synthesis of time that precedes the time put together by retentions and protentions.

I am responsible for processes in which I find myself, and which have a momentum by which they go on beyond what I willed or what I can steer. Responsibility cannot be limited to the measure of what I was able to foresee and willed. In fact real action in the world is always action in which the devil has his part, in which the force of initiative has force only inasmuch as it espouses things that have a force of their own. I am responsible for processes that go beyond the limits of my foresight and intention, that carry on even when I am no longer adding my sustaining force to them – and even when I am no longer there. Serious responsibility recognizes itself to be responsible for the course of things beyond one's own death. My death will mark the limit of my force without limiting my responsibility.

There is in this sense an infinity that opens in responsibility, not as a given immensity of its horizons, but as the process by which its bounds do not cease to extend – an infinition of infinity. The bond with the alterity of the other is in this infinity.

I am answerable before the other in his alterity – responsible before all the others for all the others. To be responsible before the other is to make of my subsistence the support of his order and his needs. His alterity commands and solicits, his approach contests and appeals; I am responsible before the other for tne other. I am responsible before the other in his alterity, that is, not answerable for his empirical and mundane being only, but for the alterity of his initiatives, for the imperative appeal with which he addresses me. I am responsible for the responsible moves of another, for the very impact and trouble with which he approaches me. To be responsible before another is to answer to the appeal by which he approaches. It is to put oneself in his place, not to observe.oneself from without, but to bear the burden of his existence and supply for its wants. I am responsible for the very faults of another, for his deeds and misdeeds. The condition of being hostage is an authentic figure of responsibility.

3. THE INNOVATIONS OF *OTHERWISE THAN BEING*

An ethical philosophy of responsibility grounded in a phenomenology of the face (or quasi-phenomenology: for a face is not so much a mode of appearing of the other, as a "trace" where alterity passes) has been the central concern of Levinas in *Totality and Infinity* and in subsequent writings that developed its theses, especially those assembled in *Humanism and the Other*. But *Totality and Infinity* was structured, classically, as a phenomenology in different strata, related as founding and founded. A sphere of pure sensibility was first disengaged, sphere of the nocturnal horror of the indeterminate, and of ipseity taking form as a relationship of immersion in the sensuous element, determining itself as pleasure or contentment. The relationship with things was carefully distinguished from this antecedent relationship of sensuous enjoyment and alimentation. It begins with inhabitation, the establishing of a dwelling, a zone of the intimate closed from the sphere of the alien. Things are apprehended as solid substances and movable goods, furnishings for a dwelling, before they are means and implements in a practical field. And there is a new form of ipseity identifying itself in these acts of inhabitation and appropriation, existence for oneself in the form of being at home with oneself, *être chez soi*. There was already a relationship with the other at this level, a relationship through cohabitation, with the other as complementary and "feminine" presence. But the relationship with the other in his alterity, the ethical relationship, breaks out in the face to face position in which language takes place. The ethical nature of the relationship with a face constituted the center and principle originality of Levinas's analyses. But Levinas described also an erotic sphere, relationship with the carnal and with the child that comes in the carnal, relationship of voluptuousness and fecundity, as "beyond" the face, a sphere over and beyond the ethical.

Otherwise than Being abandons this construction by strata. On the one hand, the highly original concepts that were elaborated to formulate the erotic relationship – the concept of closeness for the sake of closeness contrasted with that of intentional, teleological movement, the concept of "proximity" contrasted with the presence that establishes distance, the concept of contact by sensuousness contrasted with the signifying aim, even the theme of skin caressed contrasted with face addressed – are now the basic concepts with which the ethical relationship of responsibility with the other is formulated. The ethical relationship with alterity is now described with concepts opposed to those of presence, the present, aim or intentionality. These concepts will be used to formulate saying itself, and the signifyingness of speech founded on an existential structure of being for-the-other, in terms of a making-contact that precedes and supports making signs. The ethical relationship in this book thus acquires, if not an erotic, a sensuous character. Though still realized in language, it is described as sensuous contact and closeness, and not at all as a sort of Kantian rational respect.

On the other hand, this book relates sensibility with responsibility in an entirely new way. In *Totality and Infinity* the relationship with the other was presented as a contestation of the pure sensibility, in which the ego pursues its own closure and contentment. Now Levinas actually sets out to see in the exposedness to alterity in the face of another the original form of openness. It even founds and sustains the openness to things or to the elements. Not only perceptions but even sensation is seen to be wholly sustained by ethical responsibility. The sense of alterity itself maintains open every kind of openness, even that to distant terms or immediately oncoming elements. The "deepest" level of life – that of vulnerability and susceptibility to pleasure and pain– is taken to be constituted not by a relationship with death, a relationship of being with nothingness, but by a relationship with alterity.

Levinas's early work, *Existence and Existents* and to some measure still *Totality and Infinity*, was presented as an elucidation of the constitution of entities, terms or identities, not by but out of Being. But soon the alterity detected in the other was described as pure exteriority, other than the phenomenal trace it leaves in the world, never present but always already come to pass, transcending the play of absence and nonbeing which determines entities and presence. But if alterity cannot be satisfactorily formulated as an entity, nor as an event of Being, Levinas will more and more find that to be true of the ego to which it is addressed. Much of the work before us is devoted to bringing out in the ego or the ipseity, which for transcendental philosophy is the ultimate self-identifying source of identity and the absolute entity, a movement by which it too eludes presence and identity, by which it cannot be posited as an entity. In this period of Levinas's work, subjectivity is not ontologically elucidated by showing how the movement of Being issues in its constitution as an entity – or by showing how it constitutes itself as a term and a commencement by an ecstatic flight from Being. Levinas opposes the ontological philosophy which accounts for subjectivity as a locus or moment engendered by the inner movement of Being for its own exhibition. He intends to show subjectivity as the locus where alterity makes contact, a locus finally created by this movement of alterity. As support of alterity, subjectivity's final meaning is not to be a subsistent entity or moment of Being. This intention to free subjectivity from any ontic or ontological account, to inaugurate a discourse in terms of "otherwise than being," marks both the polemical context in which this book is situated, as well as the strange turns of its composition.

4. THE EXPERIENCE OF ALTERITY: ITS TEMPORAL FORMAT

The relationship with the other in his alterity consists in being appealed to, and contested, by the other. The movement comes from without; alterity is not posited by any act of my subjectivity, the imperative word that comes to bind me does not originate in a synthesis effected by my subjectivity according to its own a prioris. The approach of the other has to be conceived as an empirical and contingent event, even as an experience in a stronger sense than the experience of objects, which are objectified by their images being thematically assembled about poles of ideal identity. On the other hand, as a relationship out of which responsibility arises, exercised in initiatives, and eventually in thematizations, cognitions and actions, the relationship with the other is an a priori fact preceding the a priori forms or conditions for the possibility of experience. Somewhat as in Kant, where the subjection to law – the fact of the categorical imperative – precedes and makes possible the legislative activity of autonomous subjectivity, precedes even its intrinsic forms.

The approach of the other is an initiative I undergo. I am passive with regard to it – and even passive in a more pure sense than the sense in which a material substrate receives, with an equal and opposite reaction, the action impressed on it, and in the sense that the sensibility is passive as a receptivity that synoptically, or syndotically, receives the medley of sensation given to it. Here no form, no capacity preexisted in me to espouse the imperative and make it my own. Not being able to treat the law as a law I myself have given myself is just in what the sense of alterity consists. Not being able to arise by my own forces here is just in what the sense of an appeal made to me, an invocation or a provocation, consists. Not being able to take up the order put to me and appropriate it, and make it into my own principle, is just in what the sense of being contested consists. The sense of the law as an imperative is caught up in the obedience itself – and not in a justification of the law, where the law affecting my "rational feeling" would be converted into a law imposed upon me by myself. There is an obedience before the order has been understood, comprehended, even synthetically formulated for me – as though I find myself obedient to the law before it has been pronounced.

This is the situation of an idea put into me for which I had no capacity to contain it in myself. Alterity comes to me from without, and comes by exceeding my capacities – like the idea of infinity in Descartes, which is put into me, which I could not have accounted for out of myself – and whose very reality as infinity is in this exceeding of any capacity.

It is then not to an apprehensive or comprehensive initiative that alterity is given, but to sensibility. One is passive with regard to the approach of alterity, one sustains its impact without being able to assimilate it, one is open to it, exposed in its direction, to its sense, susceptible to being affected, being exalted and being pained. These terms locate the impact with alterity in the sensibility, but in a sensibility that is no longer being conceived as the receptive side of a synthetic and double event, where receptivity is receptive only in already being comprehensively grasped, where the receptive entity continually regains possession of itself by synoptically apprehending what affects it. Such is sensibility defined as an element of a cognitive act, an act of consciousness. The sensibility affected by alterity is not that sensibility, where identification is already at work. Precisely alterity is the unidentifiable. Its sense is the unilateral direction of an approach, caught in a being ordered, an obedience.

Thus Levinas conceives the register upon which the ethical imperative makes its impact on subjectivity not as a cognitive sensibility, but as sensuality, susceptibility to being affected, vulnerability with regard to pleasure and pain. In fact Kant already had characterised the "rational feeling" by which our nature is inclined by the law as a suffering. But Levinas concludes that sensibility in this sense is a dimension of all sensibility – that sensibility is not only apprehension of a sense, but also sensitivity, susceptibility to being nourished and pained and not only to receive a message by the datum with which one is affected. This vulnerability, this mortality, is even the basis of sensibility qua receptivity for sense. Not only is there no receptive and perceptive sensibility without susceptibility with regard to what one is exposed to, but the exposure to alterity as such – an openness opened by the outside – is at the basis of the openness by which the subject opens itself to objects and to things.

Extreme as this thesis may seem, was not something like it already implied in Kant's moral philosophy? For if in Kant there is no perception of objects without a comprehending spontaneity already at work, this spontaneity acts in order to order the material of sensation, is already under order. Then is not the "rational feeling" by which the mind is first affected with the sense of law prior to the perception of organized objects? What is new in Levinas is that the being afflicted with alterity, prior to the being affected by material being, does not issue in an ordered appropriation of the world. For Levinas will conceive even the expression that consolidates what is given to the receptive sensibility as exposure to the other – exposure of this exposedness.

While he conceives the being-affected by material being in very positive terms as sustenance, over and beyond information, it is especially as pain that Levinas conceives the impact of alterity. It is being shaken in the complacency and pleasure of contentment. Being exposed to the other is being exposed to being wounded and outraged. It is being confounded in the exultancy of one's own initiatives, which arise as from themselves, in a present without memories or inheritance. Exceeded on all sides by responsibilities beyond its control and its capacity even to fulfill, the responsible subject is depicted by Levinas in distress, in terms that equal or even exceed the desolate terms with which Kant describes the law-abiding rational entity humiliated and pained by being bent to the law, and continually frustrated in natural happiness.

The appeal and contestation of alterity then affect me without any mediation; it is the very experience of immediacy. Alterity is closer still to me than the present, even if between the presented and the subject neither the subject's own materiality nor intervening objects form a screen — for presence involves and maintains distance, indeed establishes distance. The instant by which the subject stands in itself and turns to what is at hand is already this distancing. But the subject is exposed to alterity before it can gather itself up and take a stand. This closeness without distance, this immediacy of an approach which remains approach without what approaches being circumscribable, locatable *there*, Levinas calls proximity. The other, my neighbor (*le prochain*) concerns, afflicts me with a closeness (*proximité*) closer than the closeness of entities (*prae-ens*). The relationship with alterity, which is what escapes apprehension, exceeds all comprehension, is infinitely remote, is, paradoxically enough, the most extreme immediacy, proximity closer than presence, obsessive contact.

The structure of the experience of alterity can be expressed in terms of temporality, which is the internal format of subjectivity. The openness by which subjectivity opens to things is itself opened by the internal scission of the instant of its presence, the internal movement of its moment whereby it does not hold itself together in utter identity, but splits, gets out of phase with itself, and clings to itself despite this fission. The present is already passing, bypassing itself (*se passe*). This diachrony which is already in the instant itself makes the instant of a subjective stance not a coinciding with itself, but already a gaping open of itself and a clinging on to itself. An internal openness, and a retention and protention of itself even in the instant when it coheres to itself and posits itself as present, the present is the span of time in which the data that affect it are also retained, synchronized, synthesized.

But the thesis is that there is an openness beneath or prior to that openness. There is an exposure to exteriority itself, to alterity, which is the effect of that alterity. There is an impact of alterity which comes as a shattering of the subsistent instant of the subject. This impact is a fact, has already been effected, has already come to pass. The present established by consciousness finds itself already in relationship with that past moment. It does not so much retain it as it is held by it, retained by it. The present instant is extended by a past which it cannot catch up with or coincide with or represent, render present. It exists in this internal distension. And Levinas's bold idea is that it is this distension which even accounts for the fission by which the moment gets out of phase with itself, can cohere with itself and hold on to itself only as it already passes, only in retaining itself, as it nonetheless passes irrevocably.

The phenomenology of internal time consciousness explained the past entirely by this retentional effort; the past is the represented, by recall and first by primary retention; it is held by the force of the present. In principle everything is retained, and still recoverable, representable. Yet the past passes, and passes of itself, irretrievably. There is loss, falling away irrevocably, *lapse* of time. The bond with the past is a bond with a dimension of oneself which one cannot regain possession of once more, which prevents complete self-possession – and which yet holds on to one, holds one like a bond. Ageing is this temporalization – by virtue of the temporalization of one's time, one is being carried beyond one's powers.

Levinas's bold thesis is that the relationship with alterity is the original case of this affliction of the present of consciousness with a past that it cannot render present, represent. The present is afflicted with a bond with something that comes to pass without being convertible into an initiative of the present, and that holds on, and in this hold distends one.

The thesis is as perplexing as it is audacious – should not the loss involved in the passing of time be rooted in the finitude of subjectivity, eventually to its own unilateral destination to death? Or to the facticity of its having been cast into existence without having constituted itself from bottom up – its having been born? Heidegger had already given a moral sense to this facticity – it is the original guilt of a being that has to take over an existence it has not constituted from bottom up. But does the lapse of time also express facticity of being – where the present is not solely the achievement of consciousness, but is dependent on the facticity of the primary impression? Does it not indicate the movement of withdrawal and obnubilation that belongs to being itself? How can all these senses of the facticity and irrevocable passing of time – the passive synthesis of time not entirely convertible into an active synthesis – be intelligibly subordinated to the time-structure of the relationship with alterity?

5. CREATIVE CONTACT

Conceived as an approach, the relationship with alterity is expressed as utterly a posteriori, an experience in the purest sense, contingent and not preceded by a preformed capacity for it. But also as a fact that cannot be taken up and is more a priori still than the spontaneity of the understanding, which would arise out of nothing, out of itself, more a priori still than its a priori forms which condition the possibility of experience.

The concept of creation is a traditional concept which reflects such a situation. For, as Sartre pointed out in *Being and Nothingness*, the notion of a creature involves the paradoxical idea of an entity receptive not only, like a substance, with regard to the accidents that befall it or the properties it supports, but receptive with regard to its very being. It must receive its being – without there first being anything there to receive it. Sartre rejected as inconsistent this idea of an absolute passivity of being; such a being could not sustain enough exteriority to issue out of its creator. But Kant had found this very structure in the constitution of the pure spontaneity of the rational entity when he showed that this spontaneity could be constituted in its very autonomy only by a subjection to law. The purely rational entity is morally bound to constitute itself, but it constitutes itself not on the basis of a pre-given substantiality, but on the basis of the facticity of a subjection.

In a somewhat parallel way, the exposedness to alterity is taken by Levinas to be prior to the openness to the sensible, given beings – and even to the nothingness or clearing in which they are articulated. Subjectivity is opened from the outside, by the contact with alterity. Before subjectivity is a locus posited by Being for its own manifestation, it is a support called up or provoked to respond to alterity. Before it is a devotion to Being, it is a subjection to the Good. "No one is good voluntarily" – the Good is not the correlate of an axiological option or valorization. Before finding itself a freedom in the free space opened by the play of being and nothingness, where an exercise of options is possible, subjectivity is a subjection to the force of alterity, which calls for and demands goodness of it.

Not only the powers and initiatives provoked, but even the passive affectivity, the susceptibility for pleasure and pain, will be taken now no longer as the original locus of the spontaneous eddy of an ego, but as conditioned by the impact of alterity. The most fundamental mode of affectivity, the enjoyment and anxiety by which subjectivity is affected with itself in being affected by plenary or vacuous sensuous contents, is taken to be preceded by the being thrown back upon oneself, reeling under the impact of alterity. It is the demand of alterity that throws subjectivity back upon its own resources, and this movement is what first constitutes it in-itself.

The incarnation of subjectivity, its very materiality, is no longer, as in *Existence and Existents*, taken as the primary fact by which the ego-identity, positing itself by spontaneous hypostasis, finds itself mired in itself, finds itself encumbered with the primary gravity and weight which is the weight and burden of its existence. Here the weight of existence is first of all the gravity of having to bear the burden of alien existence, and materiality is first one's existence as a maternal sustenance of another. The incarnation of subjectivity, its having an exterior, its being exposed and vulnerable in the given world, is first the necessity to exist only in exposure to alterity.

Thus it is not a repudiation of our specifically human nature, and our reconstitution as a purely rational agency, that is commanded by the moral imperative. For Levinas it is our sensibility, our passive susceptibility, and our material incarnation that is required by the ethical relationship.

6. SUBSTITUTION

The relationship with alterity is thus presented by Levinas both as an experience and as an a priori to all experience, on the "hither side" even of the a prioris that make experience possible. Thirdly, it is conceived as a behavior – that of substituting oneself for another. The approach of the other, which is a putting of the idea of alterity in me, is also a putting myself in the place of another.

The relationship with alterity is finding oneself under a bond, commanded, contested, having to answer to another for what one does and for what one is. It is also finding oneself addressed, appealed to, having to answer for the wants of another and supply for his distress. Alterity is not only remote like a height and a majesty that commands, but also like a nakedness and a destitution that calls for solicitude. It is just this appeal that is imperative, it is presented as a destitution and a pressing need and not only as an absence and a nothingness in the measure that it imperatively calls to me. And it is because the imperative put on me is the imperative need with which I am burdened that the imperative is not only the epiphany of a celestial order fixed in its imperturbable aevernity, but is an imperative that orders my action, calls for my obedience and not only my acquiescence. Thus alterity before whom I am responsible is also that for whom I am responsible.

To acknowledge the imperative force of another is to put onself in his place, not in order to appropriate one's own objectivity, but in order to answer to his need, to supply for his want with one's own substance. It is, materially, to give sustenance to another, "to give to the other the bread from one's own mouth." Thus substitution is conceived as maternal support for the material destitution of another. On the other hand, alterity is a force at the same time as this frailty and mortality, an approach at the same time as this involution and this weakness, an intervention in the world – a disturbance of its order – at the same time as a passage of transcendence beyond the world. To put oneself in the place of another is also to answer for his deeds and his misdeeds, for the trouble he causes and for his faults. It is even to be responsible for the very pain he causes me, at the limit for his persecution – the contestation he formulates against me for what I did not author or authorize. It is to bear the burden of that persecution, to endure it and to answer for it. Thus substitution is conceived as the state of being hostage, held accountable for what I did not do, accountable for the others before the others. Substitution is not to be conceived actively, as an initiative, but as this materiality and this passive condition.

Heidegger too formulated the first contraction of being with others as a substitution. To discover another Dasein is not to perceive him, that is, to objectify him; it is to take him precisely as another Dasein, like oneself, and this is effected in a virtual seeing the world from the *Da*, putting oneself in that place. But the other is conceived by Heidegger as another Dasein – another locus from which the world comes into view. Through the substitution the world-for-me becomes the world. but the world is the world from the first; from the first the world-for-me is a profile or a perspective on the world. Then from the start I am another one, locus of a clearing of the world that from the start has its equivalents. What commands is the world-order, the universal logos which ordains all the perspectives, which not only assembles them into a coherence that can hold together, but assembles them imperiously.

Commanded by the exigency for truth, substitution in Heidegger has a moral tone, according to the philosopher's morality where what is at stake is first courage and cowardice. But to Heidegger substitution appears as an unburdening of oneself, a fleeing of one's own post and one's own being in order to distract oneself with the tasks and fields of operation where the others are stationed; it is a living in the virtual rather than in the actual, a leap out of the finitude of one's own time into the quasi-ubiquity of life in general. From within Dasein's own existence calls it to singularity and to a singular predicament, isolated in the courage that faces the death to come singularly to it.

For Levinas substitution is the ethical itself; responsibility is putting oneself in the place of another. Through becoming interchangeable with anyone, I take on the weight and consistency of one that bears the burden of being, of alien being and of the world. I become substantial and a subject, subjected to the world and to the others. And because in this putting myself in the place of another I am imperiously summoned, singled out, through it I accede to singularity.

The difference finally is in that for Levinas the order that commands substitution is not the cosmic order, the order by which the world becomes the world, but is the imperious transcendence of alterity. The other is not experienced as an empty pure place and means for the world to exhibit another perspective, but as a contestation of my appropriation of the world, as a disturbance in the play of the world, a break in its cohesion.

7. THE THEORY OF SUBJECTIVITY: SENSATION AND SIGNIFICANCE

Levinas locates first the contact with alterity; it even precedes the institution of beginning which consciousness marks in the beginningless, endless happening of Being. The justification of this position requires an explanation as to how the theoretical attitude, and already the ontological exposition, is derived out of the antecedent relationship with alterity. How can thought, thematization, the exhibition of a world, truth, be shown to issue out of a relationship with alterity? But, if the relationship with alterity is to be taken to be constitutive, indeed creative, of subjectivity, how is that subjectivity to be conceived?

Levinas's account of subjectivity does not begin with the correlation of matter and form, receptivity and spontaneity. It also is not founded on the theory of intentionality. The presentational or representational act, or objectification, is no longer taken to be the essential act of subjectivity. Nor is it a will, or a freedom, freeing itself from the determination of what is in itself, or freeing beings in letting them be. Levinas's conception of subjectivity is formed around the concepts of sensibility and expression. And sensibility and expression – signifying or saying – are not two faculties, or two levels, of subjectivity. They are not even conceived as the receptive and the active sides of subjectivity. Sensibility is already referential from the start, and expression is not an exteriorization of something inwardly received, but is itself conceived as a sensitivity.

But there is also a duality in Levinas's account of sensibility. Sensation means sense-impression, the imprinting of a sense. There is a signifyingness in sensation. It also means being affected – sensitivity or susceptibility.

Levinas's conception of the signifyingness in sensation is not derived from the model of intentionality. Already in Husserl's own analyses, sensation did not fit properly into the noetico-noematic distinction. The sensuous hyle is not something transcendent and real, but something lived in consciousness. And the sensing is not an aim come from without the impression. The primary impression undergoes already an internal distension, gets out of phase with itself, and, clinging to itself across this gap, is impressed on itself. The present, presence, occurs in this continuous distension and this retention of the impression, this temporalization. This temporalizing is in fact the very movement of Be-ing, of ess-ence itself, the movement or happening by which the opaqueness lightens and clears. Through it entities can be posited in the flow of lived sensation.

Levinas thus interprets the apparently empiricist residue of sensation in the Husserlian theory of consciousness to in fact reflect the ontological process. The mutual implication – or even ambiguity – of sensing and sensed in sensation, which cannot be conceived according to the intentionality-term, act-object polarity, reflects the "amphibology" of Being and entities. Levinas will also conceive it according to the difference between, and also convertibility of, verbs and nouns in language.

For the articulation of sensation is already logos, saying. Terms, identities, take form in the flow of sensation through denomination. Denomination is a taking of this qua that; it posits and fixes the sensation in function of an ideal identity. Levinas depicts, in rather Platonic fashion, the sphere of sensuous material as a continual vibrancy of images, whose scintillation is fixed, or more exactly given direction or sense, by an identifying move, which is a pure claim or pronouncement. Denomination acts on the basis of a schematism incorporated in the system of a language – an "already said."

But the terms thus nominalized can begin again to function as flows of time, as modalities of essence. They do so in art. In art the terms lose their opacity and their qualities become vibrant and promote their own presence. In painting red reddens and green greens, forms from contours and gape open with their vacuity. In music sounds resound, in poems the verbal material becomes sonorous, in architecture buildings chant and enchant.

They do so also in the predicative proposition, where a term is predicated of another term by the action of a verb, functions adverbally, as a mode of its time and of its vibrancy. The verb, and first of all the verb to be, is just what effects this adverbalization of the terms. It makes their articulation resound. In fact they first resound in the predicative proposition, through the effect of the verb. Artworks themselves call for the verbal and propositional exegesis, in which the sensuous qualities become modes of time or vibrations of essence. Without it what they wanted to say would again relapse into fixed images, idols.

The verbal force of the verb par excellence, the verb to be, does not only link up terms and fixed properties, it verbalizes the terms themselves, or more exactly adverbalizes them, makes the terms sound like qualifications of the timeflow of the sensuous. Be-ing, distinguished from the beings, is a verb. But it is not a verb among others; it is the verb force of verbs. For a functioning verb does not simply designate an event – it effects that event, it makes terms into events. In the predicative proposition the verb is not simply the name or sign of an event, it effects the verbalization or adverbalization. This adverbalization is Being articulating entities, making images resound.

And just because the verb to be resounds silently to verbalize the nominalized terms, it does not resist being nominalized itself, and thus being dissimulated as an event named and fixed. Saying realizes this amphibology of the said, this movement of nouns into adverbs, and of verbs into nouns. And it is this that Levinas sees as the very dissimulation of Be-ing, of ess-ence, in the entities.

Sensibility is thus the sphere of an articulation of the sensuous flux into entities, a nominalization under the influence of the schematism of language, as well as the making of those entities exhibit themselves as verbal modalities in predication. The verb that temporalizes is this saying.

Yet there is also another saying. It is the projection outside of this inner articulation of sensation, by which the sensibility is expressive. But this cannot be something only added on to the flux of sensation; the sphere of sensibility is itself exposed to alterity. The articulation it pursues within the element of sensation speaks to another. There is a sensitivity to the other, a saying that is the sensibility's being-for-the-other, which sustains the saying that is nominalization and predication.

Levinas does not conceive this expressivity of sensibility as a transverse intention that would transcend the sphere of articulated sensation and add an extrinsic reference to it, making significant signs into indices. In a bold move, he identifies it with the very sensuousness of sensation. And this too is understood in strikingly new terms.

Sensibility is not only sense-ascription; it is also sensuous affection. The phenomenological terminology taking the signifying intention as a sort of emptiness seeking plenitude and contentment, a sort of hunger tending toward satisfaction, expresses this duality in sensibility. Levinas has emphasized this vital and not only cognitive function of sensation. The sensuous data are material and sustenance for life; life lives off its sensations. Sensation has to be seen not as acts of perception from the start, as acts of envisaging and viewing from a distance, objectification; but as contact, immediacy, assimilation. Heidegger had argued that the apprehension of an instrumental node is this contact and this involvement with mundane material, gear, prior to perception conceived according to the intentional model, as identification of sensuous material in function of ideal essences. But for Levinas prior even to this operative gearing-in with a field of instrumental connections, there is the sensuous contact with the material. One should conceive sensing not as sighting, nor as handling, but as savoring. In the savoring the sensuous material materializes, and life has content, sensibility becomes volume, life becomes a fullness for itself. In this assimilating of material, this contentment, sensibility becomes vibrant on itself, a plenitude and a superabundance, and not only a locus of transmission of the energies of material nature. It intensifies, becomes an intensity in this vibrancy of contentment or this involution of enjoyment. Savoring and alimentation, sensation is conceived as enjoyment. Pleasure is not a mere byproduct of sensation; it is the concord with itself of a content vibrant with its own superabundant plenitude – and the very involution of ipseity in sensation.

But sensibility as savoring is not to be conceived first of all as spontaneity and act. It is a susceptibility to being affected, in which not only a reception of messages, but the living of life is at stake. Prior to the openness of a capacity for being, there is exposedness, and vulnerability.

Affectivity with regard to alien entities involves affectivity with regard to oneself; Heidegger had described it as the condition of being passive or receptive with regard to one's own existence – in general, the condition of being born. In temporal terms, it is the relation of the essentially active actual presence of existence with its past, its being burdened with the weight of the being that has come to pass. But this being passive with regard to one's own being, this not being able to give oneself being, was also seen as a liability to nonbeing; the condition of one who is born is to be exposed to the possibility of nothingness. Thus Heidegger had seen in the sensibility of consciousness mortality. A mortal anxiety animates our sensuality; the apprehension of being begins in this apprehensiveness.

The capacity of being affected by beings is conditioned by this exposure to nothingness, and this is indeed why beings are from the first a means or a threat to our existence before they are forms surrounding it or signs supplying messages to it, why sensibility is affective concerns before it is perception. But at the same time, when Heidegger finds beneath the capacity to be affected by the impact of beings an exposure to or a projection into nothingness, he conceives of sensibility as an eddy of freedom and a self-propelled projection from the start. There is sensibility for beings and presence to beings when it is exposed to nothingness, or finds itself in emptiness, clearing or free space.

Levinas wants to locate, beneath the sensuous exposure to material and as its basis, the exposure to alterity. He wishes to see in the condition of being passive with regard to one's own existence not the de facto having being but still risking nonbeing – but the dependency on alterity. The relationship with the past that vulnerability expresses is not having to hold on to the being with which one has been afflicted, but a being held by the passage of alterity, a finding of one's substance required and one's support demanded. Our sensibility is not so much an apprehensiveness about being extinguished as a sensitivity to being wounded and outraged.

The capacity for being sustained by sensuous material is conditioned by this requisition of alterity, and that is why the sensuous is first a nourishing medium before it is a field of gear, why it is immersion and savoring before it is freedom and utilization.

It is because Heidegger conceives of the first tremor of sensibility as an eddy of freedom and an ecstasy, a self-propelled projection, that for him the being exposed to nothingness is already there. But Levinas has long seen in the first tremor of sensation not an exhilaration and ecstasy out of being, but an enjoyment, an intensity and an involution. In *Totality and Infinity* it was conceived as immersion, the immediacy of finding oneself in the sensuous element without having to first envisage it and circumscribe it by its contours. Finding oneself in the light was taken as the primary model of what happens when life becomes an illumination[8] – and not finding oneself in the emptiness of a forest clearing. Heidegger thinks of our existence being open as being in an openness – it is in the sense of the hand that has leeway to move. Levinas in this work presents the first movement of animation as an opening of the subject upon a space filled with air before being filled, or emptied, by the light. The openness upon the air is not an intention or an apprehension but inspiration, our substance being open to the core.

In the course of his writings, the notions of proximity, immediacy and contact were deepened, elucidated and contrasted with the notion of presence. They were employed to articulate the relationship with alterity, which is found in me from the start, is obsessive, and does not even admit of the distance that would be involved if the other could be present to me, could share the space of the present with me. Here the structures of freedom, a self-propelled project, a free space or a clearing of nothing are not required for the contact to take place.

The present work now relates the notion of the immediate, obsessive contact with alterity and the notion of immersion in the sensuous element in such a way as to make the first the basis for the second. No doubt this extremely audacious thesis is very difficult to understand. It involves the idea that before the material elements are true or false in themselves, they are possessed by others; that the material world is "human" even before it is a nourishing medium. That its elements are "objective" or "intersubjective," elements in themselves or open to others before they are good for me. That they are relics or traces of alterity, whose closeness to us derives from the contact with the face of another, whose mineral surfaces materialize privatively as the caress of alterity in the skin subsides into touch of the resistant.

Levinas's position is that the structure of proximity, immediacy and contact subtends the structure of space, with the presence and distance constitutive of it. The space in which the sensuous material is laid out is extended by the sense of alterity, the contact with the irremediably exterior.

It is true that already in Husserl and in Heidegger the lateral relationship with others, as other points of view, or as other "Theres" where Being pursues its exhibition, entered into the first constitution of universal space. But Levinas proposes two innovations. First, that the relationship with the other does not only enter at the point where my field, already extended by intentional perception or by the utilitarian reach, accedes to an impersonal and universal extension; for Levinas the relationship with alterity precedes and makes possible the sensuous expanse and the practical layout itself. Intersubjectivity does not only intervene for the constitution of universal or objective space, but already for the first exteriorization of the sensible and the practical. Secondly, the relationship with alterity can have this role because the relationship with the other is not itself perceptual or pragmatic, but ethical. There is then a difference of levels, and it is not empirical contact with the other that would come first, as though the other were the first object of perception, or the first instrument with which one could get one's bearings in a field of.gear.

Levinas several times proceeds by way of language to these positions. In general a language, the said, is the medium of simultaneity, the field where everything past and to come can be presented or represented; it is logos that assembles into a system, that establishes togetherness, that institutes synchrony. Space, the sphere of the simultaneous, is itself a work of temporalization, established in a synchronization. But the constituted and fixed, maintained logos itself is sustained by the saying that is a relationship with alterity. And, more particularly, the relationship with the third party. It is the entry of the third party which calls for justice, comparisons, distributive justice – and distribution in general. The very field of simultaneity would already be a context, space already a field of inscription.

There are undoubtedly missing steps in this demonstration. Just how does one deduce the contiguity of space from the ethical sense of contact and immediacy? Just how does one deduce the distance measured by the reaching hand and gauged by the perceiving eye from the inapprehendable remoteness of the other? Just how does one deduce distribution in general from the exigency for ethical justice?

But one has to remember that in Levinas the relationship with the other is first described as putting myself in his place, a substitution. Levinas does not find responsibility first on the level of conformity to cosmic law on the part of a being whose destiny is to become a purely rational entity. He seeks the responsible structure of subjectivity in our sensuous nature and our occupancy of place. It is in the incarnation of consciousness that subjectivity is exposed to the exterior and committed to alterity. It is in taking the place of another that subjectivity first comes to inhabit space.

8. THE IPSEITY

The formulations will become ever more paradoxical when Levinas sets out to formulate the identity of such a subjectivity. For he seeks the identity involved beneath the level of an identity constituted by acts of identification – as where subjectivity is defined as being for-itself. No doubt subjectivity identifies itself in its own acts as it identifies entities for itself, but it is also affected with its identity and held to it. There is something like a fatality in one's identity. There is a falling back upon oneself or a being thrown back upon oneself, a recurrence to oneself, that precedes and motivates acts of self-identification and efforts to escape oneself.

The oneself is one and selfsame; one is singled out. This singularization is neither the being determined by a specific difference, nor the result of the invention of some overall characteristic or style. It is a passive effect, which "one" does not even properly speaking receive. This singularization is the work of the exterior, of alterity. It is in being addressed and contested, in being accused that one is first singled out.

Singularization is not the result of a work of the subject itself. Every initiative of a subject already involves a taking of a distance from itself, a freeing itself of itself, a transcending of one's particularity. Levinas does not conceive singularization existentially as the process of imposing a particular line of coherence upon a disparate succession of roles and contingencies. For him singularization rather means being held to be oneself, being passive with regard to oneself. This singularity marks me entirely inasmuch as it means being held to my own existence and my own deeds, bound to bear their weight and answer for them – and in this sense being backed up against my own being and my own time. But in addition it means being burdened with being generally, in a univocal relationship of support for all the world. That the whole weight of the universe is on my shoulders, and that I cannot shift this burden upon anyone else – this is my finding myself one without a double. And this predicament is founded on the relationship with alterity; it is being answerable without limit. The approach of the other holding me responsible for everything, even for what I did not do – this unlimited accusation – is what singularizes me utterly. The (French) grammar of ipseity, where the self (*se, soi*) is an accusative without a nominative form, would reflect this situation linguistically.

This singular self is not properly speaking named: it is addressed by a pro-noun. By its pronoun identifiability, it already lends itself to being named with a noun. But the noun will designate but a semblance of identity, a mask or persona it wears. Levinas writes that what the commonality of names seems to designate is pure appearance, a pure effect of language, and of language fixed and congealed as the said.

Singularization then does not amount to an unconditional position in being. It cannot even contemplate itself, put itself in its own presence. It is out of phase with itself. Its unicity is less than identity with itself. If this inner fission is experienced as a distress, a breathlessness of one unable to catch up with itself, that is because it is somehow under obligation to catch up with itself, to be at the level of its own resources. But not in order to achieve a coinciding with itself which would be self-revelation or self-certainty, and which would be required by a supreme exigency for revelation which would be the essence of Being itself. Rather the being bound to oneself and being in deficit with regard to oneself is brought about by the moral obligation. It is the demand put on it and the contestation made of it that binds it to itself.

Less than identical with itself, in deficit with regard to itself, unable to catch up with itself, unable to achieve presence and self-presence, the self cannot be conceived as an entity. It has dropped out of being, and out of being striving for manifestation, is disinterested. It is, in Levinas's telling expression, in exile in itself. That is, driven, from the outside, into itself, but not finding a home, a position, a rest in itself.

On the other hand, this incomparable unicity and singularity is, paradoxically enough, what is universally substitutable. It even exists in this universal substitution, it is by putting itself in every place, to bear every burden. It is this movement, and not an aiming to posit itself, that is the movement of the psyche. Thus this less than identity, less than an entity, is also what figures as the universal support for all and for everything.

One is answerable before the other, for the other. One is thrown back upon itself in being called upon to answer in the place of another. These two movements, being thrown back upon oneself, being backed up against oneself, and being put in the place of another, are inseparable. The being under accusation by the other, the being afflicted by the other, converts at once into a supporting of the other, a being put in the place of another. The being wounded by the other converts at once into a being wounded for, expiating for, the other. The being singularized and constrained to one's own self converts into a putting oneself in the place of all – and is the same movement, the movement of recurrence which ipseity is. These are not even the passive and active phases of a movement. For one does not bear the burden of others as a result of one's own initiative. One is held to bear the burden of others; the substitution is a passive effect, which one does not succeed in converting into an active initiative or into one's own virtue.

Beings doubled up with an exigency to answer for them – that is the situation where, over and beyond being, there is signification. The self "exists" in this signification, rather than in being. As this need to answer for what is, the psychic is over and beyond being, and is itself otherwise than being, put in its singular position and driven in its constitutive movement by alterity.

There are then two instances which are not destined for manifestation, for inclusion within the totality of the identifiable, for presentation and representation, for synchronization. The other is not only other than me, but other than the sphere of what is presented to me, other than what can be posited as a being or than what strives to appear. And from this transcendence puts the totality under accusation. And puts under accusation oneself, the singular eddy of recurrence at the bottom of oneself, called upon to answer for all that is and for all that is not. These two instances are in an original relationship, prior to the manifestation of beings. This relationship is not a bond between two terms, but a subjection of oneself to the Good.

9. ALTERITY AND INFINITY

The movements in philosophy where the ontological theater was already conceived in relation with something beyond it are recalled by Levinas in order to formulate the ethical relationship. From his earliest writings Levinas has resisted the central position of existential philosophy, formulated in its term Being-in-the-world, conceiving the subjectivity entirely as an openness upon the world, and the world as the destiny and finally the *raison d'être* of subjectivity. In the Neo-Platonic concept of the One over and beyond Being, itself having its sources in the Platonic concepts of the One and the Good, in the opposition between totality and infinity, and in the religious word God, Levinas sees each time a philosophical position for which Being and its truth are not all-encompassing, and not even intelligible by themselves. Even the Platonic metaphysical position, by which being has to be understood by significance, which is over and beyond being, is invoked. But Levinas uses all these terms and movements of thought as material with which to formulate what for him is over and beyond Being and its truth: the other and the ethical bond to alterity. Yet for Levinas this is not just so much linguistic or conceptual material whose proper and intended meaning has died, and which can now be put to his own uses.

For he really means to show that the original sense of the one, and the final basis of all unity, lies in the singularity of the responsible subjectivity. And he holds that the sense of infinity has its origin not in a formalization and idealization of the spatial sense of horizonal openness, nor in the absolutization of the idea of truth – as Husserl had said, but in the inapprehendability of alterity and the unsatisfiability of the moral exigency. In fact the passage from the idea of a particular and pragmatic truth to the idea of absolute truth in Husserl already incorporates a recognition of the universal contestation and unrestricted claims of the other point of view – which Levinas takes to be first an ethical claim. And in transferring religious language to the ethical sphere, Levinas no doubt divinizes the relationship with alterity; indeed he will say that the description of the other in his alterity is less a phenomenology than a hagiography. But Levinas does not mean purely to employ a language now without proper object to describe human relations, in order to exalt them with the sentiments that once transcendent divinity inspired. He rather means to locate the proper meaning of God – the one God – in the ethical bond. Not so much that God would be a postulate required to render the ethical imperative intelligible, nor that God would be revealed in ethical phenomena – but that God is the very nonphenomenal force of the other, that God "exists" in his voice, which speaks in the ethical imperative. And that all responsibility bears witness to the Infinite who is God.

The development rests especially on two dimensions of the ethical structure: on the one hand, that obligation figures always as a more required than what one has accomplished. The sense of the unfinished, of infinition, is intrinsic to the sense of moral bond. Whereas the very move of Being is to present, re-present, synchronize, integrate, totalize, the approach of alterity comes as disturbance, transcendence and infinition. The movement is different, and irreducibly so. On the other hand, oneself and the other are not reversible. Alterity is irreducible in not being interchangeable with me, even if finally my whole subjective reality consists in substituting myself for him. The dimension of irreversibility in the relationship, that by which alterity, unendingly withdrawing, infinitely withdrawing, remains other, was what Levinas named illeity. Illeity is that by which the you is not the simple reverse of the I. The irreversibility is essential to the whole analysis: there can be command, imperative obligation, contestation and appeal put on me, only if not only the other is not derivative off me, but not equivalent to me.

Illeity, this movement of infinition, Levinas names God. Sacred, in a literal sense, it is the transcendent instance that contests and judges being. It is the Good that calls unto being and to expiation for the wants and faults of being. Here God figures not as a compensation for us for the wants of the universe, nor as healer of our mortality, but as judge and as imperative which calls us into question.

But this sacred instance is not only an ingredient of the face of other human beings, multiple that they are. What is at stake is God in the singular and not the divine – not an identifiable essence or condition for the possibility of the identifiable. God is not approachable through the divine, which would be his manifestation or revelation, however ciphered or mysterious – for God is there uniquely where manifestation is disturbed by alterity, in the one that addresses me. It is not even correct to say that Levinas argued for a personal conception of God against all reification, for for him the personal is not a category of which the first, second and third person would be species. We have noted that the personal identity of the first person – even if only identified as the ego – is a pure mask. And the second person eludes apprehension precisely in function of the third personality designated in him – *ille*. The *ille* is indivisible and unmultipliable as infinity, and each time singular.

And yet even these phrases already thematize God, and already dissimulate or transpose his incidence in human discourse. The other inasmuch as he lends himself to thematization and becomes a phenomenon said, becomes something present and represented – but that by which he is other is precisely the *ille* that eludes my presence, not as a telos or end already anticipated and representable, apprehendable in advance, but rather as an irrecuperable past.

Already my own identity is not something representable and identifiable by me. The first person singular enters language with the utterance "Here I am." This entry into language is not an act of self-positing; it is rather the passivity of an exposure. The words do not record exposure, and represent it or signify it, but rather effect the exposure. With them the exposedness to another is exposed. They are, in Levinas's expression, a sign given of the giving of signs – but even more, they are a sign given by which one becomes this giving and this signifying.

These words then of themselves respond to alterity, and bear witness to it. Through their passive expositional sense, they bear witness to its unending withdrawal and transcendence. God, the Infinite, is properly neither designated by words nor even indicated or named, but borne witness to in the peculiar character of the "Here I am," a pure saying unconvertible into something put forth, said.

It is then in my own words, saying "Here I am" that the Infinite touches language. God is not a voice that addresses me to reveal himself and become thematizable, but enters language only in the witness I formulate not in words that put forth my presence, but in words that expose my exposedness. The Infinite is there in the order that orders me to my neighbor. But it is in my words "Here I am" inasmuch as they formulate obedience to this order that the order is first formulated. Levinas does not express this situation according to the Kantian typology, as a veritable constitution of autonomy out of this inaugural heteronomy of the law – where I must act as though it is I myself that give myself the law to which I am subject. Yet he calls the Kantian formula remarkable, and reinterprets it to mean that the Law I recognize is first formulated in my own words of obedience – the "Here I am." Here I exist as the author of what was put to me despite myself and unbeknownst to myself.

Thus there is really not anything like an evidence, or a certainty, of God. Not only is God invisible, not manifest in the cosmic order, but his command is inaudible, or audible only in my words. The force of God, the proximity of in'finity, has all its inscription in my own voice. There is not even really a belief in God, which would supply for the inadequate evidence. Thus the proximity of God can be completely repudiated. It is even always dissimulated in the movement by which the saying itself converts into, is fixed in a said. All saying, which says Being, dissimulates this Beyond. It is only aimed at – or, more exactly, addressed – retrospectively or reductively by a critical movement back from the already-said. Yet this reduction is not a phenomenological reduction, for it does not issue in a pure intuition, does not come upon a sphere of utter plenitude that would be origin. Unlike the Kantian moral deduction, God is not attained in the demand for moral intelligibility that postulates him, for the demand for certainty and even for articulation in the coherent text of the said already deforms his witness.

10. THE ENTRY OF THE THIRD PARTY: RESPONSIBILITY AND JUSTICE

Most of the discussion conducted in this book concerns the face to face relationship with alterity, I facing the other as you. The you is eminently singular and singularizing. The entry of a third party is not simply a multiplication of the other; from the first the third party is simultaneously other than the other, and makes me one among others. This alterity is itself first ethical, and not simply numerical; it is a relation of appeal and contestation. To find that the one before whom and for whom I am responsible is responsible in his turn before and for another is not to find his order put on me relativized or cancelled. It is to discover the exigency for justice, for an order among responsibilities.

And the entry of a third party, treating me as an other alongside of the other I faced, first institutes a kind of common terrain among us. I am, thanks to him, someone to be concerned about, someone to answer for. For Levinas, then, the very structure of concern for oneself, of care for oneself, is not an ontological *conatus*, which owes its origin ultimately to the advance revelation of the menace of universal death cast over being, and to the desire of being to be, to persevere in its being. It is from the first an ethical obligation, the sense that one is answerable for one's own being too. It is then not the reversibility of the relationship with alterity that produces it, but its multiplication to the second power.

The concern about oneself then is not originally a movement back upon oneself on the part of a striving to posit oneself in being and persevere in being, which has anticipated the nothingness that threatens it. For Levinas it originates in a subjectivity whose responsibility has become a problem for itself, which has discovered the exigency for an order among responsibilities. With the entry of the third party, there arises a problem of copresence and synchronization, of distributive justice. There arises a problem of consciousness, which is con-sciousness.

The exercise of consciousness is justification. Little by little Levinas means to found reckonings, rationality, systemization, labor, the State and technology on the exigency for assembling and synchronization, which in turn is required by the exigency for justice. Even the very assembling of Being effected in all these registers is founded on this ethical exigency. "It is in view of justice that all things show themselves." It is as a text, a context and system, that things are synchronized in justice. And thus the articulated logos, the said, and the beings thus put forth and fixed in identities, and even the very movement of being that verbalizes them and promotes these identities – all this is founded on the exigency for justice, and the pluralism of ethical instances. Levinas gives an essentially human meaning to the exigency for justice. The simultaneity of the other and the third party is the original locus where this exigency for justice emerges. It is as this exigency, this purely ethical bond, that the three are compossible.

One can at once raise the objection that the assembling, arrangement or truth of the world can hardly rest only on an extra-mundane and subjective exigency; must not what is thus exhibited and said lend itself to this truth and this composition? Must one not then recognize a destination of the world to its truth, which destination would be the very striving, or essence of the world? Would we not have to recognize, beneath the said in which what is is compossible, and beneath the entities and the nonentities too, something like a *There is*, whose happening is the striving for truth?

But that is not Levinas's position. For him distinction and determination are the work of consciousness; the *There is* is of itself indetermination and interminableness, striving without end, without beginning, without direction, without sense. It is essentially nocturnal. The ethical imposition comes to subjectivity as its deliverance from this anonymity and indifference of being.

II. THE INSURMOUNTABLE SKEPTICISM

On the one hand, then, it is the ethical exigency alone that founds the assembling of being, its truth in a totality and in representation; reason and truth are the outcome of, and the proper work of, justice. But, on the other hand, if there is not a truth which Being itself pursues, if signification and truth come from beyond being, if there is not an ontological truth independent of and rivalling the ethical truth, the truth that is founded by the ethical exigency ipso facto dissimulates that exigency. The said is a fixing and a silencing of the saying that makes it significant. The ethical structure is completely covered over by the exhibition of the world.

Thus Levinas presents the disclosure of this ethical structure to which his work is devoted as requiring a reduction, a going back not to the constitutive origin of the constituted world and discourse said, but to what is prior to that origin. To what in fact is an irrecoverable past, which cannot be rendered present. Thus it is excluded that the reduction yield a proper discourse in thematic language about the structure of ethical responsibility that subtends it.

It follows then that the structure of ethical responsibility, the very nature of subjectivity, is expressible only in a thematic discourse which dissimulates it. The very sentences of this book — thematic, synchronic time, systematic language, constantly making the verb *to be* intervene in phrases that profess to express what is antecedent to the work of being — can only be a continual transposition, and dissimulation, of the prethematic alterity, the diachronic time of the contact with the other, the non-presence of one term to another, which these phrases mean to put forth. What they mean to translate into a text is always betrayed, in a translation always unfaithful to the pre-text. But it is only thus that they can be said. And the saying cannot be utterly obliterated under the said. It is also conveyed nonetheless in this unfaithful text.

But there is no way to construct a key, whereby the systematic unfaithful text could be systematically translated into a direct and univocal discourse. There is no metalanguage in which one could establish oneself so as to control the meaning and the evidence of the text and the pre-text. All one can do is live this effort to reduce the said to the saying, and be confounded by the ever-unfaithful text that that yields. Philosophy has to exist in this ambivalence, between the intelligibility of system and synchrony and the intelligibility of signifyingness itself which is assymetry and diachrony.

This situation Levinas compares to the relationship between philosophical truth and skepticism. The skeptical thesis denies the possibility of truth, the unity of orders and levels. Its refutation does not consist in counterpositing truth and coherence of orders, but in pointing out that what skepticism says itself is in contradiction with the saying that says it, and which claims to be true. There would be a mutual incompatibility between the said and the saying that says it. Skepticism is thus indeed refuted. And yet the refutation appeals to, and presupposes nonetheless, exactly what the skeptical thesis puts into question: the possibility of truth, the validity of coherence, the genuineness of unity. Thus the refutation itself presupposes itself. And skepticism returns, after the refutation. Skepticism is then somehow possible. Negation of synchronic and coherent discourse, it is itself possible only as a diachronic and noncoordinated discourse. Here there is a said, and a saying which puts it forth, which are possible because they are not on the same level or time, which the refutation forces them into. Philosophy cannot avoid the skeptical question about the possibility of truth, and has to refute skepticism, but skepticism returns. The discourse that demands truth exists in these moments which cannot be synchronized, this diachronic temporal diagram.

Such a situation would be also in effect in general in the philosophical discourse which aims to go back to, to reduce to, the saying that subtends it. Converting everything into thematic, systematic discourse, discourse of being, philosophy seems to leave nothing irreducible to the said, to reduce the saying to nothing. But its own efforts betray a saying they themselves are, addressed to another, like all discourse.

Traduire c'est trahir: all translation is unfaithful. More than in his other texts, Levinas's composition in this book reflects the understanding of the work of language the book puts forth. The thought succeeds in formulating itself without being set forth in predicative assertions. Constructions by participial clauses avoid the very use of the copula. Where he elides the verb *to be*, Levinas is forced to write in clauses rather than in sentences, and yet the French text is precise and unequivocal. Again and again the procedure is to juxtapose formulations in apposition, as though the movement is not to reduce but to disimplicate. We have first tried to produce an English version which would duplicate these grammatical artifices, but the result seemed to us to strain the expressive devices of English grammar much more than seemed to have been the case in French. We have concluded that in English Levinas's intentions would have required different grammatical distortions. Failing to find these, we have reintroduced the copula and the predicative structure everywhere, and movements preceding by enchainments of appositions have been dismembered and rephrased in declarative propositions. As a result the present English version, more than most philosophical translations, is a transposition of the original text, and does not wish to sever its dependence on and subordination to it. We here entreat the reader to be alerted to this subordination.

xlv

Acknowledgment is gratefully made to the Liberal Arts Research Office of the Pennsylvania State University, which has generously supported the work of this translation.

Alphonso Lingis
Zamboanga, Philippines
December, 1978

NOTE

It is necessary to emphasize at the beginning of this book something that will be often repeated within it, and which is necessary if its language, and its very title, are to be understood: the term *essence* here expresses *being* different from *beings*, the German *Sein* distinguished from *Seiendes*, the Latin *esse* distinguished from the Scholastic *ens*. We have not ventured to write *essance* as would be required by the history of the language, where the suffix *-ance*, deriving from *-antia* or *-entia*, gave birth to abstract nouns of action. We shall carefully avoid using the term essence or its derivates in their traditional usage. For essence, essential, essentially, we will say eidos, eidetic, eidetically, or nature, quiddity, fundamental, etc.

Several extracts from the present work have been published in journals. Under the title "La Substitution," the main part of Chapter IV appeared in *La Revue philosophique de Louvain* (October, 1968). Chapter I, which lays out the argument of this book, was published, as "Au delà de l'Essence," in the *Revue de Métaphysique et de Morale* (August-September, 1970). *Le Nouveau Commerce* (Spring, 1971) published, under the title "Le Dire et le Dit," an essential part of Chapter II. "La Proximité," taken from Chapter III, was printed in *Archives de Philosophie* (October, 1971). And in the collection *Le Témoignage*, in which was published the acts of the conference organized in January, 1972, by the Centre International d'Études Humanistes and the Institut d'Études Philosophiques de Rome, presided by Professor Enrico Castelli, there appeared important pages from Chapter V, under the title "Vérité comme dévoilement et vérité comme témoignage."

Yet this book is not a collection of articles. Built around Chapter IV, which is its centerpiece, its first version preceded the published texts. They were detached from the whole, and were finished in such a way to make them relatively autonomous. The traces of this autonomy have not always been effaced in the present version, in spite of the changes made since, and the notes added.

To see in subjectivity an exception putting out of order the conjunction of essence, entities and the "difference"; to catch sight, in the substantiality of the subject, in the hard core of the "unique" in me, in my unparalleled identity, of a substitution for the other; to conceive of this abnegation prior to the will as a merciless exposure to the trauma of transcendence by way of a susception more, and differently, passive than receptivity, passion and finitude; to derive práxis and knowledge in the world from this nonassumable susceptibility – these are the propositions of this book which names the *beyond essence*. The notion cannot claim to be original, but the access to it is as steep as in ancient times. The difficulties of the climb, as well as its failures and renewed attempts, are marked in the writing, which no doubt also shows the breathlessness of the author. But to hear a God not contaminated by Being is a human possibility no less important and no less precarious than to bring Being out of the oblivion in which it is said to have fallen in metaphysics and in onto-theology.

THE ARGUMENT

CHAPTER I

ESSENCE AND DISINTEREST

> There is something to be said, Novalis wrote, in favor of passivity. It is significant that one of Novalis' contemporaries, Maine de Brain, who wished to be the philosopher of activity, will remain essentially the philosopher of two passivities, the lower and the higher. But is the lower lower than the higher?
> Jean Wahl, *Traité de métaphysique*, 1953, p. 562.

1. BEING'S "OTHER"

If transcendence has meaning, it can only signify the fact that the *event of being*, the *esse*, the *essence*,[1] passes over to what is other than being. But what is *Being's other*? Among the five "genera" of the *Sophist* a genus opposed to being is lacking, even though since the *Republic* there had been question of what is beyond essence. And what can the *fact* of passing over mean here, where the passing over, ending at being's other, can only undo its facticity during such a passage?

Transcendence is passing over to being's *other*, otherwise than being. Not *to be otherwise*, but *otherwise than being*. And not to not-be; passing over is not here equivalent to dying. Being and not-being illuminate one another, and unfold a speculative dialectic which is a determination of being. Or else the negativity which attempts to repel being is immediately submerged by being. The void that hollows out is immediately filled with the mute and anonymous rustling of the *there is*,[2] as the place left vacant by one who died is filled with the murmur of the attendants. Being's essence dominates not-being itself. My death is insignificant – unless I drag into my death the totality of being, as Macbeth wished, at the hour of his last combat. But then mortal being, or life, would be insignificant and ridiculous even in the "irony with regard to oneself" to which it could in fact be likened.

To be or not to be is not the question where transcendence is concerned. The statement of being's *other*, of the otherwise than being, claims to state a difference over and beyond that which separates being from nothingness – the very difference of the *beyond*, the difference of transcendence.

4

But one immediately wonders if in the formula "otherwise than being" the adverb "otherwise" does not inevitably refer to the verb to be, which simply has been avoided by an artificially elliptical turn of phrase. Then what is signified by the verb to be would be ineluctable in everything said, thought and felt. Our languages woven about the verb to be would not only reflect this undethronable royalty, stronger than that of the gods; they would be the very purple of this royalty. But then no transcendence other than the factitious transcendence of worlds behind the scenes, of the Heavenly City gravitating in the skies over the terrestrial city, would have meaning. The Being of beings and of worlds, however different among themselves they may be, weaves among incomparables a common fate; it puts them in conjunction, even if the unity of Being that assembles them is but an analogical unity. Every attempt to disjoin the conjunction and the conjuncture but emphasizes them. The *there is* fills the void left by the negation of Being.

2. BEING AND INTEREST

The essence thus works as an invincible persistance in essence, filling up every interval of nothingness which would interrupt its exercise. *Esse* is *interesse*; essence is interest. This being interested does not appear only to the mind surprised by the relativity of its negation, and to the man resigned to the meaninglessness of his death; it is not reducible to just this refutation of negativity. It is confirmed positively to be the *conatus* of beings. And what else can positivity mean but this *conatus*? Being's interest takes dramatic form in egoisms struggling with one another, each against all, in the multiplicity of allergic egoisms which are at war with one another and are thus together. War is the deed or the drama of the essence's interest. No entity can await its hour. They all clash, despite the difference of the regions to which the terms in conflict may belong. Essence thus is the extreme synchronism of war. Determination is formed, and is already undone, by the clash. It takes form and breaks up in a swarming. Here is extreme contemporaneousness or immanence.

Does not essence revert into its other by peace, in which reason, which suspends the immediate clash of beings, reigns? Beings become patient, and renounce the allergic intolerance of their persistence in being; do they not then dramatize the *otherwise than being*? But this rational peace, a patience and length of time, is calculation, mediation and politics. The struggle of each against all becomes exchange and commerce. The clash of each against all in which each comes to be with all, becomes reciprocal limitation and determination, like that of matter. But the persisting in being, interest, is maintained by the future compensation which will have to equilibrate the concessions patiently and politically consented to in the immediate. The beings remain always assembled, present, in a present that is extended, by memory and history, to the totality determined like matter, a present without fissures or surprises, from which becoming is expelled, a present largely made up of re-presentations, due to memory and history. Nothing is gratuitous. The mass remains permanent and interest remains. Transcendence is factitious and peace unstable. It does not resist interest. And the ill-kept commitment to recompense virtue and chastise vices, despite the assurances of those who claim it was made for a term more distant than the distance that separates the heavens from the earth, will accredit strange rumors about the death of God or the emptiness of the heavens. No one will believe in their silence.

Commerce is better than war, for in peace the Good has already reigned. And yet we must now ask if even the difference that separates essence in war from essence in peace does not presuppose that *breathlessness of the spirit*, or the spirit holding its breath, in which since Plato what is beyond the essence is conceived and expressed? And ask if this breathlessness or holding back is not the extreme possibility of the Spirit, bearing a sense of what is beyond the essence?

3. THE SAID AND THE SAYING

Is not the inescapable fate in which being immediately includes the statement of being's *other* not due to the hold the *said* has over the *saying*, to the *oracle* in which the said is immobilized? Then would not the bankruptcy of transcendence be but that of a theology that thematizes the *transcending* in the logos, assigns a term to the passing of transcendence, congeals it into a "world behind the scenes," and installs what it says in war and in matter, which are the inevitable modalities of the fate woven by being in its interest?

It is not that the essence qua persistance in essence, qua *conatus* and interest, would be reducible to a word-play. Saying is not a game. Antecedent to the verbal signs it conjugates, to the linguistic systems and the semantic glimmerings, a foreword preceding languages, it is the proximity of one to the other, the commitment of an approach, the one for the other, the very signifyingness of signification. (But is approach to be defined by commitment, and not rather commitment by approach? Perhaps because of current moral maxims in which the word *neighbor* occurs, we have ceased to be surprised by all that is involved in proximity and approach.) The original or pre-original saying, what is put forth in the foreword, weaves an intrigue of responsibility. It sets forth an order more grave than being and antecedent to being. By comparison being appears like a game. Being is play or detente, without responsibility, where everything possible is permitted. But is play free of interest? Right off a stakes, money or honor, is attached to it. Does not disinterestedness, without compensation, without eternal life, without the pleasingness of happiness, complete gratuity, indicate an extreme gravity and not the fallacious frivolity of play? By anticipation let us ask: does not this gravity, where being's *esse* is inverted, refer to this pre-original language, the responsibility of one for the other, the substitution of one for the other, and the condition (or the uncondition) of being hostage which thus takes form?

But this pre-original saying does move into a language, in which saying and said are correlative of one another, and the saying is subordinated to its theme. It can be shown that even the distinction between Being and entities is borne by the amphibology of the said, though this distinction and this amphibology are not thereby reducible to verbal artifices. The correlation of the saying and the said, that is, the subordination of the saying to the said, to the linguistic system and to ontology, is the price that manifestation demands. In language qua said everything is conveyed before us, be it at the price of a betrayal.[3] Language is ancillary and thus indispensable. At this moment language is serving a research conducted in view of disengaging the *otherwise than being* or *being's other* outside of the themes in which they already show themselves, unfaithfully, as being's *essence* – but in which they do show themselves. Language permits us to utter, be it by betrayal, this *outside of being*, this *ex-ception* to being, as though being's other were an event of being. Being, its cognition and the said in which it shows itself signify in a saying which, relative to being, forms an exception; but it is in the said that both this exception and the birth of cognition [la naissance de la connaissance] show themselves. But the fact that the ex-ception shows itself and becomes truth in the *said* can not serve as a pretext to take as an absolute the apophantic variant of the saying, which is ancillary or angelic.

An ancillary or angelic variant, however sublime it be, the apophantic form of the saying is only mediating. For thematization, in which being's essence is conveyed before us, and theory and thought, its contemporaries, do not attest to some fall of the saying. They are motivated by the pre-original vocation of the saying, by responsibility itself. We will see more of this further.[4]

But apophansis does not exhaust what there is in saying. The apophansis presupposes the language that answers with responsibility, and the gravity of this response is beyond the measure of being. The impossibility of declining responsibility is reflected only in the scruple or remorse which precedes or follows this refusal. The reality of the real ignores scruples. But, though naturally superficial, essence does not exclude the retreats of responsibility in the way that being excludes nothingness. And the gravity of the responsible saying retains a reference to being, whose nature will have to be made clear. Moral impossibility is not of lesser gravity; it does not situate responsibility in some low tension zone, at the confines of being and non-being. This gravity of the *otherwise than being* shows now, in a still confused way, its affinity with ethics. We have been seeking the *otherwise than being* from the beginning, and as soon as it is conveyed before us it is betrayed in the said that dominates the saying which states it. A methodological problem arises here, whether the pre-original element of saying (the anarchical, the non-original, as we designate it) can be led to betray itself by showing itself in a theme (if an an-archeology is possible), and whether this betrayal can be reduced; whether one can at the same time know and free the known of the marks which thematization leaves on it by subordinating it to ontology. Everything shows itself at the price of this betrayal, even the unsayable. In this betrayal the indiscretion with regard to the unsayable, which is probably the very task of philosophy, becomes possible.

When stated in propositions, the unsayable (or the an-archical) espouses the forms of formal logic;[5] the beyond being is posited in doxic theses, and glimmers in the amphibology of *being* and *beings* – in which beings dissimulate being. The *otherwise than being* is stated in a saying that must also be unsaid in order to thus extract the *otherwise than being* from the said in which it already comes to signify but a *being otherwise*. Does the beyond being which philosophy states, and states by reason of the very transcendence of the *beyond*, fall unavoidably into the forms of the ancillary statement?

Can this *saying* and this *being unsaid* be assembled, can they be at the same time? In fact to require this simultaneity is already to reduce being's *other* to *being* and *not being*. We must stay with the extreme situation of a diachronic thought. Skepticism, at the dawn of philosophy, set forth and betrayed the diachrony of this very conveying and betraying. To conceive the *otherwise than being* requires, perhaps, as much audacity as skepticism shows, when it does not hesitate to affirm the impossibility of statement while venturing to *realize* this impossibility by the very statement of this impossibility. If, after the innumerable "irrefutable" refutations which logical thought sets against it, skepticism has the gall to return (and it always returns as philosophy's illegitimate child), it is because in the contradiction which logic sees in it the "at the same time" of the contradictories is missing, because a secret diachrony commands this ambiguous or enigmatic way of speaking, and because in general signification signifies beyond synchrony, beyond essence.

8

4. SUBJECTIVITY

To conceive the otherwise than being we must try to articulate the break-up of a fate that reigns in essence, in that its fragments and modalities, despite their diversity, belong to one another, that is, do not escape the same order, do not escape Order, as though the bits of the thread cut by the Parque were then knotted together again. This effort will look beyond freedom. Freedom, an interruption of the determinism of war and matter, does not escape the fate in essence and takes place in time and in the history which assembles events into an *epos* and synchronizes them, revealing their immanence and their order.

The task is to conceive[6] of the possibility of a break out of essence. To go where? Toward what region? To stay on what ontological plane? But the extraction from essence contests the unconditional privilege of the question "where?"; it signifies a null-site [non-lieu]. The essence claims to recover and cover over every ex-ception – negativity, nihilation, and, already since Plato, non-being, which "in a certain sense is." It will then be necessary to show that the exception of the "other than being," beyond not-being, signifies subjectivity or humanity, the *oneself* which repels the annexations by essence. The ego is an incomparable unicity; it is outside of the community of genus and form, and does not find any rest in itself either, unquiet, not coinciding with itself. The outside of itself, the difference from oneself of this unicity is non-indifference itself, and the extraordinary recurrence of the pronominal or the reflexive, the *self* (*se*) – which no longer surprises us because it enters into the current flow of language in which things show *themselves*, suitcases fold and ideas are understood (les choses *se* montrent, les bagages *se* plient et les idées *se* comprennent). A unicity that has no site, without the ideal identity a being derives from the kerygma that identifies the innumerable aspects of its manifestation, without the identity of the ego that coincides with itself, a unicity withdrawing from essence – such is man.

The history of philosophy, during some flashes, has known this subjectivity that, as in an extreme youth, breaks with essence. From Plato's One without being to Husserl's pure Ego, transcendent in immanence, it has known the metaphysical extraction from being, even if, betrayed by the said, as by the effect of an oracle, the exception restored to the essence and to fate immediately fell back into the rules and led only to worlds behind the scenes. The Nietzschean man above all was such a moment. For Husserl's transcendental reduction will a putting between parentheses suffice – a type of writing, of commiting oneself with the world, which sticks like ink to the hands that push it off? One should have to go all the way to the nihilism of Nietzsche's poetic writing, reversing irreversible time in vortices, to the laughter which refuses language.

The philosopher finds language again in the abuses of language of the history of philosophy, in which the unsayable and what is beyond being are conveyed before us. But negativity, still correlative with being, will not be enough to signify the *other than being*.

5. RESPONSIBILITY FOR THE OTHER

But how, at the still temporal breaking point where being *comes to pass*, would being and time fall into ruins so as to disengage subjectivity from its essence? Do not the falling into ruins and the disengagement last; do they not occur in being? The *otherwise than being* cannot be situated in any eternal order extracted from time that would somehow command the temporal series. Kant has shown the impossibility of that in the antithesis of the fourth Antinomy. It is then the temporalization of time, in the way it signifies being and nothingness, life and death, that must also signify the *beyond being and not being*; it must signify a difference with respect to the couple being and nothingness. Time is essence and monstration of essence. In the temporalization of time the light comes about by the instant falling out of phase with itself – which is the temporal flow, the differing of the identical. The differing of the identical is also its manifestation. But time is also a recuperation of all divergencies, through retention, memory and history. In its temporalization, in which, thanks to retention, memory and history, nothing is lost, everything is presented or represented, everything is consigned and lends itself to inscription, or is synthetized or, as Heidegger would say, assembled, in which everything is crystallized or sclerosized into substance – in the recuperating temporalization, without time lost, without time to lose, and where the being of substance comes to pass – there must be signaled a lapse of time that does not return, a diachrony refractory to all synchronization, a transcending diachrony.

The meaning of this signalling will have to be clarified. Can it preserve a relationship across the break of the diachrony, without, however, restoring to representation this "deep formerly" as a past that had flowed on, without signifying a "modification" of the present and thus a commencement, a principle that would be thematizable, and therefore would be the origin of every historical or recallable past? Can it, on the contrary, remain foreign to every present, every representation, and thus signify a past more ancient than every representable origin, a pre-original and anarchical *passed*? The signalling of this pre-original past in the present would not again be an ontological relation.

But if time is to show an ambiguity of being and the otherwise than being, its temporalization is to be conceived not as essence, but as saying. Essence fills the said, or the epos, of the saying, but the saying, in its power of equivocation, that is, in the enigma whose secret it keeps, escapes the epos of essence that includes it and signifies beyond in a signification that hesitates between this beyond and the return to the epos of essence. This equivocation or enigma is an inalienable power in saying and a modality of transcendence.[7] Subjectivity is a node and a denouement – of essence and essence's other.

But how is the saying, in its primordial enigma, said? How is time temporalized such that the dia-chrony of transcendence, of the other than being, is signalled? How can transcendence withdraw from *esse* while being signalled in it? In what concrete case is the singular relationship with a past produced, which does not reduce this past to the immanence in which it is signalled and leaves it be past, not returning as a present nor a representation, leaves it be past without reference to some present it would have "modified," leaves it be a past, then, which can not have been an origin, a pre-original past, anarchical past?

A linear regressive movement, a retrospective back along the temporal series toward a very remote past, would never be able to reach the absolutely diachronous pre-original which cannot be recuperated by memory and history. But it may be that we have to unravel other intrigues of time than that of the simple succession of presents. Men have been able to be thankful for the very fact of finding themselves able to thank; the present gratitude is grafted onto itself as onto an already antecedent gratitude. In a prayer in which the worshipper asks that his prayer be heard, the prayer as it were precedes or follows itself.

But the relationship with a past that is on the hither side of every present and every re-presentable, for not belonging to the order of presence, is included in the extraordinary and everyday event of my responsibility for the faults or the misfortune of others, in my responsibility that answers for the freedom of another, in the astonishing human fraternity in which fraternity, conceived with Cain's sober coldness, would not by itself explain the responsibility between separated beings it calls for. The freedom of another could never begin in my freedom, that is, abide in the same present, be contemporary, be representable to me. The responsibility for the other can not have begun in my commitment, in my decision. The unlimited responsibility in which I find myself comes from the hither side of my freedom, from a "prior to every memory," an "ulterior to every accomplishment," from the non-present par excellence, the non-original, the anarchical, prior to or beyond essence. The responsibility for the other is the locus in which is situated the null-site of subjectivity, where the privilege of the question "Where?" no longer holds. The time of the *said* and of *essence* there lets the pre-original saying be heard, answers to transcendence, to a dia-chrony, to the irreducible divergency that opens here between the non-present and every representable divergency, which in its own way – a way to be clarified – makes a sign to the responsible one.

6. ESSENCE AND SIGNIFICATION

But is not the relationship with this pre-original a recuperation? Let us look into this more closely. The response of the responsible one does not thematize the diachronical as though it were retained, remembered or historically reconstructed. It can not thematize or comprehend. Not out of weakness; to what could not be contained there corresponds no capacity. The non-present is in-comprehendable by reason of its immensity or its "superlative" humility or. for example, its goodness, which is the superlative itself. The non-present here is invisible, separated (or sacred) and thus a non-origin, an-archical. The Good cannot become present or enter into a representation. The present is a beginning in my freedom, whereas the Good is not presented to freedom; it has chosen me before I have chosen it. No one is good voluntarily. We can see the formal structure of nonfreedom in a subjectivity which does not have time to choose the Good and thus is penetrated with its rays unbeknownst to itself. But subjectivity sees this nonfreedom redeemed, exceptionally, by the goodness of the Good. The exception is unique. And if no one is good voluntarily, no one is enslaved to the Good.[8]

Immemorial, unrepresentable, invisible, the past that bypasses the present, the pluperfect past, falls into a past that is a gratuitous lapse. It can not be recuperated by reminiscence not because of its remoteness, but because of its incommensurability with the present. The present is essence that begins and ends, beginning and end assembled in a thematizable conjunction; it is the finite in correlation with a freedom. Diachrony is the refusal of conjunction, the non-totalizable, and in this sense, infinite. But in the responsibility for the Other, for another freedom, the negativity of this anarchy, this refusal of the present, of appearing, of the immemorial, commands me and ordains me to the other, to the first one on the scene, and makes me approach him, makes me his neighbor. It thus diverges from nothingness as well as from being. It provokes this responsibility against my will, that is, by substituting me for the other as a hostage. All my inwardness is invested in the form of a despite-me, for-another. Despite-me, for-another, is signification par excellence. And it is the sense of the "oneself," that accusative that derives from no nominative;[9] it is the very fact of finding oneself while losing oneself.

What is exceptional in this way of being signalled is that I am ordered toward the face of the other. In this order which is an ordination the non-presence of the infinite is not only a figure of negative theology. All the negative attributes which state what is beyond the essence become positive in responsibility, a response answering to a non-thematizable provocation and thus a non-vocation, a trauma. This response answers, before any understanding, for a debt contracted before any freedom and before any consciousness and any present, but it does answer, as though the invisible that bypasses the present left a trace by the very fact of bypassing the present. That trace lights up as the face of a neighbor, ambiguously him *before whom* (or *to whom*, without any paternalism) and him *for whom* I answer. For such is the enigma or ex-ception of a face, judge and accused.

What is positive in responsibility, outside of essence, conveys the infinite. It inverses relationships and principles, reverses the order of interest: in the measure that responsibilities are taken on they multiply. This is not a *Sollen* commanding the infinite pursuit of an ideal. The infinity of the infinite lives in going backwards. The debt increases in the measures that it is paid. This divergency perhaps deserves the name glory. The positivity of the infinite is the conversion of the response to the infinite into responsibility, into approach of the other. The Infinite is non-thematizable, gloriously exceeds every capacity, and manifests, as it were in reverse, its exorbitance in the approach of a neighbor, obedient to its measure. Subjectivity, prior to or beyond the free and the non-free, obliged with regard to the neighbor, is the breaking point where essence is exceeded by the infinite.

It is the breaking-point, but also the binding place; the glow of a trace is enigmatic, equivocal. It is so in still another sense, which distinguishes it from the appearing of phenomena. It cannot serve as the point of departure for a demonstration, which inexorably would bring it into immanence and essence. A trace is sketched out and effaced in a face in the equivocation of a saying. In this way it modulates the modality of the transcendent.[10]

The infinite then cannot be tracked down like game by a hunter. The trace left by the infinite is not the residue of a presence; its very glow is ambiguous. Otherwise, its positivity would not preserve the infinity of the infinite any more than negativity would.

The infinite wipes out its traces not in order to trick him who obeys, but because it transcends the present in which it commands me, and because I cannot deduce it from this command. The infinite who orders me is neither a cause acting straight on, nor a theme, already dominated, if only retrospectively, by freedom. This detour at a face and this detour from this detour in the enigma of a trace we have called illeity.[11]

Illeity lies outside the "thou" and the thematization of objects. A neologism formed with *il* (he) or *ille*, it indicates a way of concerning me without entering into conjunction with me. To be sure, we have to indicate the element in which this *concerning* occurs. If the relationship with illeity were a relationship of consciousness, "he" would designate a theme, as the "thou" in Buber's I-thou relation does, probably – for Buber has never brought out in a positive way the spiritual element in which the I-thou relationship is produced. The illeity in the beyond-being is the fact that its coming toward me is a departure which lets me accomplish a movement toward a neighbor. The positive element of this departure, that which makes this departure, this diachrony, be more than a term of negative theology, is my responsibility for the others. Or, one may say, it is the fact that the others show themselves in their face. There is a paradox in responsibility, in that I am obliged without this obligation having begun in me, as though an order slipped into my consciousness like a thief, smuggled itself in, like an effect of one of Plato's wandering causes. But this is impossible in a consciousness, and clearly indicates that we are no longer in the element of consciousness. In consciousness this "who knows where" is translated into an anachronical overwhelming, the antecedence of responsibility and obedience with respect to the order received or the contract. It is as though the first movement of responsibility could not consist in awaiting nor even in welcoming the order (which would still be a quasi-activity), but consists in obeying this order before it is formulated. Or as though it were formulated before every possible present, in a past that shows itself in the present of obedience without being recalled, without coming from memory, being formulated by him who obeys in his very obedience.

But this is still perhaps a quite narrative, epic, way of speaking. Am I the interlocutor of an infinity lacking in straightforwardness, giving its commands indirectly in the very face to which it ordains me? Illeity, which does not simply designate an oblique presentation to a squinting look, may indeed first signify such a disposition of personages. But we must go all the way. The infinite does not signal itself to a subjectivity, a unity already formed, by its order to turn toward the neighbor. In its *being* subjectivity undoes *essence* by substituting itself for another. Qua one-for-another, it is absorbed in signification, in saying or the verb form of the infinite. Signification precedes essence. It is not a stage of cognition calling for the intuition that would fulfill it, nor the absurdity of nonidentity or of impossible identity. It is the glory of transcedence.

Substitution is signification. Not a reference from one term to another, as it appears thematized in the said, but substitution as the very subjectivity of a subject, interruption of the irreversible identity of the essence. It occurs in the taking charge of, which is incumbent on me without any escape possible. Here the unicity of the ego first acquires a meaning – where it is no longer a question of the ego, but of me. The subject which is not an ego, but which I am, cannot be generalized, is not a subject in general; we have moved from the ego to me who am me and no one else.[12] Here the identity of the subject comes from the impossibility of escaping responsibility, from the taking charge of the other. Signification, saying – my expressivity, my own signifyingness qua sign, my own verbality qua verb – cannot be understood as a modality of being; the disinterestedness suspends essence. As a substitution of one for another, as me, a man, I am not a transubstantiation, a changing from one substance into another, I do not shut myself up in another identity, I do not rest in a new avatar. As signification, proximity, saying, separation, I do not fuse with anything. Have we to give a name to this relationship of signification grasped as subjectivity? Must we pronounce the word expiation, and conceive the subjectivity of the subject, the otherwise than being, as an expiation? That would perhaps be bold and premature. At least we can ask if subjectivity qua signification, qua one-for-another, is not traceable back to the vulnerability of the ego, to the incommunicable, non-conceptualizable, sensibility.

7. SENSIBILITY

Man is not to be conceived in function of being and not-being, taken as ultimate references. Humanity, subjectivity – the excluded middle, excluded from everywhere, null-site – signify the breakup of this alternative, the one-in-the-place-of-another, substitution, signification in its signifyingness qua sign, prior to essence, before identity. Signification, prior to being, breaks up the assembling, the recollection or the present of essence. On the hither side of or beyond essence, signification is the breathlessness of the spirit expiring without inspiring, disinterestedness and gratuity or gratitude; the breakup of essence is ethics. This beyond is said, and is conveyed in discourse, by a saying out of breath or retaining its breath, the extreme possibility of the spirit, its very epoché, by which it *says* before resting in its own theme and therein allowing itself to be absorbed by essence. This breakup of identity, this changing of being into signification, that is, into substitution, is the subject's subjectivity, or its subjection to everything, its susceptibility, its vulnerability, that is, its sensibility.

Subjectivity, locus and null-site of this breakup, comes to pass as a passivity more passive than all passivity. To the diachronic past, which cannot be recuperated by representation effected by memory or history, that is, incommensurable with the present, corresponds or answers the unassumable passivity of the self. "*Se passer*" – to come to pass – is for us a precious expression in which the *self* (*se*) figures as in a past that bypasses itself, as in ageing without "active synthesis." The response which is responsibility,

responsibility for the neighbor that is incumbent, resounds in this passivity, this disinterestedness of subjectivity, this sensibility.

Vulnerability, exposure to outrage, to wounding, passivity more passive than all patience, passivity of the accusative form, trauma of accusation suffered by a hostage to the point of persecution, implicating the identity of the hostage who substitutes himself for the others: all this is the self, a defecting or defeat of the ego's identity. And this, pushed to the limit, is sensibility, sensibility as the subjectivity of the subject. It is a substitution for another, one in the place of another, expiation.[13]

Responsibility for the other, in its antecedence to my freedom, its antecedence to the present and to representation, is a passivity more passive than all passivity, an exposure to the other without this exposure being assumed, an exposure without holding back, exposure of exposedness, expression, saying. This exposure is the frankness, sincerity, veracity of saying. Not saying dissimulating itself and protecting itself in the said, just giving out words in the face of the other, but saying uncovering itself, that is, denuding itself of its skin, sensibility on the surface of the skin, at the edge of the nerves, offering itself even in suffering – and thus wholly sign, signifying itself. Substitution, at the limit of being, ends up in saying, in the giving of signs, giving a sign of this giving of signs, expressing oneself. This expression is antecedent to all thematization in the said, but it is not a babbling or still primitive or childish form of saying. This stripping beyond nudity, beyond forms, is not the work of negation and no longer belongs to the order of being. Responsibility goes beyond being. In sincerity, in frankness, in the veracity of this saying, in the uncoveredness of suffering. being is altered. But this saying remains, in its activity, a passivity, more passive than all passivity, for it is a sacrifice without reserve, without holding back, and in this non-voluntary – the sacrifice of a hostage designated who has not chosen himself to be hostage, but possibly elected by the Good, in an involuntary election not assumed by the elected one. For the Good can not enter into a present nor be put into a representation. But being Good it redeems the violence of its alterity, even if the subject has to suffer through the augmentation of this ever more demanding violence.

8. BEING AND BEYOND BEING

The proximity of one to the other is here conceived outside of ontological categories in which, in different ways, the notion of the *other* also figures, whether as an obstacle to freedom, intelligibility or perfection, or as a term that confirms a finite being, mortal and uncertain of itself, by recognizing

.

it, or as a slave, collaborator or God able to succour. Everywhere proximity is conceived ontologically, that is, as a limit or complement to the accomplishment of the adventure of essence, which consists in persisting in essence and unfolding immanence, in remaining in an ego, in identity. Proximity remains a distance diminished, an exteriority conjured. The present study sets out to not conceive proximity in function of being. The *otherwise than being* which, to be sure, is understood in a being, differs absolutely from essence, has no genus in common with essence, and is said only in the breathlessness that pronounces the extra-ordinary word *beyond.* Alterity figures in it outside any qualification of the other for the ontological order and outside any attribute. It figures as what is near in a proximity that counts as sociality, which "excites" by its pure and simple proximity. We have sought to analyze this relation without resorting to categories that dissimulate it, by conceiving it in terms of proximity qua saying, contact, sincerity of exposure, a saying prior to language, but without which no language, as a transmission of messages, would be possible.

The way of thinking proposed here does not fail to recognize being or treat it, ridiculously and pretentiously, with disdain, as the fall from a higher order or disorder. On the contrary, it is on the basis of proximity that being takes on its just meaning. In the indirect ways of illeity, in the anarchical provocation which ordains me to the other, is imposed the way which leads to thematization, and to an act of consciousness. The act of consciousness is motivated by the presence of a third party alongside of the neighbor approached. A third party is also approached; and the relationship between the neighbor and the third party cannot be indifferent to me when I approach. There must be a justice among incomparable ones. There must then be a comparison between incomparables and a synopsis, a togetherness and contemporaneousness; there must be thematization, thought, history and inscription. But being must be understood on the basis of *being's other.* To be on the ground of the signification of an approach is to be *with another* for or against a third party, with the other and the third party against oneself, in justice. This way of thinking is against a philosophy which does not see beyond being, and reduces, by an abuse of language, saying to the said and all sense to interest. Reason, to which the virtue of arresting violence is ascribed, issuing in the order of peace, presupposes disinterestedness, passivity or patience. In this disinterestedness, when, as a responsibility for the other, it is also a responsibility for the third party, the justice that compares, assembles and conceives, the synchrony of being and peace, take form.

17

9. SUBJECTIVITY IS NOT A MODALITY OF ESSENCE

The problem of transcendence and of God and the problem of subjectivity irreducible to essence, irreducible to essential immanence, go together. Without resorting to the truism that all reality that is in any way recognized is subjective, a truism that goes with the one that says that everything that is in any way recognized presupposes the comprehension of being, Kant, by distinguishing in the course of the solution of the Antinomies the temporal series of experience from the in-temporal (or synchronic?) series conceived by the understanding of the other, has shown in the very objectivity of an object its phenomenality: a reference to the fundamental incompletion of the succession, and hence to the subjectivity of the subject.

But is subjectivity thus conceived in what is irreducibly its own? Hegel and Heidegger try to empty the distinction between the subject and being of its meaning. In reintroducing time into being they denounce the idea of a subjectivity irreducible to essence, and, starting with the object inseparable from the subject, go on to reduce their correlation, and the anthropological order understood in these terms, to a modality of being. In the Introduction to the *Phenomenology of Mind*, in treating as a "pure presupposition" the thesis that knowing is an instrument to take hold of the Absolute (a technological metaphor) or a medium through which the light of truth penetrates the knower (a dioptic metaphor), Hegel denies that there is a radical break between subjectivity and the knowable. It is in the midst of the Absolute that the *beyond* takes on meaning; essence, understood as the immanence of a knowing, is taken to account for subjectivity, which is reduced to a moment of the concept, of thought or of absolute essence. Heidegger says, in a remark at the end of his *Nietzsche* (Vol. II, p. 451), that the "current term subjectivity immediately and too obstinately burdens thought with deceptive opinions that take as a destruction of objective being any reference from Being to man and especially to his egoity." Heidegger tries to conceive subjectivity in function of Being, of which it expresses an "epoque":[14] subjectivity, consciousness, the ego presuppose Dasein, which belongs to essence as the mode in which essence manifests itself. But the manifestation of essence is what is essential in essence; experience and the subject having the experience constitute the very manner in which at a given "epoque" of essence, essence is accomplished, that is, is manifested. Every overcoming as well as every revaluing of Being in the subject would still be a case of Being's essence.

Our inquiry concerned with the *otherwise than being* catches sight, in the very hypostasis of a subject, its subjectification, of an ex-ception; a null-site on the hither side of the negativity which is always speculatively recuperable, an *outside* of the absolute which can no longer be stated in terms of being. Nor even in terms of entities, which one would suspect modulate being, and thus heal the break marked by the hypostasis. The subject already resists this ontologization when it is conceived as a saying. Behind every statement of being as being, the saying overflows the very being it thematizes in stating it to the other. It is being which is understood in the – first or last – word, but the last saying goes *beyond* the being thematized or totalized. Irreducible to being's essence is the substitution in responsibility, signification or the one-for-another, or the defecting of the ego beyond every defeat, going countercurrent to a *conatus*, or goodness. In it the other is imposed quite differently from the reality of the real: he imposes himself because he is other, because this alterity is incumbent on me with a whole charge of indigence and weakness. Can substitution and goodness in turn be interpreted as a "movement" or a modality of being's essence? Would it yet move in the light of being? But is the sight of a face in the light of being? Is not sight here immediately a taking charge? The intention *toward another*, when it has reached its peak, turns out to belie intentionality. *Toward another* culminates in a *for another*, a suffering for his suffering, without light, that is, without measure, quite different from the purely negative blinding of Fortune which only seems to close her eyes so as to give her richess arbitrarily. Arising at the apex of essence, goodness is *other* than being. It no longer keeps accounts; it is not like negativity, which conserves what it negates, in its history. It destroys without leaving souvenirs, without transporting into museums the altars raised to the idols of the past for blood sacrifices, it burns the sacred groves in which the echoes of the past reverberate. The exceptional, extra-ordinary, transcendent character of goodness is due to just this break with being and history. To reduce the good to being, to its calculations and its history, is to nullify goodness. The ever possible sliding between subjectivity and being, of which subjectivity would be but a mode, the equivalence of the two languages, stops here. Goodness gives to subjectivity its irreducible signification.

The human subject – me – called on the brink of tears and laughter to responsibility, is not an avatar of nature or a moment of the concept, or an articulation of "being's presence to us," or parousia. It is not a question of assuring the ontological dignity of man, as though essence sufficed for dignity, but of contesting the philosophical privilege of being, of inquiring after what is beyond or on its hither side. To reduce men to self-consciousness and self-consciousness to the concept, that is, to history, to deduce from the concept and from history the subjectivity and the "I" in order to find meaning for the very singularity of "that one" in function of the concept, by neglecting, as contingent, what may be left irreducible after this reduction, what residue there may be after this deduction, is, under the pretext of not caring about the inefficacity of "good intentions" and "fine

souls" and preferring "the effort of concepts" to the facilities of psychological naturalism, humanist rhetoric and existentialist pathetics, to forget
what is better than being, that is, the Good.

The beyond being, *being's other* or the *otherwise than being*, here situated in diachrony, here expressed as infinity, has been recognized as the
Good by Plato. It matters little that Plato made of it an idea and a light
source. The beyond being, showing itself in the said, always shows itself
there enigmatically, is already betrayed. Its resistance to assemblage, conjunction and conjuncture, to contemporaneousness, immanence, the present of manifestation, signifies the diachrony of responsibility for another
and of the "deep formerly," more ancient than all freedom, which commands it, while, in a present statement, they are synchronized. This diachrony is itself an enigma: the beyond being does and does not revert to
ontology; the statement, the beyond, the infinite, becomes and does not
become a meaning of being.

10. THE ITINERARY

The different concepts that come up in the attempt to state transcendence
echo one another. The necessities of thematization in which they are said
ordain a division into chapters, although the themes in which these concepts present themselves do not lend themselves to linear exposition, and
cannot be really isolated from one another without projecting their shadows and their reflections on one another. Perhaps the clarity of the exposition does not suffer here only from the clumsiness of the expounder.

The exposition is worked out between the present argument, which
introduces it, and the final chapter, which, as conclusion, elucidates it in a
different way.

It aims to disengage the subjectivity of the subject from reflections on
truth, time and being in the amphibology of being and entities which is
borne by the said; it will then present the subject, in saying, as a sensibility
from the first animated by responsibilities (Chapter II). Then it will set out
to show proximity to be the sense of the sensibility (Chapter III), substitution as the *otherwise than being* at the basis of proximity (Chapter IV),
and as a relationship between a subject and infinity, in which infinity
comes to pass (Chapter V). In bringing out substitution in the saying which
is in responsibility, it will then have to justify, starting with this saying
which is in substitution, the order of the said, thought, justice and being,
and to understand the conditions in which philosophy, in the said, in
ontology, can signify truth. It will do so by linking to the alternating fate
of skepticism in philosophical thought – refuted and coming back

again – the alternatings or diachrony, resisting assemblage, of the *otherwise than being* or transcendence, and its exposition.

Is the itinerary whose stages we have just indicated sufficiently reliable? Is its beginning indeed accessible? Will the reproach not be made that this movement is not sufficiently warned of the dangers on the way and has not provided itself with means to ward them off? No doubt it is not completely disengaged from pre-philosophical experiences, and many of its byways will appear well-worn, many of its thrusts imprudent. But a fine risk is always something to be taken in philosophy. That the beginning of the silent discourse of the soul with itself can be justified only by its end is a still optimistic conception of philosophical discourse which a genius, and a synthetic genius, such as Hegel can permit himself, assured as he is of being able to complete the cycle of thought. Hegel will ask, no doubt rightly, if a preface in which the project of a philosophical enterprise is formulated is not superfluous or even obscurantist, and Heidegger will contest the possibility of an introduction where the movement begins in Being instead of coming from man, where it is not a question of leading man to the presence of Being, but where Being is in the presence of man in parousia. Should we not think with as much precaution of the possibility of a conclusion or a closure of the philosophical discourse? Is not its interruption its only possible end? More modestly, Husserl will have taught us that every movement of thought involves a part of naivety, which, in the Hegelian enterprise, lies at least in its pretention to include the Real. Husserl will have taught us that the reduction of naivety immediately calls for new reductions, that the grace of intuition involves gratuitous ideas, and that, if philosophizing consists in assuring onself of an absolute origin, the philosopher will have to efface the trace of his own footsteps and unendingly efface the traces of the effacing of the traces, in an interminable methodological movement staying where it is. Unless, that is, the naivety of the philosopher not call, beyond the reflection on oneself, for the critique exercized by *another* philosopher, whatever be the imprudences that that one will have committed in his turn, and the gratuity of his own saying. Philosophy thus arouses a drama between philosophers and an intersubjective movement which does not resemble the dialogue of teamworkers in science, nor even the Platonic dialogue which is the reminiscence of a drama rather than the drama itself. It is sketched out in a different structure; empirically it is realized as the history of philosophy in which new interlocutors always enter who have to restate, but in which the former ones take up the floor to answer in the interpretations they arouse, and in which, nonetheless, despite this lack of "certainty in one's movements" or because of it, no one is allowed a relaxation of attention or a lack of strictness.

THE EXPOSITION

CHAPTER II

INTENTIONALITY AND SENSING

1. QUESTIONING AND ALLEGIANCE TO THE OTHER

A philosopher seeks, and expresses, truth. Truth, before characterizing a statement or a judgment, consists in the exhibition of being. But what shows itself, in truth, under the name of being? And who looks? What shows itself under the name being? This name is not unequivocal. Is it a noun or a verb? Does the word being designate an entity, ideal or real, that is, or this entity's *process of being*, its *essence*?[1] And does this word *designate*? No doubt it does designate. But does it only designate? For if it only designates, then, even taken as a verb, it is a noun. And the process captured by the designation, even if it is a movement, shows itself, but is immobilized and fixed *in the said*. Does the mystery of being and entities, their difference, disturb us already? The distinction and the amphibology of being and entities will turn out from the start to be important and to be determinant for truth, but this distinction is also an amphibology and does not signify the ultimate. If this difference shows itself in the said, in words (which are not epiphenomenal), if it belongs to *monstration* as such, it belongs on the same plane as being, whose hide-and-seek game is indeed essential. But if monstration is a modality of signification, we would have to go back from the *said* to the *saying*. The said and the non-said do not absorb all the saying, which remains on this side of, or goes beyond, the said.

But let us for the moment stay with what is implied in the general meaning of truth. The question "*what* shows itself?" is put by him *who* looks, even before he thematically distinguishes the difference between being and entities. The question enunciates a "what?" "what is it?" "what is it that it is?" Concerning what is it wants to know *what* it is. The "what?" is already wholly enveloped with being, has eyes only for being, and already sinks into being. Concerning the *being* of what is, it wants to know what it is. The question – even "what is being?" – then questions with respect to being, with respect to what is precisely in question. The answer required is from the start in terms of being, whether one understands by it *entity* or *being of entities*, entity or being's *essence*. The question "what?" is thus correlative of what it wishes to discover, and already has recourse to it. Its quest occurs entirely within being, in the midst of what it is seeking. It is ontology, and at the same time has a part in the effectuation of the very being it seeks to understand. If the question "what?" in its adherence to being is at the origin of all thought (can it be otherwise, as long as thought proceeds by determinate terms?), all research and all philosophy go back to ontology, to the understanding of the being of entities, the understanding of essence. Being would be not only what is most problematical; it would be what is most intelligible.

And yet, this intelligibility is questionable. That intelligibility would become questionable is something surprising. Here is a problem preliminary to the questions "who?" and "what?"[2] Why is there a question in exhibition?

One could immediately answer that there is a question because there is an inquiry, and because the appearing of being is also the possibility of its appearance, and appearance dissimulates being in its very disclosure. The search for truth has to draw being out of appearance. Or else – but is it not the same thing? – there is a question because every manifestation is partial, and in that sense apparent, whereas truth cannot be fractioned without being altered. Consequently truth is a progression, and is exposed in several moments, remaining problematical in each. Yet the question about the question is more radical still. Why does research take form as a question? How is it that the "what?", already steeped in being so as to open it up the more, becomes a demand and a prayer, a special language inserting into the "communication" of the given an appeal for help, for aid addressed to another?

The problem is not aroused, like a bad quarrel, by a capricious or curios or industrious subject approaching being, which would be non-problematical in itself. But it is not necessary to take literally the metaphor of the interpellation of the subject by being which manifests itself. The manifestation of being, the appearing, is indeed the primary event, but *the very primacy of the primary is in the presence of the present.* A past more ancient than any present, a past which was never present and whose anarchical antiquity was never given in the play of dissimulations and manifestations, a past whose *other* signification remains to be described, signifies over and beyond the manifestation of being, which thus would convey but a moment of this signifying signification. In the diachrony which turned up under our pen above, with regard to the progressiveness of manifestation, one can suspect there is the interval that separates the same from the other, an interval that is reflected in manifestation. For manifestation, which one might have thought to be by right a fulgurating instant of openness and intuition, is discontinuous, and lasts from a question to the response. But this leads us to surprise the Who that is looking, the identical subject, allegedly placed in the openness of Being, as the crux of a diachronic plot (which remains to be determined) between the same and the other. The silent coming and going from question to response, with which Plato characterized thought, already refers to a plot in which is tied up the node of subjectivity, by the other commanding the same. The reference is there even when, turned toward being in its manifestation, thought knows itself. Asking oneself and questioning oneself does not undo the torsion of the same and the other in subjectivity; it refers to it. There is an intrigue of the other in the same which does not amount to an openness of the other to the same. The other to whom the petition of the question is addressed does not belong to the intelligible sphere to be explored. He stands in proximity. Here is where the *quis*-nity of the "what" excepts itself from the ontological quiddity of the "what" sought which orients the research. The same has to do with the other before the other appears in any way to a consciousness. Subjectivity is structured as the other in the same, but in a way different from that of consciousness. Consciousness is always correlative with a theme, a present represented, a theme put before me, a being which is a phenomenon. The way subjectivity is structured as the other in the same differs from that of consciousness, which is consciousness of being, however indirect, tenuous and inconsistent this relationship between consciousness and its theme "placed" before it may be – a perception of a presence "in flesh and bone," – a figuration of an image, symbolization of a symbolized, a transparency and a veiling of the fugitive and the unstable in an allusion, a divination incapable of objectification, but aspiring to objectification and thus a consciousness – and thus consciousness of being.

Subjectivity is the other in the same, in a way that also differs from that of the presence of interlocutors to one another in a dialogue, in which they are at peace and in agreement with one another. The other in the same determinative of subjectivity is the restlessness of the same disturbed by the other. This is not the correlation characteristic of intentionality, nor even that of dialogue, which attests to essence by its essential reciprocity. The folding back of being upon itself, and the self formed by this fold, where the effect of being remains correlative with being, also does not go to the crux of subjectivity.

The knot tied in subjectivity, which when subjectivity become a consciousness of being is still attested to in questioning, signifies an allegiance of the same to the other, imposed before any exhibition of the other, preliminary to all consciousness — or a being affected by the other whom I do not know and who could not justify himself with any identity, who as other will not identify himself with anything. This allegiance will be described as a responsibility of the same for the other, as a response to his proximity before any question. In this responsibility the latent birth of consciousness itself as a perception or listening in to being, can be surprised, and dialogue based on questioning.

Being then would not be the construction of a cognitive subject, contrary to what idealism claims. The subject opening to the thought and truth of being, as it incontestably does, opens upon a way quite different from that which lets the subject be seen as an ontology or an understanding of being. Being would not derive from cognition. This not coming from cognition has a quite different meaning than ontology supposes. Being and cognition together signify in the proximity of the other and in a certain modality of my responsibility for the other, this response preceding any question, this saying before the said.

Being signifies on the basis of the one-for-the-other, of substitution of the same for the other. Both being and the vision of being refer to a subject that has risen earlier than being and cognition, earlier than and on this side of them, in an immemorial time which a reminiscene could not recuperate as an a priori. The "birth" of being in the questioning where the cognitive subject stands would thus refer to a *before the questioning*, to the anarchy of responsibility, as it were on this side of all birth. We will try, with the notion of the saying without the said, to expose such a modality of the subjective, an *otherwise than being*. How many conditionals here! What singular eventualities! We will have to answer for the liberties that we are thus taking with the eventual as though there were no risks, forgetting the first pages and the warnings of the Introduction to the *Phenomenology of Mind*. At least the first indications of these eventualities permit us to announce the orientation of this chapter, which does not begin by running up against the finitude of the subject devoted to the relativity of a forever unfinished science. Instead, in this very finitude, taken as an outcome of the-one-for-the-other structure characteristic of proximity, we already catch sight of the excellence, the height and the signification, of responsibility, that is, of sociality, an order to which finite truth – being and consciousness – are subordinate.

2. QUESTIONING AND BEING: TIME AND REMINISCENCE

If one is deaf to the petition that sounds in questioning and even under the apparent silence of the thought that questions itself, everything in a question will be oriented to truth, and will come from the essence of being. Then one will have to stay with the design of this ontology, even if in certain of its implications inflexions of forgotten voices resound. To ontology, the exposition of being in its amphibology of being and entitles, belong time and language, inasmuch as language, assembling the dispersion of duration into nouns and propositions, lets being and entities be heard. In this said, we nonetheless surprise the echo of the saying, whose signification cannot be assembled.

We have shown that the question "What shows itself in truth?" questions the being that exhibits itself in terms of this being. The question "who is looking?" is also ontological. Who is this *who*? In this form the question asks that "the looker" be identified with one of the beings already known, even if the answer to the question "Who is looking?" should be stated in the monosyllabic "Me," without any content, wholly an emission of signs, from the first a "me who...," but in fact "me who am known to you," "me whose voice you find in your memories," or "me who could situate myself in the system of your history." If the question "who?" tends to discover the situation of the subject, that is, the place of a person in a conjuncture, a conjunction of beings and things – or if it consists in asking, as Plato puts it in the *Phaedrus* (denouncing those who, already philologists, instead of listening to a statement, ask about the one that states it) "who is it?" "from what land does he come?" – then the question "who?" asks about being. Such a "who?" amounts to a "what?", to "what about him?" It goes back to that, or gets lost in it. The difference between "who?" and "what?" which is reflected in vocabulary and grammar would be only eidetic or essential, motivated by the nature or mode of being of the entity that is problematical. And the logical supremacy of the "what?" in the said abolishes this difference. The logos as said, a revelation of being in its amphibology of being and entities, lets the "who?" get lost in the "what?" It lets it get lost in it still more evidently in our questioning "who is looking?", which does not ask about such a one or other, but about the essence of the "who that is looking" in its generality. In the "who is this *who*?" it asks "what about this *who*?" to which the look turned on being is given. Thus on all sides the privilege of the question "what?", or the ontological nature of the problem is affirmed.

This privilege means that, in all cases, in asking ourselves, with regard to truth: "who is looking at being manifesting itself in truth?", the welcoming of the manifestation of being could not take place outside of the being that manifests itself. The response to the question "who is looking?" then could in its turn signify only the exposition of essence: the subject of the look will be a thinking being, in a strict correlation with its object, belonging to the subject-object unity. Moreover, how, if one starts with the notion of the truth, could one place the welcoming of the manifestation of being outside of the being that manifests itself? Can he that looks place himself outside of the Absolute, and the look withdraw from the event of being, by hollowing out the fold of inwardness, in which knowledge is deposited, accumulates and is formulated? But then things would happen outside of being, and there would still be being there, which seems to be contradictory in its terms. We are not yet in a position to see clearly in this semblance, still less to reduce it, even if we suspect that there is in the position in which the folding back of being upon itself, or subjectivity, is produced something else than this reflection. It is then necessary that the one to whom being shows itself still belongs to being, and that looking amounts to being.

The exposition or exhibition of being would, however, then be falsified. The spectator and the speculation "would not be in on it," would be excluded from what shows itself, dissimulated in a "hither side." The "hither side" would indeed not be a region in which the "who" aroused by the exhibition would get lost, but it would remain a modality of being, a way of withdrawing, of excepting oneself, of drawing back without disappearing, of drawing back into the night of a oneself. Is the "who" – the spectator, the subjectivity, the soul – exhausted in this process of interiorization? Or is interiorization all there is in the negativity of "not showing oneself?" That is in fact our problem: what does "who?" mean? But if the inwardness were an absolute exception, the being discovered in truth would be truncated of its inwardness; it would be in truth partly dissimulated, apparent and non-true.

It is then necessary, in order that truth come about, that in one way or another this ex-ception of inwardness be recuperated, that the exception enter under the rule, that within the being exposed be found the subject of knowledge, and the pulsation and respiration of the "soul" belong to or come back to being as a whole. Truth can consist only in the exposition of being to itself, in self-consciousness. The upsurge of a subjectivity, a soul, a "who," remains correlative with being, that is, simultaneous and one with it. The mutation of the exhibition into knowledge has to be interpretable as a certain inflexion of this exhibition. The soul would live only for the disclosure of being which arouses it or provokes it; it would be a moment of the life of the Spirit, that is, of Being-totality, leaving nothing outside of itself, the same finding again the same. But the manifestation of being to itself would imply a separation in being. The manifestation cannot occur as a fulguration in which the totality of being shows itself to the totality of being, for this "showing itself to" indicates a getting out of phase which is precisely time, that astonishing divergence of the identical from itself!

The getting out of phase of the instant, the "all" pulling off from the "all" – the temporality of time – makes possible, however, a recuperation in which nothing is lost. There is a disclosing of being; disengaged from its identity, from itself (what we are here calling a getting out of phase) and rediscoveries of truth; between what shows itself and the aim it fulfills, there is monstration. There is the same as this aim and the same as discovered, only discovered and *amounting to the same* — truth. Time is needed, the remission of the immobile eternity, of the immanence of the whole in the whole, in order that there be established the new tension, unique in its kind, through which intentionality or thought is awakened in being. Truth is rediscovery, recall, reminiscence, reuniting under the unity of apperception. There is remission of time and tension of the recapture, relaxation and tension without a break, without a gap. There is not a pure distancing from the present, but precisely re-presentation, that is, a distancing in which the present of truth *is* already or *still is*; for a representation is a recommencement of the present which in its "first time" is for the second time; it is a retention and a protention, between forgetting and expecting, between memory and project. Time is reminiscence and reminiscence is time, the unity of consciousness and essence.

But in the totality of being temporally getting out of phase, which alone could be sufficient for truth, would the totality, diverging from itself, go "beyond totality"? Yet totality should not leave anything outside.[3] Then the transcendence of the totality thematized in truth is produced as a division of the totality into parts. How can these parts still be equivalent to the whole, as is implied when exposition is truth? By reflecting the whole. The whole reflected in a part is an image. Truth then would be produced in the images of being. It is nonetheless true that time and reminiscence and the astonishing diastasis of identity and its rediscoveries, by which essence "puts in its time" of being essence, is beyond essence and truth, even if in understanding and expounding it we say that they *are* beyond essence, that is, that beyond essence *they are*. Beyond essence, signification, an excluded middle between being and non-being, signifies.

An image is both a term of the exposition, a figure that shows itself, the immediate, the sensible, and a term in which truth is not at its term, since in it the whole of being does not show itself in itself, but is only reflected in it.[4] In an image, the sensible, the immediate, is intentionally turned in a search for a more complete presence. But if exposition implies a partition of the totality of being, exposition cannot be completed without being put out. Truth is something promised. Always promised, always future, always loved, truth lies in the promise and the love of wisdom,[5] even if it is not forbidden to catch sight, in the time of disclosure, of the structured work of history and of a progression in the successive up to the limits of non-philosophy.

Philosophy is disclosure of being, and being's *essence* is truth and philosophy. Being's essence is the temporalization of time, the diastasis of the identical and its recapture or reminiscence, the unity of apperception. *Essence* does not first designate the edges of solids or the moving line of acts in which a light glimmers; it designates this "modification" without alteration or transition, independent of all qualitative determination, more formal than the silent using up of things which reveals their becoming, already weighted down with matter, the creaking of a piece of furniture in the silence of the night. This modification by which the same comes unstuck or parts with itself, undoes itself into this and that, no longer covers over itself and thus is disclosed (like in Dufy's paintings, where the colors spread out from their contours and do not rub up against them), becomes a phenomenon – is the *esse* of every being. Being's essence designates nothing that could be a nameable content, a thing, event or action; it names this mobility of the immobile, this multiplication of the identical, this diastasis of the punctual, this lapse. This modification without alteration or displacement, being's essence or time, does not await, in addition, an illumination that would allow for an "act of consciousness." This modification is precisely the visibility of the same to the same, which is sometimes called openness. The work of being, essence, time, the lapse of time, is exposition, truth, philosophy. Being's essence is a dissipating of opacity, not only because this "drawing out" of being would have to have been first understood so that truth could be told about things, events and acts that *are*; but because this drawing out is the *original dissipation* of opaqueness. In it forms are illuminated where knowledge is awakened; in it being leaves the night, or, at least, quits sleep, that night of night, for an unextinguishable insomnia of consciousness. Thus every particular knowledge, every factual exercise of understanding – ideology, faith, or science – every perception, every disclosing behavior whatever it be, would owe their light to essence, the first light, and to philosophy which is its dawn or its twilight. Temporality, in the divergence of the identical from itself, is *essence* and original light, that which Plato distinguished from the visibility of the visible and the clairvoyance of the eye. The time of the essence unites the three moments of knowing. Is the light of essence which makes things seen itself seen? It can to be sure become a theme; essence can show itself, be spoken of and described. But then light presents itself in light, which latter is not thematic, but resounds for the "eye that listens," with a resonance unique in its kind, a resonance of silence. Expressions such as the eye that listens to the resonance of silence are not monstrosities, for they speak of the way one approaches the temporality of the true, and in temporality being deploys its essence.

Does temporality go beyond essence? The question remains: are this night or this sleep which being would "quit" by means of time so as to manifest itself still *essence*, simple negations of light and wakefulness? Or "are" they an "otherwise" or a "hither side"? By virtue of a temporality beyond reminiscence, in diachrony, beyond essence, are they on this side of, or beyond, *otherwise than being*, indeed liable to being shown in the said, but then immediately reduced? Is the subject completely comprehensible out of ontology? That is one of the principle problems of the present research – or, more exactly, that is what it puts into question.

3. TIME AND DISCOURSE

a. Sensuous Lived Experience
The disclosure of all things depends on their insertion in this light, or this resonance, of the time of essence. Things are discovered in their qualities, but the qualities are in lived experience, which is temporal. The exposition, the phenomenality of being, can not be separated from time. We can then understand the justification of a philosophical tradition which reflects on sensation, and which goes back from Kant, Berkeley and Descartes to antiquity. "Common act of the feeling and the felt," sensation is the ambiguous unity of the temporal flow of the lived element and the identity of beings and events, designated by words.

This ambiguousness has not been dissipated by the notion of intentionality such as it was affirmed in Husserl's polemics against psychologism, where what was important was to distinguish radically between the psychic life of the logician, the intentional *Erlebnis*, and the ideality of the thematized logical formation, which transcends the psychic and lived experience. There it would have been natural to admit that sensation belongs to the lived becoming, the *Erleben*, only qua sensing, and that the sensing consists in a set of lived noeses, that its nature is exhausted in intentional functions of welcome extended to the qualities called sensorial, in view of identifying them. These qualities would be distinguishable from every other given by their immediate presence, their fullness of content, their richness. Though changing, they would vary only outside of the lived experience, on the plane of the sensed, *beyond* the sensing. The lived and the sensed, the lived and the sensible qualities, would thus be separated by an "open chasm of meaning," as Husserl put it.

And yet this schema does not hold. The sensible is not revealed in the exposition that would be the fulgurating instant of a noesis, would be pure welcome. The noesis itself has a temporal stretching in it, and is constituted in time; it refers in its intention to the materiality of a ὑλή. The sensible qualities – sounds, colors, hardness, softness – are attributes of things; but they also seem to be lived in time in the form of a psychic life, stretching out or dividing in the succession of temporal phases, and not only lasting or being altered in the measurable time of physicists. Husserl agrees, and emphasizes this more than anyone today, rehabilitating the teachings of a venerable philosophical tradition which he seems to contest by certain aspects of the theses he puts forth. The sensorial qualities are not only the sensed: as affective states, they are the sensing. Berkeley always taught this. One can very well attribute to sensing an intentionality that identifies colors and objective sounds, still it is itself an abridged version of these colors and sounds. It "resembles" the sensed. There is something common to the objective and the lived. It is as though the sensible – whose meaning is *multiple* and whose status in consciousness was fixed only on the basis of *knowledge* as receptivity – were an element *sui generis*, into which identical entities dissolve and from which they emerge, but in which their opacity and fixity as substances turn into duration, while the flow of the lived is always on the verge of coagulating into ideal identities.[6]

In Husserl internal time consciousness, and consciousness as such, are described in the temporality of sensation: "sensing is what we hold to be the originary consciousness of time,"[7] and "without the impression consciousness is nothing."[8] Time, the sensorial impression and consciousness are put together. Even at this primordial level which is that of lived experience, in which the flow, reduced to pure immanence, should exclude even any suspicion of objectification, consciousness remains an intentionality, an "intentionality of a specific kind,"[9] to be sure, but unthinkable without an apprehended correlate. This specific intentionality is time itself. There is consciousness insofar as the sensible impression differs from itself without differing; it differs without differing, is other within identity. The impression is illuminated by "opening up," as though it plugged itself up; it undoes that coincidence of self with self in which the "same" is smothered under itself, as under a candle extinguisher. It is not in phase with itself; *just* past, *about to* come. But to differ within identity, to maintain the moment that is being altered, is "protaining" and "retaining"! Differing within identity, modifying itself without changing, consciousness glows in an impression inasmuch as it diverges from itself, to *still* be expecting itself, or *already* recuperating itself. Still, already – are time, time in which nothing is lost. The past itself is modified without changing its identity, diverges from itself without letting go of itself, "becomes older," sinking into a deeper past: it remains identical with itself through retention of retention, and so on. Then memory recuperates in images what retention was not able to preserve, and historiography reconstructs that whose image is lost. To speak of consciousness is to speak of time.

It is in any case to speak of a time that can be recuperated. At a level which for Husserl is originary, temporality involves a consciousness that is not even intentional in the "specific" sense of retention. Despite the complete overlapping of the perceived and the perception in the *Ur-impression*, the originary or primal impression, which ought to no longer let the light pass through, despite their strict contemporaneousness which is the pres-

ence of the present,[10] despite the non-modification of this "absolute beginning of this generation – the primal source, that from which all others are
continually generated,"[11] this today without a yesterday or a tomor-
row – the primal impression is nonetheless not *impressed* without consciousness.[12] Does not the originary impression · "non-modified,"
self-identical, but without retention – precede every protention, and thus
precede its own *possibility*? Husserl seems to say this, in calling the
"primal impression" the "absolute beginning" of every modification that is
produced as time, a primal source which "is not generated" and is born
"through spontaneous generation." "It does not grow up (it has no seed); it
is primal creation."[13] Would not the "real" that precedes and surprises the
possible be the very definition of the *present*, which in this description is
indifferent to protention ("generation has no seed!), but would nonetheless
be conscious of it? That is certainly the most remarkable point of this
philosophy in which intentionality "constitutes" the universe, the prototype
of theoretical objectification commands all the modes of intentional positing, be they axiological or practical, and in which in every case a rigorous
parallelism between the doxic, axiological and practical theses is constantly
affirmed. Husserl will then have liberated the psyche from the primacy of
the theoretical neither in the order of know-how with equipment nor in
that of axiological emotion, nor in the thought of Being, different from the
metaphysics of entities. Rather, objectifying consciousness, the hegemony
of re-presentation, is paradoxically surmounted in the consciousness of the
present.[14] And this makes understandable indeed the underlying or commanding importance of the still so little explored manuscripts concerning
the "living present" in the whole corpus of his research. Though it be a
rehabilitation of the "sensorial given" of empiricist sensualism, the primal
impression finds again in the context of intentionality (which for Husserl
remains all-encompassing) its power to surprise. Here consciousness is produced outside of all negativity in Being (which still operates in the temporality of retentions and protentions). Through the notion of the living
present, the notion of origin and of creation, a spontaneity in which activity and passivity are completely one, tend to become intelligible. When it
turns out that this consciousness in the living present, *originally* non-
objectifying and not objectified, is thematizable and thematizing in retention, without thereby losing the "temporal place" which gives
"individuation,"[15] then we see the non-intentionality of the primal impression fitted back in the normal order, not leading to the hither side of the
same or of the origin. Nothing enters incognito into the same, to interrupt
the flow of time and interrupt the consciousness that is produced in the
form of this flow. A putting the self-identity of the living present out of
phase, a putting of the phases themselves out of phase, in the intentionality

of retentions and protentions, the flow looks like a multiplication of modification dispersing from the living present. In Husserl the time structure of sensibility is a time of what can be recuperated. The thesis that the non-intentionality of the primal retention is not a loss of consciousness, that nothing can be produced in a clandestine way,[16] what nothing can break the thread of consciousness,[17] excludes from time the irreducible diachrony whose meaning the present study aims to bring to light, behind the *exhibiting* of being.

Varying in its identity, and identical in its difference; retained, remembered or reconstructed; accumulating, according to the so admirably phenomenological Kantian formulas, through the "synthesis of apprehension in intuition" (that is, in the sensible becoming cognition), and by the synthesis of "recognition in imagination," the impression is temporalized and opens upon itself.

Rather than being a metaphor taken from the movement of waters in a river, would not flowing be the very temporality of time and the "science" of which "consciousness" (*conscience*) is made? To speak of time in terms of flowing is to speak of time in terms of time and not in terms of temporal events.[18] The temporalization of time – the openness by which sensation manifests itself, is felt, modifies itself without altering its identity, doubling itself up by a sort of diastasis of the punctual, putting itself out of phase with itself – is neither an attribute nor a predicate expressing a causality "sensed" as a sensation. The temporal modification is not an event, nor an action, nor the effect of a cause. It is the verb to be.

b. Language

The verb understood as a noun designating an event, when applied to the temporalization of time, would make it resound as an event, whereas every event already presupposes time. Time's modification without change, the putting of the identical out of phase with itself, teems behind the transformations and the endurance, and, as ageing, even within endurance. And yet a verb perhaps comes into its very verbalness by ceasing to name actions and events, ceasing to name. It is here that a word "has its own ways," unique of their kind, irreducible to symbolization which names or evokes. The verb *to be* tells the flowing of time as though language were not unequivocally equivalent to denomination, as though in *to be* the verb first came to function as a verb, and as though this function refers to the teeming ar.d mute itching of that modification without change that time operates. This time can, to be sure, be recuperated in retention, memory, "tales," and books. The relationship between the verb and being, or being's essence is not that between genus and species. Essence, temporalization, is the verbalness of a verb. To suggest the difference between Being and entities, and the strange temporal itch, a modification without change, one resorts to metaphors taken from the temporal and not from time – such as process, act of being, disclosure or effectuation of being, or its passage. But being is the verb itself. Temporalization is the verb form to be. Language issued from the verbalness of a verb would then not only consist in making being understood, but also in making its essence vibrate.

Language is thus not reducible to a system of signs doubling up beings and relations; that conception would be incumbent on us if words were nouns. Language seems rather to be an excrescence of the verb. And qua verb it already bears sensible life – temporalization and being's essence. The lived sensation, being and time, is already understood in a verb. In sensibility the qualities of perceived things turn into time and into consciousness, independently of the soundless space in which they seem to unfold in a mute world. But has not then sensibility already been *said*? Do not its qualitative variations make the *how* of the verb stated in it understood? Do not the sensations in which the sensible qualities are lived resound *adverbially*, and, more precisely, as adverbs of the verb to be?

But then if they could be surprised on the hither side of the said, would they not reveal another meaning?

But language is also a system of nouns. Denomination designates or constitutes identities in the verbal or temporal flow of sensation. Through the opening that temporalization works in the sensible, disclosing it by its very passing, assembling it by retention and memory (an assembling which Kant caught sight of in the diverse syntheses of the imagination, before every idealization of the sensible), the word identifies "this *as* that," states the ideality of the same in the diverse. This identification is a supplying with meaning: "this as that." In their meaning entities show themselves to be identical unities. "The consciousness of time is the originary locus of the constitution of the unity of identity in general," Husserl writes.[19] The "identical unities" are not given or thematized first, and then receive a meaning; they are given through this meaning. The "this as that" is not lived; it is said. Identification is understood on the basis of a mysterious schematism, of the already said, an antecedent *doxa* which every relationship between the universal and the individual presupposes. For this relationship evidently can not be based on resemblance.

Identification is kerygmatical. The said is not simply a sign or an expression of a meaning; it proclaims and establishes this as that. The surplus of this "spontaneity"[20] over the reflexion which, in its reflection, thought involves, is not accurately suggested by the notion of *action* which is customarily opposed to the pure receptivity of the sensible.[21] This surplus, situated between passivity and activity, is in the language that enters into a *hearsay*, an *already said*, a doxa, without which the identifying, naming language would not have been able to approach the sensible. In the doxa, the *already said*, tale, epos, the given is held in its theme. Is not its temporal accumulation doxic, since even in Husserl it is from the first presented to the prepredicative judgment as an *Urdoxa*, an originary doxa?[22] A word is a nomination, as much as a denomination, a consecrating of the "this as this" or "this as that" by a saying which is also *understanding* and *listening*, absorbed in the said. It is an obedience in the midst of the will ("I hear this or that said"), a kerygma at the bottom of a *fiat*.[23] Before all receptivity an *already said* before languages exposes or, in all the sense of the term, signifies (proposes and orders) experience, giving to historical languages spoken by peoples a locus, enabling them to orient or polarize the diversity of the thematized as they choose.

In the sensible as lived, identity shows itself, becomes a phenomenon, for in the sensible as lived is heard and "resounds" essence, the lapse of time and the memory that recuperates it, consciousness; the time of consciousness is the resonance and understanding of time. But this ambiguity and this gnoseological function of sensibility, this ambiguity of the understanding and intuition that does not exhaust the signifyingness of the sensible and of immediacy, is its play, logical and ontological, as consciousness. This play does not begin by caprice; we will have to show the horizon in which it occurs. But this play does not undo the responsibilities that arouse it. In analyzing the sensible in the ambiguity of duration and identity, which is already the ambiguity of the verb and the noun that scintillates in the said, we have found it *already said*. Language has been in operation, and the saying that bore this said, but goes further, was absorbed and died in the said, was inscribed. Or, if one likes, our analysis concerned the time that marks historiography, that is, the recuperable time, the recoverable time, the lost time that can be found again. As the time narrated becomes, in the narrative and in writing, a reversible time, every phenomenon is said, characterized by the simultaneity of the successive in a theme. In the remission or detente of time, the same modified retains itself on the verge of losing itself, is inscribed in memory and is identified, is said. The lived, a "state of consciousness," a being, designated by a substantive, is distended, in the time of lived experience, into life, into *essence*, into a verb but across the opening that the diastasis of identity works, across time, the same finds again the same modified. Such is consciousness. These rediscoveries are an identification – of this as this or as that. Identification is ascription of meaning. Entities show themselves in their meanings to be identical entities. They are not first given and thematized, and then receive a meaning; they are given by the meaning they have. But these rediscoveries by identification occur in an *already said*. The said, the word, is not simply a

37

sign of a meaning, nor even only an *expression* of a meaning (contrary to Husserl's analysis in the first *Logical Investigation*); the word at once proclaims and establishes an identification of this with that in the *already said*.

c. The Said and the Saying
The identity of entities refers to a saying teleologically turned to the kerygma of the said, absorbing itself in it to the extent of being forgotten in it. It refers to a saying that would be *correlative* with the said, or that would idealize the identity of entities. This saying would thus constitute that identity, and recuperate the irreversible, coagulate the flow of time into a "something," thematize, ascribe a meaning. It would take up a position with regard to this "something," fixed in a present, re-present it to itself, and thus extract it from the labile character of time. The saying extended toward the said[24] and absorbed in it, correlative with it, names an entity, in the light or resonance of lived time which allows a *phenomenon* to appear. This light and resonance can in turn be identified in another said. The designation and resonance are not just added on to a phenomenon from the outside, by the effect of a conventional code which regulates the usage of a system of signs. It is through the *already said* that words, elements of a historically constituted vocabulary, will come to function as signs and acquire a usage,[25] and bring about the proliferation of all the possibilities of vocabulary.

The entity that appears *identical* in the light of time *is* its essence in the *already said*. The phenomenon itself is a phenomenology. It is not that a discourse, coming from one knows not where, arbitrarily arranges the phases of temporality into a "this as that." The very exposition of Being, its manifestation, essence qua essence and entities qua entities, are spoken. It is only in the said, in the epos of saying, that the diachrony of time is synchronized into a time that is recallable, and becomes a theme. The *epos* is not added to the identical entities it exposes; it exposes them as identities illuminated by a memorable temporality. The identical with respect to which temporality comes to be analyzed as a divergency making possible the rediscoveries of an act of consciousness (as though the identical were independent of time, and "then" becomes a flowing) has meaning only through the kerygma of the said,[26] in which temporality which illuminates resounds for the "listening eye" in the verb to be. And it is for that that man is a being of truth, belonging to no other genus of being. *But is the power to say in man, however strictly correlative to the said its function may be, in the service of being?* If man were only a saying correlative with the logos, subjectivity could as well be understood as a function or as an argument of being. But the signification of saying goes beyond the said. It is not ontology that raises up the speaking subject; it is the signifyingness of saying going beyond essence that can justify the exposedness of being, ontology.[27]

For the lapse of time is also something irrecuperable, refractory to the simultaneity of the present, something unrepresentable, immemorial, prehistorical. Before the syntheses of apprehension and recognition, the absolutely passive "synthesis" of ageing is effected. Through it time passes (*se passe*). The immemorial is not an effect of a weakness of memory, an incapacity to cross large intervals of time, to resuscitate pasts too deep. It is the impossibility of the dispersion of time to assemble itself in the present, the insurmountable diachrony of time, a beyond the said. It is diachrony that determines the immemorial; a weakness of memory does not constitute diachrony. But then we have this problem: is not diachrony characterizable only negatively? Is it pure loss? Has it no signification? For such a signification what is signified would not be a "something" identified in the theme of the said, a "this as that" illuminated in the memorable time of essence. Need temporalization signify only by letting itself be understood in the said, in which its diachrony is exposed to synchronization? If saying is not only the correlative of a said, if its signifyingness is not absorbed in the signification said, can we not find beyond or on the hither side of the saying that tells being the signifyingness of diachrony? Behind being and its monstration, there is now already heard the resonance of other significations forgotten in ontology, which now solicit our inquiry.

But before entering into this inquiry concerning the saying, let us return to the structure of the said, in which identical entities, beings, are shown.[28]

d. The Amphibology of Being and Entities

Time and the *essence* it unfolds by manifesting *entities*, identified in the themes of statements or narratives, resound as a silence without becoming themes themselves. They can, to be sure, be named in a theme, but this naming does not reduce to definitive silence the mute resonance, the murmur of silence, in which essence is identified as an entity. Once again for the "listening eye" a silence resounds about what had been muffled, the silence of the parcelling out of being, by which entities in their identities are illuminated and show themselves.

In a predicative proposition, an apophansis, an entity can make itself be understood verbally, as a "way" of essence, as the *fruitio essendi* itself, as a *how*, a modality of this essence or this temporalization.

Already the tautological predication, A is A, in which an entity is both subject and predicate, does not only signify the inherence of A in itself or the fact that A possesses all the characteristics of A. A is A is to be understood also as "the sound resounds" or "the red reddens" – or as "A As." In "the red reddens" the verb does not signify an event, some dynamism of the red opposed to its rest as a quality, or some activity of the red, for example, turning red, the passage from non-red to red or from less red to more red, an alteration. Nor in the verb to redden is there stated some metaphor of action or alteration, founded on an analogy with the dynamism of action, which would have the preeminent right to be designated by a verb.

Is this verb to redden, in which the immediate coincidence of the nominalized adjective, the red, with itself is abruptly diachronized, only a sign that, like a noun, designates a process, a succession of states, to the interlocutor, and doubles up the totality of entities and events with the system of signs of a language? It is probably this function of signs, designation (which words incontestably exercise within the said), that is implicitly ascribed to a verb when one tries to reduce the function of a verb to the "expression" of events, actions or alterations. If being's essence is spelled out, scanned, resounds or temporalizes in the verb to be and thereby becomes discourse and apophansis, this is not by analogy with actions and processes (in which the massive turns into energy), which verbs would first designate. It is the verbalness of the verb that resounds in the predicative proposition; the dynamism of entities is designated and expressed by verbs secondarily, by reason of its privileged exposure in time. The effort to reduce verbs to the function of signs naively presupposes the division of entities into substances and events, into statics and dynamics, to be original. But the connection between the said and being is not simply reducible to designation. The imperative kerygma of identification over and above the sign, is already visible in a noun.

Apophansis – the red reddens, or *A is A* – does not double up the real. In predication the essence of the red, or the reddening as an essence, becomes audible for the first time. The nominalized adjective is first understood as an essence, and a temporalization properly so called, in predication. *Essence* is not only conveyed in the said, is not only "expressed" in it, but originally – though amphibologically – resounds in it qua essence. There is no essence or entity behind the said, behind the Logos. The said, as a verb, is the essence of essence. Essence is the very fact that there is a theme, exhibition, doxa or logos, and thus truth. Essence is not only conveyed, it is temporalized in a predicative statement.

To affirm that being is a verb then does not simply, or only, mean that a certain word, a sonorous or graphic reality belonging to cultural reality, classified by grammarians among verbs, is a sign designating a fundamental process or action, which in themselves would do without language – no more than language qua denomination, doubling up the entity designated, is indifferent to this entity and only lets it be seen. And to affirm that being is a verb does not mean that language, an exterior denomination, remains foreign to the essence it names, and only lets this essence be seen. The noun that doubles up the entity it names is necessary for its identity. And so also the verb: not only is it not the name of being, but in the predicative proposition it is the very resonance of being understood as being. Temporalization resounds as essence in the apophansis.

Language qua said can then be conceived as a system of nouns identifying entities, and then as a system of signs doubling up the beings, designating substances, events and relations by substantives or other parts of speech derived from substantives, designating identities – in sum, *designating*. But also, and with as much right, language can be conceived as the verb in a predicative proposition in which the substances break down into modes of being, modes of temporalization. Here language does not double up the being of entities, but exposes the silent resonance of the essence.

But identical entities, things and qualities of things, begin to resound with their essence in a predicative proposition not as a result of psychological reflection about subjectivity and the temporality of sensation, but out of art. Art is the pre-eminent exhibition in which the said is reduced to a pure theme, to absolute exposition, even to shamelessness capable of holding all looks for which it is exclusively destined. The said is reduced to the Beautiful, which supports Western ontology. Through art essence and temporality begin to resound with poetry or song. And the search for new forms, from which all art lives, keeps awake everywhere the verbs that are on the verge of lapsing into substantives. In painting, red reddens and green greens, forms are produced as contours and vacate with their vacuity as forms. In music sounds resound; in poems vocables, material of the said, no longer yield before what they evoke, but sing with their evocative powers and their diverse ways to evoke, their etymologies;[29] in Paul Valéry's *Eupalinos* architecture makes buildings sing. Poetry is productive of song, of resonance and sonority, which are the verbalness of verbs or essence.

In the inexhaustible diversity of works, that is, in the *essential renewal* of art, colors, forms, sounds, words, buildings – already on the verge of being identified as entities, already disclosing their nature and their qualities in the substantives that bear adjectives — recommence being. There the essence they modulate is temporalized. The palette of colors, the gamut of sounds, the system of vocables and the meandering of forms are realized as a pure *how*; in the touch of color and pencil, the secrecy of words, the sonority of sounds – all these modal notions – there is resonance of essence. The research of modern art, or, perhaps more exactly, art in the stage of search, a stage never overcome, seems in all its aesthetics to look for and understand this resonance or production of essence in the form of works of art. It is as though the differences of pitch, register and timber, color and forms, words and rhythms, were but temporalization, sonority and key. Writing about writing would be poetry itself. Music, for example in Xenakis' "Nomos Alpha for Unaccompanied Cello," bends the quality of the notes emitted into adverbs. Every quiddity becomes a modality, the strings and woods turn into sonority. What is taking place? Is a soul complaining or exulting in the depth of the sounds that break up or between the notes which hitherto in their identities succeeded one another and contributed to the harmony of the whole, silencing their grating, but which now no longer melt into a melodic line? What misleading anthropomorphism or animism! The cello *is* a cello in the sonority that vibrates in its strings and its wood, even if it is already reverting into notes, into identities that settle into their natural places in gamuts from the acute to the grave, according to the different pitches. Thus the essence of the cello, a modality of *essence*, is temporalized in the work.

But it does so in isolation: every work of art is in this sense exotic, without a world, essence in dissemination. To fail to recognize the said *properly so-called* (relative as it may be) in the predicative propositions which every artwork — plastic, sonorous or poetic — awakens and makes resound in the form of *exegesis* is to show oneself to be as profoundly deaf as in the deafness of hearing only nouns in language. It is this call for exegesis that is also brought out by the *essential* function of the verbal said in the emergence and presentation of artworks in the form of prefaces, manifestos, titles or aesthetic canons – a non-eliminatable meta-language. It is this call, bringing the modality of the essence said in the work back to the depth of the essence *properly so-called*, such as it is heard in the predicative statement, that is justified by the notion of world. The essence properly so-called, is the verb, the logos, that resounds in the *prose* of predicative propositions. The exegesis is not something laid on to the resonance of essence in the artwork; the resonance of essence vibrates within the said of the exegesis. In the verb of the apophansis, which is the verb properly so called, the verb *to be*, essence resounds and is heard. *A is A* but also *A is B* are taken as a way A's essence resounds, vibrates, or is temporalized. All the attributes of individual beings, of entities that are fixed in or by nouns, as predicates can be understood as modes of being; such are the qualities of which the entities make a show, the typical generalities by which they are ordered, the laws that regulate them, the logical forms that contain and deliver them. The very individuality of an individual is a way of being. Socrates socratizes, or Socrates is Socrates, is the *way* Socrates is. Predication makes the time of essence be heard.

But in the said, the essence that resounds is on the verge of becoming a noun. In the copula *is* scintillates or sparkles an ambiguousness between the essence and the nominalized relation. The said as a verb is essence or temporalization. Or, more exactly, the logos enters into the amphibology in which being and entities can be understood and identified, in which a noun can resound as a verb and a verb of an apophansis can be nominalized.

The discoursing of the essence which dissipates opacity ensures the brilliance of every image, and thus the very light of intuition,[30] making possible the exposition of entities and of essence itself. The exposition of the temporal diastasis, that is, the exposition of exposition, exposition of the phenomenality of phenomena, is the verb stated in a predicative proposition.

But yet, through the ambiguousness of the logos, in the space of an identification, to be, the verb par excellence in which essence resounds, is exposed, is nominalized, becomes a word designating and sanctioning identities, assembling time (and that which modulated the temporalization of time in the apophansis, such as adverbs) into a conjuncture. The verb to be – field of synchronizable diachrony, of temporalization, that is, field of memory and historiography – becomes a quasi structure and is thematized and shows itself like an entity. Phenomenality, essence, becomes a phenomenon, is fixed, assembled in a tale, is synchronized, presented, lends itself to a noun, receives a title. An entity or a configuration of entities emerge thematized and are identified in the synchronism of denomination (or in the unity of a tale which cannot be out of phase). They become history, are delivered over to writing, to books, in which the time of the narrative, without being reversed, recommences. They become states of affairs, Sachverhalte, in which words designate idealities identified first, substrates, as Husserl calls them, nuclei of things. But they are still in an amphibology: identification at any level implies the temporalization of the lived, essence. Things and all substrates come from a narrative and refer to the logos, to the said; already an entity named is dissolved in the time of essence which resounds in the apophansis that illuminates it.

Logos is the ambiguousness of being and entities, the primordial amphibology. Every "lived state" (Erlebnis), lived in "temporal modification," in a parcelling out of essence, is memorable, and thus can be named, identified, appear, be represented. There does not exist a verb that is refractory to nominalization. The verb to be in predication (which is its "natural place") makes essence resound, but this resonance is collected into an entity by the noun. To be thenceforth designates instead of resounding. It designates then an entity having as its whole quiddity only the essence of entities, a quiddity identified like the quiddity of every other named entity. The birthplace of ontology is in the said. Ontology is stated in the amphibology of being and entities. Fundamental ontology itself, which denounces the confusion between Being and entities, speaks of Being as an identified entity. And the mutation is ambivalent, every nameable identity can turn into a verb.

To affirm that this mutation in the amphibology of being and entities is an amphibology of the logos, that it is due to the status of the said, is not to reduce the difference between being and entities to a frivolous play of syntax. It is to measure the pre-ontological weight of language instead of taking it only as a code (which it is also). But also, by interpreting the fact that essence exposes and is exposed, that temporalization is stated, resounds, is said, it is to not give priority to the said over the saying. It is first to awaken in the said the saying which is absorbed in it and, *thus absorbed, enters into the history that the said imposes*. To the extent that the saying would have no other meaning than this enunciation of the said, that it would be strictly "correlative" with the said, it would justify the thesis that the subject is dependent on being, as well as the thesis that being refers to the subject. We must go back to what is prior to this correlation. Is not saying but the active form of the said? Does not to tell oneself amounts to being said ("*Se* dire," revient-il à "*être dit*")? The reflexive pronoun *oneself* and the recurrence it denotes raise a problem; they can not be understood solely on the basis of the said. The originally accusative form of this singular pronoun is hardly perceptible when it is joined to verbs and used to confer on them a passive form, in the said. We must go back to their signification beyond or on the hither side of the comprehending activity or passivity in being, the said, the logos and the amphibology of being and entities. The "reduction" is made in this movement. It involves a positive phase: to show the signification proper to the saying on the hither side of the thematization of the said.

e. The Reduction
It is clear that the verb *to be*, or the verb *to consist*, is used in the formulas from these first pages that name the hither side of being. It is also clear that being makes its apparition, shows itself, in the said. As soon as saying, on the hither side of being, becomes dictation, it expires, or abdicates, in fables and in writing. If being and manifestation go together in the said, it is in fact natural that if the saying on the hither side of the said can show itself, it be said already in terms of being. But is it necessary and is it possible that the saying on the hither side be thematized, that is, manifest itself, that it enter into a proposition and a book? It is necessary. The responsibility for another is precisely a saying prior to anything said. The surprising saying which is a responsibility for another is against "the winds and tides" of being, is an interruption of essence, a disinterestedness imposed with a good violence. But one has to say that the gratuity none-

theless required of substitution, that miracle of ethics before the light, this astonishing saying, comes to light through the very gravity of the questions that assail it. It must spread out and assemble itself into essence, posit itself, be hypostasized, become an eon in consciousness and knowledge, let itself be seen, undergo the ascendancy of being. Ethics itself, in its saying which is a responsibility, requires this hold. But it is also necessary that the saying call for philosophy in order that the light that occurs not congeal into essence what is beyond essence, and that the hypostasis of an eon not be set up as an idol. Philosophy makes this astonishing adventure – showing and recounting as an essence – intelligible, by loosening this grip of being. A philosopher's effort, and his unnatural position, consists, while showing the hither side, in immediately reducing the eon which triumphs in the said and in the monstrations, and, despite the reduction, retaining an echo of the reduced said in the form of ambiguity, of diachronic expression. For the saying is both an affirmation and a retraction of the said. The reduction could not be effected simply by parentheses which, on the contrary, are an effect of writing. It is the ethical interruption of essence that energizes the reduction.

To expose an otherwise than being will still give an ontological said, in the measure that all monstration exposes an essence. The reduction of this said unfolds in stated propositions, using copulas, and virtually written, united anew into structures; it will let the destructuring it will have operated *be*. The reduction then will once again let the otherwise than being be as an eon. As the truth of what does not enter into a theme, it is produced out of time or in two times without entering into either of them, as an endless critique, or skepticism, which in a spiralling movement makes possible the boldness of philosophy, destroying the conjunction into which its saying and its said continually enter. The said, contesting the abdication of the saying that everywhere occurs in this said, thus maintains the diachrony in which, holding its breath, the spirit hears the echo of the *otherwise*. The hither side, the preliminary, which the pre-originary saying animates, refuses the present and manifestation, or lends itself to them only out of time. The unsayable saying lends itself to the said, to the ancillary indiscretion of the abusive language that divulges or profanes the unsayable. But it lets itself be reduced, without effacing the unsaying in the ambiguity or the enigma of the transcendent, in which the breathless spirit retains a fading echo.

But one can go back to this signification of the saying, this responsibility and substitution, only from the said and from the question: "What is it about ... ?", a question already within the said in which everything shows itself. One can go back to it through reduction only out of what shows itself, that is, the essence and the thematized eon, of which alone there is a manifestation. But in it the questioning look is only the impossible synchronization of the unassemblable, Merleau-Ponty's fundamental historicity, which the diachrony of proximity has already escaped.

The reduction, the going back to the hither side of being, to the hither side of the said, in which being shows itself, in which the eon is hypostatized, could nowise mean a rectification of one ontology by another, the passage from some apparent world to a more real world. It is only in the order of being that rectification, truth and error have meaning, and that the betrayal is the lack of a fidelity. The hither side of or the beyond being is not an entity on the hither side of or beyond being; but it also does not signify an exercise of being, an essence, that is truer or more authentic that the being of entities. The entities *are*, and their manifestation in the said is their true *essence*. The reduction nowise means to dissipate or explain some "transcendental appearance." The structures with which it begins are ontological. That the really true being and entities are in the said, or that they lend themselves to expression and writing, takes nothing from their truth and only describes the level and the seriousness of language. To enter into being and truth is to enter into the said; being is inseparable from its meaning! It is spoken. It is in the logos. But the reduction is reduction of the said to the saying beyond the logos, beyond being and non-being, beyond essence, beyond true and non-true. It is the reduction to signification, to the one-for-the-other involved in responsibility (or more exactly in substitution), to the locus or non-lieu, locus and non-lieu, the utopia, of the human. It is the reduction to restlessness in the literal sense of the term, or to its diachrony, which, despite all its assembled forces, despite all the simultaneous forces in its union, being can not eternalize. The subjective and its Good can not be understood out of ontology. On the contrary, starting with subjectivity in the form of saying, the signification of the said will be interpretable. It will be possible to show that there is question of the said and being only because saying or responsibility require justice. Thus only will justice be done to being, will the affirmation, the, to take it literally, strange affirmation that through injustice "all the foundations of the earth are shaken" will be understandable. Thus alone will the terrain of disinterestedness that allows us to separate truth from ideology be given its truth.

4. SAYING AND SUBJECTIVITY

a. The Saying without the Said

From the amphibology of being and entities in the said we must go back to the saying which signifies prior to essence, prior to identification, on the hither side of this amphibology. Saying states and thematizes the said, but signifies it to the other, a neighbor, with a signification that has to be distinguished from that borne by words in the said. This signification to the other occurs in proximity. Proximity is quite distinct from every other relationship, and has to be conceived as a responsibility for the other; it might be called humanity, or subjectivity, or self. Being and entities weigh heavily by virtue of the saying that gives them light. Nothing is more grave, more august, than responsibility for the other, and saying, in which there is no play, has a gravity more grave than its own being or not being.

This saying has to be reached in its existence antecedent to the said, or else the said has to be reduced to it. We must fix the meaning of this antecedence. What does saying signify before signifying a said? Can we try to show the crux of a plot that is not reducible to phenomenology, that is, to the thematization of the said, and to the description of the saying as having its function purely correlative with the said, a function that consists of thematizing the saying and opening being to itself, arousing an appearing, and then, in themes that arouse nouns and verbs, operating the "putting together," the synchronization or structure – the putting into a world and putting into a history for a historiography? Saying signifies otherwise than as an apparitor presenting essence and entities. This is one of the central theses of the present text.

Our task is to show that the plot proper to saying does indeed lead it to the said, to the putting together of structures which make possible justice and the "I think." The said, the appearing, arises in the saying. Essence then has its hour and its time. Clarity occurs, and thought aims at themes. But all that is in function of a prior signification proper to saying, which is nither ontological nor ontic. Our task is to establish its articulation and signifyingness antecedent to ontology.[31] In correlation with the said (in which saying runs the risk of being absorbed as soon as the said is formulated), the saying itself is indeed thematized, exposes in essence even what is on the *hither side of ontology*, and flows into the temporalization of essence. And this thematization of saying does indeed bring out in it the characteristics of consciousness: in the correlation of saying and said the said is understood as a noema of an intentional act, language contracts into thought, into thought which conditions speaking, thought that in the said shows itself to be an act supported by a subject, an *entity* as it were put in the "nominative," in a proposition. The saying and the said in their correlation delineate the subject-object structure.

But the manifestation of saying out of the said, in which it is thematized, does not still dissimulate, does not irrevocably "falsify" the signifyingness proper to the said. The plot of the saying that is absorbed in the said is not exhausted in this manifestation. It imprints its trace on the thematization itself, which hesitates between, on the one hand, structuration, order of a configuation of entities, world and history for historiographers and, on the other hand, the order of non-nominalized apophansis of the other, in which the said remains a *proposition*, a proposition made to a neighbor, "a signifyingness dealt" (*significance baillée*) to the other. Being, the verb of a proposition, is, to be sure, a theme, but it makes essence resound without entirely deadening the echo of the saying that bears it and brings it to light. This resonance is always ready to congeal into nouns, where being will be congealed into a copula and the *Sachverhalt* "nominalized." But the apophansis is still a modality of saying. The predicative statement – a metalanguage necessary for the intelligibility of its own jetsam in a state of dissemination, and of its integral nominalization in mathematics – stands on the frontier of a dethematization of the said, and can be understood as a modality of approach and contact.[32] Over and beyond the thematization and the content exposed in it – entities and relations between entities shown in the theme – the apophansis signifies as a modality of the approach to another. It refers to a saying on the hither side of the amphibology of being and entities. This saying, in the form of responsibility for another, is bound to an irrecuperable, unrepresentable, past, temporalizing according to a time with separate epochs, in a diachrony. An analysis that starts with proximity, irreducible to consciousness of . . . , and describable, if possible, as an inversion[33] of its intentionality, will recognize this responsibility to be a substitution.

To maintain that the relationship with a neighbor, incontestably set up in saying, is a responsibility for the neighbor, that saying is to respond to another, is to find no longer any limit or measure for this responsibility, which "in the memory of man" has never been contracted, and is found to be at the mercy of the freedom and the fate, unverifiable by me, of the other man. It is to catch sight of an extreme passivity, a passivity that is not assumed, in the relationship with the other, and, paradoxically, in pure saying itself. The act of saying will turn out to have been introduced here from the start as the supreme passivity of exposure to another, which is responsibility for the free initiatives of the other. Whence there is an "inversion" of intentionality which, for its part, always preserves before deeds accomplished enough "presence of mind" to assume them. There is an abandon of the sovereign and active subjectivity, of undeclined self-consciousness, as the subject in the nominative form in an apophansis. And there is in subjectivity's relationship with the other, which we are here striving to describe, a quasi-hagiographic style that wishes to be neither a sermon nor the confession of a "beautiful soul."

It is not the discovery that "it speaks" or that "language speaks" that does justice to this passivity. One must show in saying, qua approach, the very de-posing or desituating of the subject, which nonetheless remains an irreplacable uniqueness, and is thus the subjectivity of the subject. This passivity is more passive still than any receptivity, in which for philosophers the supreme model of the passivity of the subject resides.

b. Saying as Exposure to Another

To say is to approach a neighbor, "dealing him signifyingness." This is not exhausted in "ascriptions of meaning," which are inscribed, as tales, in the said. Saying taken strictly is a "signifyingness dealt the other," prior to all objectification; it does not consist in giving signs. The "giving out of signs" would amount to a prior representation of these signs, as though speaking consisted in translating thoughts into words and consequently in having been first *for-oneself* and *at home with oneself*, like a substantial consistency. The relationship with the other would then extend forth as an intentionality, out of a subject posited in itself and for itself, disposed to play, sheltered from all ills and measuring by thought the being disclosed as the field of this play. Saying is communication, to be sure, but as a condition for all communication, as exposure. Communication is not reducible to the phenomenon of truth and the manifestation of truth conceived as a combination of psychological elements: thought in an ego – will or intention to make this thought pass into another ego – message by a sign designating this thought – perception of the sign by another ego – deciphering of the sign. The elements of this mosaic are already in place in the antecedent exposure of the ego to the other, the non-indifference to another, which is not a simple "intention to address a message." The ethical sense of such an exposure to another, which the intention of making signs, and even the signifyingness of signs, presuppose, is now visible. The plot of proximity and communication is not a modality of cognition.[34] The unblocking of communication, irreducible to the circulation of information which presupposes it, is accomplished in saying. It is not due to the contents that are inscribed in the said and transmitted to the interpretation and decoding done by the other. It is in the risky uncovering of oneself, in sincerity, the breaking up of inwardness and the abandon of all shelter, exposure to traumas, vulnerability.

Saying approaches the other by breaking through the noema involved in intentionality, turning inside out, "like a cloak," consciousness which, by itself would have remained for-itself even in its intentional aims. Intentionality remains an aspiration to be filled and fulfilment, the contripetal movement of a consciousness that coincides with itself, recovers, and rediscovers itself without ageing, rests in self-certainty, confirms itself, doubles itself up, consolidates itself, thickens into a substance. The subject in saying approaches a neighbor in expressing itself, in being expelled, in the literal sense of the term, out of any locus, no longer *dwelling*, not stomping any ground. Saying uncovers, beyond nudity, what dissimulation there may be under the exposedness of a skin laid bare. It is the very *respiration* of this skin prior to any intention. The subject is not *in itself*, at home with itself, such that it would dissimulate itself in itself or dissimulate itself in its wounds and its exile, understood as *acts* of wounding or exiling itself. Its bending back upon itself is a turning inside out. Its being "turned to another" is this being turned inside out. A concave without a convex. The subject of saying does not give signs, it becomes a sign, turns into an allegiance.

Here exposure has a sense radically different from thematization. The one is exposed to the other as a skin is exposed to what wounds it, as a cheek is offered to the smiter. On the hither side of the ambiguity of being and entities, prior to the said, saying uncovers the one that speaks, not as an object disclosed by theory, but in the sense that one discloses oneself by neglecting one's defenses, leaving a shelter, exposing oneself to outrage, to insults and wounding. But saying is a denuding of denuding, a giving a sign of its very signifyingness, an expression of exposure, a hyperbolic passivity that disturbs the still waters, in which, without saying, passivity would be crawling with secret designs. There is denuding of denuding, without this "reflection" or this iteration having to be added afterwards to the denuding. The passivity of the exposure responds to an assignation that identifies me as the unique one, not by reducing me to myself, but by stripping me of every identical quiddity, and thus of all form, all investiture, which would still slip into the assignation. The saying signifies this passivity; in the saying this passivity signifies, becomes signifyingness, exposure in response to . . . , being at the question before any interrogation, any problem, without clothing, without a shell to protect oneself, stripped to the core as in an inspiration of air, an ab-solution to the *one*, the one without a complexion. It is a denuding beyond the skin, to the wounds one dies from, denuding to death,[35] being as a vulnerability. It is a fission of the nucleus opening the bottom of its punctual nuclearity, like to a lung at the core of oneself. The nucleus does not open this depth as long as it remains protected by its solid crust, by a form, not even when it is reduced to its punctuality, for it identifies itself in the temporality of its essence, and thus covers itself over again. The limit of the stripping bare, in the punctual core, has to continue to be torn from itself. The one assigned has to open to the point of separating itself from its own inwardness, adhering to *esse*; it must be dis-interested. This being torn up from oneself in the core of one's unity, this absolute noncoinciding, this diachrony of the instant, signifies in the form of one-penetrated-by-the-other. The pain, this underside of skin, is a nudity more naked than all destitution. It is sacrificed rather than sacrificing itself, for it is precisely bound to the adversity or suffering of pain. This existence, with sacrifice imposed on it, is without conditions. The subjectivity of a subject is vulnerability, exposure to affection, sensibility, a passivity more passive still than any passivity, an irrecuperable time, an unassemblable diachrony of patience, an exposedness always to be exposed the more, an exposure to expressing, and thus to saying, thus to giving.

Saying, the most passive passivity, is inseparable from patience and pain, even if it can take refuge in the said, finding again in a wound the caress in which pain arises, and then the contact, and beyond it the knowing of a hardness or a softness, a heat or a cold, and then the thematization. Of itself saying is the sense of patience and pain. In saying suffering signifies in the form of *giving*, even if the price of signification is that the subject run the risk of suffering without reason. If the subject did not run this risk, pain would lose its very painfulness. Signification, as the one-for-the-other in passivity, where the other is not assumed by the one, presupposes the possibility of pure non-sense invading and threatening signification. Without this folly at the confines of reason, the one would take hold of itself, and, in the heart of its passion, recommence essence. How the adversity of pain is ambiguous! The for-the-other (or sense) turns into by-the-other, into suffering by a thorn burning the flesh, but *for nothing*. It is only in this way that the *for-the-other*, the passivity more passive still than any passivity, the emphasis of sense, is kept from being *for-oneself.*

Saying is a denuding, of the unqualifiable *one*, the pure *someone*, unique and chosen; that is, it is an exposedness to the other where no slipping away is possible. In its sincerity as a sign given to another, it absolves me of all identity, which would arise again like a curd coagulating for itself, would coincide with itself. This absolution reverses essence. It is not a negation of essence, but a disinterestedness, an "otherwise than being" which turns into a "for the other," burning for the other, consuming the bases of any position for oneself and any substantialization which would take form in this consummation, consuming even the ashes of this consummation, in which there would be a risk that everything be born again. Here identity lies in the total patience of the one assigned, who, patient, despite himself, dies continually, lasts in his instant, "whitens under the harness." The reverting of the ego into a self, the de-posing or de-situating of the ego, is the very modality of dis-interestedness. It has the form of a corporeal life devoted to expression and to giving. It is devoted, and does not devote itself: it is a self despite itself, in incarnation, where it is the very possibility of offering, suffering and trauma. Then the for-the-other involved in saying must not be treated in terms of consciousness of . . . , thematizing intentionality, nor in terms of commitment. The signifyingness of saying does not refer to commitment; for commitment presupposes saying.[36] How then are we to understand the *despite oneself*?

c. Despite Oneself

The *despite oneself* marks this life in its very living. Life is life despite life – in its patience and its ageing.

The *despite* is here not opposed to a wish, a will, a nature, a subsistence in a subject, which a foreign power would contrary. The passivity of the "for-another" expresses a sense in it in which no reference, positive or negative, to a prior will enters. It is the living human corporeality, as a possibility of pain, a sensibility which of itself is the susceptibility to being hurt, a self uncovered, exposed and suffering in its skin. In its skin it is stuck in its skin, not having its skin to itself, a vulnerability. Pain is not simply a *symptom* of a frustrated will, its meaning is not adventitious. The painfulness of pain, the malady or malignity of illness (*mal*), and, in the pure state, the very patience of corporeality, the pain of labor and ageing, are adversity itself, the against oneself that is in the self. The good or bad pleasure of the will presupposes this patience and this adversity, and this primordial lassitude. It is in terms of this adversity of suffering that one has to speak of the will, instead of reducing the "despite oneself" which is in suffering to a prior will. The passivity proper to patience, more passive thus than any passivity that is correlative to the voluntary, signifies in the "passive" synthesis of its temporality.

The temporalization of time, as it shows itself in the said, is indeed recuperated by an active ego which recalls through memory and reconstructs in historiography the past that is bygone, or through imagination and prevision anticipates the future, and, in writing, synchronizing the signs, assembles into a presence, that is, represents, even the time of responsibility for the other. But it is not possible that responsibility for another devolve from a *free* commitment, that is, a present; it exceeds every actual or represented present. It is thus in a time without beginning. Its anarchy cannot be understood as a simple return from present to prior present, an extrapolation of presents according to a memorable time, that is, a time assemblable in a recollection of a representable representation. This anarchy, this refusal to be assembled into a representation, has its own way to concern me: the *lapse*. But the lapse of time irrecuperable in the temporalization of time is not only negative like the immemorial.

Temporalization as lapse, the loss of time, is neither an initiative of an ego, nor a movement toward some telos of action.[37] The loss of time is not the work of a subject. Already the synthesis of retentions and protentions in which Husserl's phenomenological analysis, through an abuse of language, recuperates the lapse, bypasses the ego. Time passes (*se passe*). This synthesis which occurs *patiently*, called with profundity passive synthesis, is ageing. It breaks up under the weight of years, and is irreversibly removed from the present, that is, from re-presentation. In self-consciousness there is no longer a *presence* of self to self, but senescence. It is as senescence beyond the recuperation of memory that time, lost time that does not return, is a diachrony, and concerns me.

This diachrony of time is not due to the length of the interval, which representation would not be able to take in. It is a disjunction of identity where the same does not rejoin the same: there is non-synthesis, lassitude. The for-oneself of identity is now no longer for itself. The identity of the same in the ego comes to it despite itself from the outside, as an election or an inspiration, in the form of the uniqueness of someone assigned. The subject is for another; its own being turns into for another, its being dies away turning into signification. Subjectivity in ageing is unique, irreplaceable, me and not another; it is despite itself in an obedience where there is no desertion, but where revolt is brewing. These traits exclude one another, but they are resolved in responsibility for another, older than any commitment. In such a resolution not a world but a kingdom is signified. But a kingdom of an invisible king, the kingdom of the Good whose idea is already an eon. The Good that reigns in its goodness cannot enter into the present of consciousness, even if it would be remembered. In consciousness it is an anarchy. The Biblical notion of the Kingdom of God – kingdom of a non-thematizable God, a non-contemporaneous, that is, non-present, God – must not be conceived as an ontic image of a certain "époque" of the "history of Being," as a modality of essence. Rather, essence is already an Eon of the kingdom. One has to go back from the Eon to the kingdom of God, which signifies in the form of subjectivity, of the unique one assigned in the passive synthesis of life. It signifies in the form of the proximity of a neighbor and the duty of an unpayable debt, the form of a finite condition. Temporality as ageing and death of the unique one signifies an obedience where there is no desertion.

Thus the passage of the *Phaedo* which condemns suicide (*Phaedo* 61c-62c) is meaningful, and not only pious. Being for death is patience, non-anticipation, a duration despite onself, a form of obedience. Here the temporality of time is an obedience. The subject as a *one* discernible from the other, as an entity, is a pure abstraction if it is separated from this assignation.

But if we here formulate the subject as a being, it is not to call attention to the verb to be, which this participle will in the end refer to. Prior to this participation, and as an element necessary for the participation in the verb which is realized in the participle, there is signalled the purely formal eventuality of the nominal form of the individual. The nominal form, the form of the term as a term, of the *one* in this term, is irreducible to the verbal form. This nominal form comes from somewhere else than the verbalness of essence.[38] It is inseparable from the appeal one cannot elude, the assignation. Its irreducibility to a verb, even the verb to be, is significant. The subject as a term, as a noun, is someone. (Perhaps the "something" thematized in the direction of the finger that points, or Kant's "transcendental object," already owes its formal structure to it.) It is someone who, in the absence of anyone is called upon to be someone, and cannot slip away from this call. The subject is inseparable from this appeal or this election, which cannot be declined. It is in the form of the *being* of this entity, the diachronic temporality of ageing, that there is produced despite myself the response to an appeal, direct and like a traumatizing blow. Such a response cannot be converted into an "inward need" or a natural tendency. This response answers, but with no eroticism, to an absolutely heteronomous call.

d. Patience, Corporeality, Sensibility

The subject then cannot be described on the basis of intentionality, representational activity, objectification, freedom and will; it has to be described on the basis of the passivity of time. The temporalization of time, the lapse irrecuperable and outside of all will, is quite the contrary of intentionality. Not that time would be a less distinct intentionality than representation, heading in a direction less definite than that which goes to an object, to exteriority. Temporalization is the contrary of intentionality in the passivity of its patience. In it what is a subject is the inverse of a thematizing subject: a subjectivity in ageing which the identification of the ego with itself could not reckon on, *one* without identity, but unique in the unexceptionable requisition of responsibility. This requisition signifies as unexceptionable in the form of its *conatus existendi*, where its effort is an undergoing, a passive form of the self in "that comes to pass" (cela *se passe*). In the patience of senescence what is unexceptionable in proximity is articulated, the responsibility for the other man, "contracted" as it were on the hither side of memorable time, behind the "synthesis of apprehension" which is recognized to be identical in the said and in what is written. One has to go back to that hither side, starting from the trace retained by the said, in which everything shows itself. The movement back to the saying is the phenomenological reduction. In it the indescribable is described. The subject is described as a self, from the first in the accusative form, (or under accusation!), already presupposed by "the infinite freedom of the equal" with which Hegel characterizes the return to self involved in consciousness and time. This is produced already in a tale, in the said. The subject will be described denuded and stripped bare, as *one* or *someone*, expelled on the hither side of being, vulnerable, that is, sensible, to which – like the One of Plato's *Parmenides* – being can not be attributed.

The temporalization prior to the verb, or in a verb without a subject, or in the patience of a subject that lies as it were on the underside of the active ego, is the patience of ageing. It is not a position taken with regard to one's death, but a lassitude,[39] a passive exposure to being which is not assumed, an exposure to death – which thus is invisible, premature, always violent. Lassitude is that peculiar "being too much" which is also a failing but in a deficiency in which the *conatus* is not relaxed, where suicide is a desertion. Here it is as though a being, in being alienated, were only an eon of the kingdom, a modality of the necessities of being of service which characterize the "being for another," the "one for the other" involved in proximity. These necessities are more serious than being or not being. Such service is not slavery. But it is a necessity, because this obedience is prior to any voluntary decision which could have assumed it. This necessity overflows the same that is at rest, the life that enjoys life, since it is the necessity of a service. But, in this non-repose, this restlessness, it is better than rest. Such an antinomy bears witness to the Good.[40]

The self is characterized by a passivity that cannot be taken up. In this passivity no act comes to double up, commit, or multiply the one. The passivity of the subject in saying is not the passivity of a "language that speaks" without a subject (*Die Sprache spricht*). It is an offering oneself which is not even assumed by its own generosity, an offering oneself that is a suffering, a goodness despite oneself. The "despite" cannot be decomposed into a will contraried by an obstacle. It is life, ageing of life, and unexceptionable responsibility, saying. The subjectivity of subjection of the self is the suffering of suffering, the ultimate offering oneself, or suffering in the offering of oneself. Subjectivity is vulnerability, is sensibility. Sensibility, all the passivity of saying, cannot be reduced to an experience that a subject would have of it, even if it makes possible such an experience. An exposure to the other, it is signification, is signification itself, the-one-for-the-other to the point of substitution, but a substitution in separation, that is, responsibility. Our analysis will have to show that. It will examine the proximity which vulnerability signifies.

The corporeality of the subject is the pain of effort, the original adversity of fatigue, which arises in the upsurge of movement and in the energy involved in labor. In order to describe the passivity of the subject, one should not start with its opposition to a matter which resists it outside of it, or resists it in the body with which it would be incomprehensibly afflicted, and whose organization gets out of order. Nor should one start with the opposition between a man and a society that binds him to labor, while depriving him of the products of his labor. This passivity is, to be sure, an exposedness of the subject to another, but the passivity of the subject is more passive still than that which the oppressed one determined to struggle undergoes. The most passive, unassumable, passivity, the subjectivity or the very subjection of the subject, is due to my being obsessed with responsibility for the oppressed who is other than myself. Due to it the struggle remains human, and passivity does not simulate essence through a recapture of the self by the ego, in a will for sacrifice or generosity. The exposure to another is disinterestedness, proximity, obsession by the neighbor, an obsession despite oneself, that is, a pain. Pain must be not interpreted right off as an action undergone but assumed, that is, as an experience of pain by a subject that would be for itself. Pain is a pure deficit, an increase of debt in a subject that does not have a hold on itself, does not "join up the two ends." The subjectivity of the subject is precisely this non-recapture, an increasing of the debt beyond the *Sollen*. The adversity is assembled in corporeality which is susceptible to pain called physical, exposed to outrage and wounding, to sickness and ageing, but adversity is already there in the fatigue of the body's first efforts.[41] It is because my passivity as a subject, my exposedness to the other is physical pain itself that I can be exploited; it is not because I am exploited that my exposure to the another is absolutely passive, that is, excludes all assumption, is despite myself. In the form of corporeality, whose movements are fatigue and whose duration is ageing, the passivity of signification, of the one-for-another, is not an act, but patience, that is, of itself sensibility or imminence of pain.

Imminence in what sense?

Here imminence does not designate a pure possibility in neutrality. Imminence as pain arises in sensibility lived as well-being and enjoyment. If the for-another is a despite-oneself, if this despite-oneself is not a pure undergoing, the pure and simple passivity of an effect, if in a sense it is more humble than undergoing, and thus concerns the subject that undergoes in its uniqueness, this is because the for-another arises in the enjoyment in which the ego is affirmed, is complacent, and posits itself.

In corporeality are united the traits we have enumerated: for the other, despite oneself, starting with oneself, the pain of labor in the patience of ageing, in the duty to give to the other even the bread out of one's own mouth and the coat from one's shoulders. As a passivity in the paining of the pain felt, sensibility is a vulnerability, for pain comes to interrupt an enjoyment in its very isolation, and thus tears me from myself. It would be to fail to recognize the non-anonymousness of the for-another, which nonetheless does not imply anything voluntary, to think that the giving can remain a simple expenditure of the acquisitions accumulated. If giving is proximity itself, it takes on its full meaning only in stripping me of what is more my own than possession. Pain penetrates into the very heart of the for-oneself that beats in enjoyment, in the life that is complacent in itself, that lives of its life.[42] To give, to-be-for-another, despite oneself, but in interrupting the for-oneself, is to take the bread out of one's own mouth, to nourish the hunger of another with one's own fasting. The for-another characteristic of sensibility is enacted already in the enjoying and savoring, if we can express ourselves in this way. For sensibility does not enact the play of essence, does not play any game, is the very seriousness that interrupts the pleasure and complacency of games. It is with savoring and enjoying that the analysis of sensibility will have to begin.

e. The One

The exposure to the other is not something added to the one to bring it from the inward to the outside. Exposedness is the one-in-responsibility, and thus the one in its uniqueness, stripped of all protection that would multiply it. The "otherwise than being" is not a play, it is the relaxation more serious than being.

There is an extreme passivity of saying even in its last refuge; there is exposure to the other, a being required where no slipping away is possible. Uniqueness signifies through the non-coinciding with oneself, the non-repose in onself, restlessness. It is the reverse of certainty that falls back on itself; it does not identify itself and does not appear to knowing. It is in deficit, a point of pain. But, like the unity of the Kantian "I think," it is undeclinable in this passivity without any play. As an exception, and by abuse of language, one can name it me or I. But the denomination here is only a pronomination; there is *nothing* that is named *I*; the I is said by him that speaks. The pronoun already dissimulates the unique one that is speaking, subsumes it under a concept. But it designates only the mask or the person of the unique one, the mask that leaves the I evading concepts, the I involved in saying in the first person, absolutely unconvertible into a noun. For it is a sign given of this giving of signs, the exposure of oneself to another, in proximity and in sincerity. The subject in responsibility, like the unity of transcendental apperception, is not the semelfacticity of a unique exemplar, such as it manifests itself to be in the said, in tales; "once upon a time . . . ." Here uniqueness means the impossibility of slipping away and being replaced, in which the very recurrence of the I is effected. The uniqueness of the chosen or required one, who is not a chooser, is a passivity not being converted into spontaneity. This uniqueness not assumed, not subsumed, is traumatic; it is an election in persecution.

Chosen without assuming the choice! If this passivity is not reducible to the passivity of an effect in a causal relation, if it can be conceived to be on the hither side of freedom and non-freedom, it must have the meaning of a *"goodness despite itself,"* a goodness always older than the choice. Its value, that is, its excellence or goodness, the goodness of goodness, is alone able to counterbalance the violence of the choice (and, beyond counterbalancing, be for the better!). Goodness is always older than choice; the Good has always already chosen and required the unique one. As chosen without choosing its election, absent from the investiture received, the one is a passivity more passive still than all the passivity of undergoing. The passivity of the one, its responsibility or its pain, do not begin in consciousness – that is, do not begin. On the hither side of consciousness, they consist in this pre-original hold of the Good over it, always older than any present, any beginning. This diachrony prevents the one from joining up with itself and identifying itself as a substance, contemporary with itself, like a transcendental ego. Uniqueness is without identity. Not an identity, it is beyond consciousness, which is in itself and for itself. For it is already a substitution for the other.

The diachrony by which the uniqueness of the one has been designated, is the fact that the one is required, on the hither side of essence, by responsibility, and is always wanting with respect to itself, always insufficiently divested, in deficit, like a painful point. This diachrony of the subject is not a metaphor. The subject said as properly as possible (for the ground of saying is never properly said) is not in time, but is diachrony itself. In the identification of the ego, there is the ageing of him that one will never "catch up with there again." It is the diachrony of an election without identification, an election that impoverishes and denudes, a goodness that demands. This goodness consequently is not an attribute that would multiply the One, for if it were to multiply, if the One could be distinguished from the Goodness that sustains it, the One could take up a position with regard to its goodness, know itself to be good, and thus lose its goodness.

f. Subjectivity and Humanity
Concepts are ordered and unfold in truth (whose presuppositions, like conventions, make the combinations of concepts like a game), according to the logical possibilities of thought and the dialectical structures of being. Anthropology cannot lay claim to the role of a scientific or privileged philosophical discipline, with the pretext, formerly put forth, that the whole of the thinkable passes through human consciousness. This passage appears to the sciences of man to be liable to the greatest risks of deformation. Hegelianism, anticipating all the modern forms of distrust of the immediate data of consciousness, has accustomed us to think that truth no longer resides in the evidence acquired by myself, that is, in the evidence

sustained by the exceptional form of the *cogito*, which, strong in its first person form, would be first in everything. It has made us think that it rather resides in the unsurpassable plenitude of the content thought. In our days truth is taken to result from the effacing of the living man behind the mathematical structures that *think themselves out* in him, rather than he be thinking them.

For it is said in our day that nothing is more *conditioned* than the allegedly originary consciousness and the ego. The illusion that human subjectivity is capable of falling into is said to be particularly insidious. In approaching man the scientist remains a man, despite all the asceticism to which qua scientist he subjects himself. He runs the risk of taking his desires as realities without realizing it, of letting himself be guided by interests which introduce an inadmissible trickery into the play of concepts (despite the control and criticism that his partners or team-members can exercise), and of thus expounding an ideology as a science. The interests that Kant discovered in theoretical reason itself subordinated it to practical reason, which becomes reason pure and simple. It is just these interests that are contested by structuralism, which is perhaps to be defined by the primacy of theoretical reason. But disinterestedness is beyond essence.

It turns out, as we will see in the course of this study, that, even if one neglects the fact that cognition makes its way in it, the human sphere approached as an object among others takes on significations that link up and implicate one another in such a way as to lead to extreme and irreducible conceptual possibilities, possibilities that go beyond the limits of a description, even if it is dialectical, of order and being, lead to the extraordinary, to what is beyond the possible. Such conceptual possibilities are *substitution of one for another, the immemorable past that has not crossed the present, the positing of the self as a deposing of the ego, less than nothing as uniqueness, difference with respect to the other as nonindifference.* One is not obliged to subordinate to these possibilities the truth of sciences which bear on material or formal being or on being's essence. The dogmatism of mathematical and dialectical relations (attenuated only by a strange sensitivity for a certain apocalyptic poetry) is taken as necessary to exclude from the play of structures, called science (and still bound to being by the very rules of the game), the extreme possibilities of human significations, extra-vagant for precisely leading to something like issues. In these significations, far from any game and more strictly than in being itself, men stand who have never been more moved (whether in holiness or in guilt) than by other men in whom they recognize an identity even in the indiscernibility of their mass presence, and before whom they find themselves irreplaceable and unique in responsibility.

One can, to be sure, invoke, against the signifyingness of the extreme situations to which the concepts formed on the basis of human reality lead, the conditioned nature of the human. The suspicions engendered by psychoanalysis, sociology and politics[43] weigh on human identity such that we never know to whom we are speaking and what we are dealing with when we build our ideas on the basis of human facts. But we do not need this knowledge in the relationship in which the other is a neighbor, and in which before being an individuation of the genus *man*, a *rational animal*, a *free will*, or any essence whatever, he is the persecuted one for whom I am responsible to the point of being a hostage for him, and in which my responsibility, instead of disclosing me in my "essence" as a transcendental ego, divests me without stop of all that can be common to me and another man, who would thus be capable of replacing me. I am then called upon in my uniqueness as someone for whom no one else can substitute himself. One can ask if anything in the world is less conditioned than man, in whom the ultimate security a foundation would offer is absent. Is there then anything less unjustified than the contestation of the human condition? Does anything in the world deliver more immediately, beneath its alienation, its non-alienation, its separation, its holiness, which may define the anthropological over and beyond its genus? For reasons that are not transcendental but purely logical, should not the object man figure at the beginning of all knowing? The influences, complexes and dissimulation that cover over the human do not alter this holiness, but sanction the struggle for exploited man. Thus it is not as a freedom, impossible in a will that is inflated and altered, sold or mad, that subjectivity is imposed as an absolute. It is sacred in its alterity with respect to which, in an unexceptionable responsibility, I posit myself deposed of my sovereignty. Paradoxically it is qua *alienus* – foreigner and other – that man is not alienated.

The present study aims to disengage this holiness, not in order to preach some way of salvation (which there would be no shame in seeking), but in order to understand on the basis of the supreme abstractness and the supreme concreteness of the face of the other man those tragic or cynical accents, but always that acuteness, that continue to mark the sober description of the human sciences, in order to account for the impossible indifference with regard to the human which does not succeed in dissimulating itself in the incessant discourse about the death of God, the end of man and the disintegration of the world (no one is able to minimize the chances of that), but in which the wreckage preceding the catastrophe itself, like rats abandoning the ship before the shipwreck, come to us in the already insignificant signs of a language in dissemination.

CHAPTER III

SENSIBILITY AND PROXIMITY

I. SENSIBILITY AND COGNITION

Truth can consist only in the exposition of being to itself, in a singular inadequacy with itself which is also an equality, a partition in which the part counts for the whole, is the image of the whole. The image immediately welcomed without undergoing modifications is a sensible image. But the divergency between the image and the whole prevents the image from remaining in its fixity; it must stand at the confines of itself or beyond itself, so that truth not be incomplete or one-sided. The image has to symbolize the whole. Truth consists in a being whose images are its reflection, but also its symbol, being identified through new images. A symbol is apperceived or set up, and receives its *determination* in passivity and immediacy, or sensible concretion. But this immediacy is, in the knowing of the truth, always repressed. Knowing is then indirect and torturous. It is produced on the basis of the sensible intuition, which is already the sensible oriented toward that which, in the midst of the image, is announced as beyond the image, this as this or as that, this stripping itself of the halo of sensibility in which it nonetheless is reflected and abides. The intuition is already a sensibility becoming an *idea*, of another this as this, *aura* of another idea, openness in the openness. This dovetailing of ideas nowise prejudges the analytical, synthetical, dialectical spring which enables us to bring one idea out of another. Nor does it prejudge the hard work of "experimental" or "rational" research (which, in the concrete, is always divination and invention) which makes these implications explicit, draws one "content" out of another, identifies this and that. The subjective movement of cognition thus belongs to being's very essence, to its temporalization in which essence takes on sense, in which the image is already an idea, a symbol of another image, both theme and openness, pattern and transparency. This subjective movement, however, belongs to the very indifference of a noema to a noesis and to the thinker that is absorbed and forgotten in it.

Knowing, identification which understands or claims this as that, understanding, then does not remain in the pure passivity of the sensible.

Already the sensible as an intuition of an image is a claim. The intention that animates the identification of this as this or as that is a proclamation, a promulgation, and thus a language, a stating of the said. The first break with the passivity of the sensible is a saying in correlation with a said.[1] This is why all knowing is symbolic, and ends up in a linguistic formula.

Here we touch on an ambiguous point, about which all our discussion is organized. The saying that states a said is in the sensible the first "activity" that sets up this as that. This activity of sentencing and judgement, thematization and theory, occurs in the saying as a pure for-another, a pure giving of signs, making oneself a sign, expression of self, sincerity, passivity. But one can show the turning of this saying, this pure self-expression in a giving of signs to another (language prior to the said), into a saying stating a said. We will see the nominalization of the statement, which cuts it from the proposition it makes to another. Through it, the saying is absorbed in the said, offering in a "tale" a structure in which the words of living language inventoried in dictionaries (but which form a synchronic system for a speaker) find their connections.

Be that as it may, the said is not added on to a preexisting knowing, but is the most profound activity of knowing, its very symbolism. Then symbolism in knowing is not an effect of a frustration, a substitute for a missing intuition, Husserl's non-fulfilled signitive thought. It is *beyond* the sensible already in intuition, and *beyond* intuition in ideas. That knowing be conceptual and symbolic is then not a makeshift of a thought which would be incapable of opening intuitively upon the things themselves. Of itself the openness upon being is imagination and symbolism. The disclosed qua disclosed overflows itself as a symbol of this in that; it is identified in the this as that. It is then from the first claimed and said. Thus knowing is always a priori; it is beyond the play of reflections to which the intuition called sensible is usually reduced. Understanding, without which the image would be immobilized, has the authority of a supreme and sovereign instance, proclaiming, promulgating the identity of this and that. This has long been recognized in philosophy, when it spoke of the spontaneity of understanding.

If all openness involves understanding, the image in sensible intuition has already lost the immediacy of the sensible. The exposedness to affection, vulnerability, has doubtless not the signification of *reflecting being*. As discovery and knowing, sensible intuition is already of the order of the said; it is an ideality. An idea is not a simple sublimation of the sensible. The difference between the sensible and an idea is not the difference between more or less exact cognitions or between cognitions of the individual and of the universal. An individual inasmuch as it is known is already desensibilized and referred to the universal in intuition. The signification proper to the sensible has to be described in terms of enjoyment and wounding, which are, we will see, the terms of proximity.

Proximity, which should be the signification of the sensible, does not belong to the movement of cognition. Cognition is the operation in which the idea which a word substitutes for the image of an entity "enlarges the horizon" of the appearing, and reabsorbs the shadow whose opacity the consistency of the given projects on to the transparency of intuition. Intuition, which has been opposed to a concept, is already the sensible conceptualized. Sight, by reason of its distance and its totalizing embrace, imitates or prefigures the "impartiality" of the intellect and its refusal to hold to what the immediacy of the sensible would dispose, or what it would constitute. The proper sense of this disposition moreover is in fact something different; it is not at all exhausted in arresting the movement and dynamism of knowledge.

Even when unformed, or deformed, by knowing, sensible intuition can revert to its own meaning. Sensation already functions as sensible intuition; it is the unity of the sensing and the sensed in the divergency, and recoveries, of temporality, where the past is rememberable. It is an identity in the discursiveness of the this and the that, the this as that, which ensures a being's presence to itself. Sensation is already the element of consciousness, and as such is the source of idealism, while at the same time breaking with idealism. Berkeley's idealist sensualism, whose vigorous positions Husserl's phenomenology prolongs in our day, consists in reducing the sensible qualities of objects into contents experienced, in which, in an adequate possession of the sensed by the sensing, the immanent essence of consciousness, the coinciding of being with its manifestation, is found again. This is in fact the essence of idealism. It is also affirmed in contemporary ontology, in another form.

But sensation, which is at the basis of sensible experience and intuition, is not reducible to the clarity or the idea derived out of it. Not because it would involve an opaque element resistant to the luminousness of the intelligible, but still defined in terms of light and sight. It is vulnerability, enjoyment and suffering, whose status is not reducible to the fact of being put before a spectator subject. The intentionality involved in disclosure, and the symbolization of a totality which the openness of being aimed at by intentionality involved, would not constitute the sole or even the dominant signification of the sensible. The dominant meaning of sensibility should indeed enable us to account for its secondary signification as a sensation, the element of a cognition. We have already said that the fact that sensibility can become "sensible intuition" and enter into the adventure of cognition is not a contingency. The dominant signification of sensibility is already caught sight of in vulnerability, and it will be shown in the respon-

64

sibility characteristic of proximity, in its restleness and its insomnia; it contains the motivation for its cognitive function.

In knowing, which is of itself symbolic, is realized the passing from the image, a limitation and a particularity, to the totality. Consequently, being's essence is moved into the whole content of abstraction. Western philosophy has never doubted the gnoseological, and consequently ontological, structure of signification. To say that in sensibility this structure is secondary, and that sensibility qua vulnerability nonetheless signifies, is to recognize a sense somewhere else than in ontology. It is even to subordinate ontology to this signification beyond essence. The immediacy on the surface of the skin characteristic of sensibility, its vulnerability, is found as it were anaesthetized in the process of knowing. But also, no doubt, repressed or suspended. By contrast with this vulnerability (which presupposes enjoyment differently than as its antithesis), knowing, being's disclosure to itself, marks a break with the immediate, and in a certain sense an abstraction. The immediacy of the sensible which is not reducible to the gnoseological role assumed by sensation is the exposure to wounding and to enjoyment, an exposure to wounding in enjoyment, which enables the wound to reach the subjectivity of the subject complacent in itself and positing itself for itself. This immediacy is first of all the ease of enjoyment, more immediate than drinking, the sinking into the depths of the element, into its incomparable freshness, a plenitude and a fulfilment. It is pleasure, that is, the complacency in itself of life loving life even in suicide. The complacency of subjectivity, a complacency experienced for itself, is its very "egoity," its substantiality. But at the same time there is a coring out (*dénucléation*), of the imperfect happiness which is the murmur of sensibility. There is a non-coinciding of the ego with itself, restlessness, insomnia, beyond what is found again in the present. There is the pain which confounds the ego or in vertigo draws it like an abyss, and prevents it from assuming the other that wounds it in an intentional movement when it posits itself in itself and for itself. Then there is produced in this vulnerability the reversal whereby the other inspires the same, pain, an overflowing of meaning by nonsense. Then sense bypasses nonsense – that sense which is the-same-for-the-other. The passivity or patience of vulnerability has to go that far! In it sensibility is sense; it is by the other and for the other, for another. Not in elevated feelings, in "belles lettres," but as in a tearing away of bread from the mouth that tastes it, to give it to the other. Such is the coring out (*dénucléation*) of enjoyment, in which the nucleus of the ego is cored out.

2. SENSIBILITY AND SIGNIFICATION

A thermal, gustative or olfactory sensation is not primarily a cognition of a pain, a savor, or an odor. No doubt it can take on this signification of being a discovery by losing its own sense, becoming an experience of .., a consciousness of . . . , "placing itself" before the being exposed in its theme, in discourse, in which every commencement begins. But then it is already a saying correlative with and contemporary with a said. The present characteristic of manifestation, origin of the very fact of origins, is an origin for philosophy. And it is again in a thematizing discourse that sensation issues.

But does sensation succeed in staying between its beginning an its outcome? Does it not signify outside of these terms? Philosophy, which is born with appearing, with thematization, tries, in the course of its phenomenology, to reduce the manifest and the manifestation to their preoriginal signification, a signification that does not signify manifestation. There is room to think that this preoriginal signification includes the motifs of origin and appearing. Yet it is not thereby shut up in a present or a representation. If it also signifies the dawning of a manifestation in which it can indeed shine forth and show itself, its signifying is not exhausted in the effusion or dissimulation of this light.

It is from this commencement or this outcome of philosophy, conceived as a *nec plus ultra*, that Husserl is inspired in his interpretation of subjectivity as a consciousness of . . . , his theory of the priority of the "doxic thesis," bearing all intentionality whatever be its quality, his theory about the possible transformation of every non-theoretical intentionality into a theoretical intentionality which would be founding, a transformation that would be effected without recourse to reflection on the act involved, which reflection would objectify non-theoretical intentionality. Despite the great contribution of Husserl's philosophy to the discovery, through the notion of non-theoretical intentionality, of significations other than those of appearing, and of the subjectivity as a source of significations, defined by this upsurge and connection of meanings, a fundamental analogy is constantly affirmed by Husserl between the cognitive consciousness of . . . , on the one hand, and axiological or practical intentions, on the other. Between the experience of being, on the one hand, and action and desire, on the other, a rigorous parallelism is maintained. Axiology becomes a "cognition" of values or of what ought to be, and practice becomes the cognition of what is to be done or of usage objects. Sensation, a "primary content" in the *Logical Investigations*, or a *hylè* in the *Ideas*, participates in the meaningful only inasmuch as it is *animated* by intentionality, or constituted immanent time according to the schema of theoretical consciousness of . . . in retention and protention, in memory and expectation. Of course no one would deny that in the olfactory or the gustatory sensation the openness upon..., consciousness of..., or experience of... is not the dominant, that the enjoying or suffering which these sensations are do not *signify* like knowings, even if their signification shows itself in knowing. The distinction between a representational content and the content called affective in sensation belongs to the most ordinary psychology. But how does a signification signify, if its presentation in a theme, its shining forth, is not its signifyingness or its intelligibility, but only its manifestation, if its breakthrough into the light is not all there is to its signifyingness? This signifyingness is then conceived in the philosophical tradition of the West as a modality of its manifestation, a light "of another color" than that which fills the theoretical intentionality, but still a light. The structure of intentionality still remains that of thought or comprehension. The affective remains an information: about oneself, about values (as in Max Scheler), about a disposition in being's essence, and at the same time, through this disposition, an understanding of essence (as in the *Stimmung* of Heidegger), an ontology, whatever be the modalities and structures of existence that overflow all that the intellectualist tradition understood by thought, but which are nonetheless packed into a logos of being. But perhaps this prior cognition and comprehension in intentionality seem to so easily accommodate themselves to significations different from thematization only because Husserl himself imperceptively introduces into his description of intention an element that is different from pure thematization: intuition fills (that is, contents or satisfies) or deceives an aim aiming emptily as its object. From the emptiness that a symbol involves with respect to the image which illustrates the symbolized, one passes to the emptiness of hunger. Here there is a *desire* outside of the simple consciousness of...It is still an intention, but intention in a sense radically different from theoretical aim, and the practice that theory involves. Intention is now taken as desire, such that intention, occurring between deception and *Erfüllung*, already reduces the "objectifying act" to a specification of a tendency, rather than hunger being a particular case of "consciousness of..."

Consciousness of..., correlative with manifestation, a structure of every intentionality, would, on the other hand, be, in Husserl, founding of everything that shows itself, or even the essence of all that shows itself. Does not Heidegger himself maintain the founding primacy of cognition inasmuch as being's essence which stamps every entity, and outside of which one cannot go, a mystery ungraspable in itself, conditions, by its very withdrawal, the entry of light, and manifests its own mystery by the disclosure of entities? The cognition that is stated in predicative judgments is naturally founded on it. Since being's essence makes truth possible, by this very essence, the subject (whatever be the name one gives it) is inseparable from

knowing and the showing effected by intentionality. But cannot significations beyond essence, which do not signify phosphorescence and appearing, show themselves[2] even if only by betraying themselves in their
manifestation by their appearing taking on the appearances of essence,
which, however, call for a reduction? Does the fact of showing oneself
exhaust the *sense* of what does indeed show itself, but, being non-
theoretical, does not function, does not signify as a monstration? Where
are we to situate the residue which is neither what shows itself in the openness, nor the disclosure itself, the openness, idea or truth of what shows
itself? Is it certain that manifestation *founds* all that manifests itself? And
must it not itself be justified by what manifests itself?

The interpretation of sensible signification in terms of consciousness
of . . . , however little intellectualist one means it, does not account for the
sensible. It does indeed mark a progress over sensualist atomism, for it
avoids the mechanization of the sensible through the "abyss of meaning"
or transcendence that separates the lived experience from the "intentional
object." Indeed in the transcendence of intentionality diachrony is
reflected, that is, the psyche itself, in which the inspiration of the same by
the other is articulated as a responsibility for another, in proximity. Sensibility is in this way situated back in the human exception. But one has to
go back from this reflection to the diachrony itself, which is the-one-for-
the-other in proximity. It is then not a particular signification. The-one-
for-another has the form of sensibility or vulnerability, pure passivity or
susceptibility, passive to the point of becoming an inspiration, that is,
alterity in the same, the trope of the body animated by the soul, psyche in
the form of a hand that gives even the bread taken from its own mouth.
Here the psyche is the maternal body.

When interpreted as openness of disclosure, as consciousness of . . . , sensibility would be already reduced to sight, idea and intuition, a synchrony
of thematized elements and their simultaneity with the look. But there is
room to ask if sight itself is exhausted in openness and cognition? Are
expressions such as "enjoying a spectacle," or "eating up with one's eyes"
purely metaphorical? To show the way non-representational sensations signify is to describe their psyche before identifying it with consciousness
of . . . , thematizing consciousness, before finding in it the reflection of this
diachrony. Thematizing consciousness in the privileged role of manifestation that belongs to it takes on its meaning in the psyche which it does not
exhaust, and which has to be described positively. Otherwise ontology is
imposed not only as the beginning of thematizing thought – which is inevitable – and as its term in a writing, but as signifyingness itself.

We will then try to show here that signification is sensibility. The fact
that one could not philosophize before the monstration in which sense is

already a said, a something, a thematized, does not at all imply that monstration does not justify itself by signification. Signification may motivate monstration and be manifested in it as something betrayed, something to be reduced, that is, would be manifested in the said. The fact that one could not philosophize before the manifestation of something also does not imply that the signification "being," correlative of every manifestation, would be the source of this manifestation and of all signification, as one could think when one starts with Heidegger – or that monstration would be the foundation of everything that manifests itself, as Husserl thinks. We have to begin again to reflect about the very sense of a psyche which in the Western tradition is in play between being and its manifestation, or in the correlation of being with its manifestation.

Nothing is changed when one enlarges the notion of consciousness of . . . , and describes it as an "access to Being." The exteriority that this way of speaking presupposes is already borrowed from thematization, consciousness of . . . , the self sufficient correlation of the saying and the said. The "access to being" states a notion as tautological as the "manifestation of being," or ontology. Manifestation remains the privileged and ultimate sense of the subjective; the very idea of ultimate or primary sense, which is ontological, remains. The notion of access to being, representation, and thematization of a said presuppose sensibility, and thus proximity, vulnerability and signifyingness. Between the signification proper to the sensible and that of thematization and the thematized as thematized, the abyss is much greater than the parallelism constantly affirmed by Husserl between all the "qualities" or "theses" of intentionality would allow one to suppose. This parallelism would imply the equivalence of the psyche and the intentional. In renouncing intentionality as a guiding thread toward the eidos of the psyche, which would command the eidos of sensibility, our analysis will follow sensibility in its prenatural signification to the maternal, where, in proximity, signification signifies before it gets bent into *perseverance in being* in the midst of a Nature.

3. SENSIBILITY AND PSYCHE

The psyche involved in intentionality does not lie in consciousness of . . . , its power to thematize, or in the "truth of Being," which is discovered in it through different significations of the said. The psyche is the form of a peculiar dephasing, a loosening up or unclamping of identity: the same prevented from coinciding with itself, at odds, torn up from its rest, between sleep and insomnia, panting, shivering. It is not an abdication of the same, now alienated and slave to the other, but an abnegation of oneself fully responsible for the other. This identity is brought out by responsibility and is at the service of the other. In the form of responsibility, the psyche in the soul is the other in me, a malady of identity, both accused and *self*, the same for the other, the same by the other.[3] Qui pro quo, it is a substitution, extraordinary. It is neither a deception nor truth, but the preliminary intelligibility of signification. But it is an overwhelming of the order of the thematizable being in the said, of the simultaneity and reciprocity of the relations said. Such a signification is only possible as an incarnation. The animation, the very pneuma of the psyche, alterity in identity, is the identity of a body exposed to the other, becoming "for the other," the possibility of giving. The non-assemblable duality of the elements of this trope is the diachrony of the one for the other, the signifyingness of intelligibility which does not arise out of presence or out of the simultaneity of essence, of which it would be the subsiding. Intentionality is not a psyche through the thematizing it operates,[4] whatever role manifestation has in the commencement of philosophy, and whatever necessity light has for the very signification of responsibility. The psyche in intentionality, beyond the correlation of the said and the saying, is due to the signifyingness of the saying and the incarnation, the diachrony; for intentionality never makes itself simultaneous with the theme it aims at, except by losing its sense, betraying itself, *appearing* according to the intelligibility of a system.[5] The signification which animates the affective, the axiological, the active, the sensible, hunger, thirst, desire, admiration, is not due to the thematization one can find in them, nor to a variation or a modality of thematization. The-one-for-the-other which constitutes their signifyingness is not a knowing of being, nor some other access to essence. These significations do not draw their signifyingness from knowing nor from their condition of being known. The signifyingness they bear in a system, in the said, in the simultaneity of a particular language, is borrowed from this prior psyche, which is signifyingness par excellence. In a system signification is due to the definition of terms by one another in the synchrony of a totality, where the whole is the finality of the elements. It is due to the system of the language on the verge of being spoken. It is in this situation that universal synchrony is effected. In the said, to have a meaning is for an element to be in such a way as to turn into references to other elements, and for the others to be evoked by it. It is indeed clear that the psyche can thus have a sense like any other term of the language stated, showing itself in the said, in tales or writing. A psychic fact can have sense as referred to another psychic fact, like any element of the world of the experience called exterior. Perception is understood by reference to memory and expectation, and perception, memory and expectation are united by their cognitive essence, their "impassiveness," and can be understood by opposition to the will, need, hunger – actively or passively restless. And these in turn are understood with reference to the serenity of the theoretical. Formulas like "every consciousness is a consciousness of something" and "every perception is a perception of the perceived" can be understood in this synchronic sense and express the most flat banalties, taking their meaning from a system, signifying in function of its more or less worked out articulation. The meaning of perception, hunger, sensation, etc. as notions signifies through the correlation of terms in the simultaneity of a linguistic system. It has to be distinguished from the signifyingness of the-one-for-the-other, the psyche that animates perception, hunger and sensation. Here animation is not a metaphor, but, if we can put it thus, a designation of the irreducible paradox of intelligibility: the other in the same, the trope of the for-the-other in its antecedent inflexion. This signification in its very signifyingness, outside of every system, before any correlation, is an accord or peace between planes which, as soon as they are thematized, make an irreparable cleavage, like vowels in a dieresis, maintaining a hiatus without elision. They then mark two Cartesian orders, the body and the soul, which have no common space where they can touch, and no logical *topos* where they can form a whole. Yet they are in accord prior to thematization, in an accord, a chord, which is possible only as an arpeggio. Far from negating intelligibility, this kind of accord is the very rationality of signification in which the tautological identity, the ego, receives the other, and takes on the meaning of an irreplaceable identity by giving to the other.

The said shows, but betrays (shows by betraying) the dieresis, the disorder of the psyche which animates the *consciousness of*, and which, in the philosophical order of the said, is called transcendence. But it is not in the said that the psyche signifies, even though it is manifested there. Signification is the-one-for-the-other which characterizes an identity that does not coincide with itself. This is in fact all the gravity of an animate body, that is, one offered to another, expressed or opened up! This opening up, like a reverse *conatus*, an inversion of essence, is a relationship across an absolute difference. It is not reducible to any synchronic and reciprocal relationship which a totalizing and systematic thought would seek in it, the thought concerned with understanding the "unity of the soul and the body." It is neither a structure, nor an inwardness of a content in a container, nor a causality, nor even a dynamism, which still extends in a time that could be collected into a history. Merleau-Ponty's "fundamental historicity," the assembling into a world of the subject and of its world, is enacted in the said.[6] The psyche or animation is the way a relationship between uneven terms, without any common time, arrives at relationship. Non-objectifiable, non-contemporaneous, it can only signify non-indifference. An animate body or an incarnate identity is the signifyingness of this non-indifference.

Animation is not better expressed by the metaphor of inhabitation, the presence of a pilot in the helm of his boat, a vital principle immediately assimilated with a directive principle, or the virility of a logos and a command. Animation can be understood as an exposure to the other, the passivity of the for-the-other in vulnerability, which refers to maternity, which sensibility signifies. Sensibility cannot be better expressed by starting with receptivity, where sensibility has already been made into representation, thematization, assembling of the same and the other into a present, into essence. Nor by starting with consciousness of . . . , which retains aspects of this present in the form of knowings, information and messages, but divests being only of images like innumerable pelts (which makes possible the multiplication of a being on innumerable screens) under which the skin of a being, present "in flesh and bone," remains intact.

The modification of the sensibility into intentionality is motivated by the very signification of sensing as a for-the-other. One can show the latent birth of justice in signification. Justice, which must become a synchronic consciousness of being, is present in a theme in which the intentionality of consciousness itself shows itself. As manifestation, consciousness of . . . can be expressed in terms of subjectivity as well as in terms of being; there is strict correlation here. The psyche no longer signifies as the-one-for-the-other, but is neutralized into serenity, equity, as though consciousness belonged to the simultaneity of the said, to themes, to being. To knowledge as symbolic aim corresponds being showing itself symbolically, significatively, in Husserl's sense, on the basis of an other than itself, and to intuition – being in its image as a presence (perception) or as an absence (imagination and memory). Then the whole of the psyche can be interpreted as a knowing; the axiological and the practical, hunger and thirst, the gustative and the olfactory sensation, etc., show themselves as modalities of consciousness . . . , reaching objects cloaked with attributes of value. Then the psyche is latent in intentionality; its correlation is understood as a simultaneity of the act of consciousness with its intentional correlative spread out in the system of the said. Hunger then is hunger of the edible, perception consciousness of the perceived, like "four is twice two." The phenomenological, that is, *reductive*, description, should distrust such a presentation of the psychic, making it constitute a system, a set of specifications or variations of consciousness of . . . . One forgets justice, in which this simultaneity is aroused. Justice refers to a psyche, not, to be sure, as a thematization, but as the diachrony of the same and the other in sensibility.

When not reduced, sensibility is the duality of the sensing and the sensed, a separation, and at once a union, in time, a putting of the instant out of phase, and already a retention of the separated phase. As reduced, sensibility is animated, a signification of the one for the other, a duality not assemblable of the soul and the body, the body being inverted into a for-the-other by animation, a diachrony other than that of representation.

The signification of the gustatory and the olfactory, of eating and enjoying, has to be sought on the basis of the signifyingness of signification, the-one-for-the-other. For we have shown that the one-for-the-other characteristic of the psyche, signification, is not an ordinary formal relation, but the whole gravity of the body extirpated from its *conatus*. It is a passivity more passive still than any passivity that is antithetical to an act, a nudity more naked than all "academic" nudity, exposed to the point of outpouring, effusion and prayer. It is a passivity that is not reducible to exposure to another's gaze. It is a vulnerability and a paining exhausting themselves like a hemorrhage, denuding even the aspect that its nudity takes on, exposing its very exposedness, expressing itself, speaking, uncovering even the projection that the very form of identity confers upon it. It is the passivity of being-for-another, which is possible only in the form of giving the very bread I eat. But for this one has to first enjoy one's bread, not in order to have the merit of giving it, but in order to give it with one's heart, to give oneself in giving it. Enjoyment is an ineluctable moment of sensibility.

4. ENJOYMENT

In a gustative sensation, sensibility does not consist in confirming the aim of hunger with an image or an aspect of a presence. The description of all sensibility as a fulfilment, an *Erfüllung*, or a deception of consciousness of . . . implies a hunger, which, without constituting the ultimate sense of the sensibility, still troubles the sensation now become a knowing. In a gustative sensation there is not produced some covering over of the sense aimed at by its illustration, by a presence "in flesh and bone." In it a hunger is satisfied. To fill, to satisfy, is the sense of the savor, and it is precisely to leap over the images, aspects, reflections or silhouettes, phantoms, phantasms, the hides of things that are enough for the consciousness of . . . . The emptiness of hunger is emptier than all curiosity, cannot be compensated for with the mere hearsay of what it demands. This leap over the images devours the distance more radically than when the distance between a subject and its object is suppressed. A sinking in that never goes far enough, the impatience of being sated by which it has to be defined, can be discerned in the fusion of the sensing and the sensed. The suppression goes so far as to break up the form that the content apprehended in tasting still has, the form which makes the quality belong to the category of quality. Informed by this form, quality is capable of being "reflected," of having "aspects," of being multiplied in images and information. Savor inasmuch as it satisfies a hunger, savor as quenching, is a breaking up of the form of a phenomenon which becomes amorphous and turns into "prime matter." Matter carries on, "does its job" of being matter, "materializes" in the satisfaction, which fills an emptiness before putting itself into a form and presenting itself to the knowing of this materiality and the possession of it in the form of goods.[7] Tasting is first satisfaction. Matter "materializes" in satisfaction, which, over and beyond any intentional relationship of cognition or possession, of "taking in one's hands," means "biting into...." It is irreducible to a taking in one's hands, for it is already an absorption of a "within" including the ambiguity of two inwardnesses: that of a recipient of spatial forms, and that of an ego assimilating the other in its identity, and coiling in over itself.

A gustative sensation is not a knowing accompanying the physico-chemical or biological mechanism of consuming, a consciousness of the objective filling of a void, a spectacle miraculously interiorized in the tasting; it is not an epiphenomenal echoing of a physical event, nor the "reflection" of the spatial structure of filling, nor the idealist constitution, in the psyche involved in sensation, of an object that would be the tooth that bites on the bread. To bite on the bread is the very meaning of tasting. The taste is the way a sensible subject becomes a volume, or the irreducible event in which the spatial phenomenon of biting becomes the identification called me, in which it becomes me through the life that lives from its very life in a *frueri vivendi*. Satisfaction satisfies itself with satisfaction. Life enjoys its very life, as though it nourishes itself with life as much as with what makes it live, or, more exactly, as though nourishing oneself had this twofold reference. Before any reflection, any return upon oneself, enjoyment is an enjoying of enjoyment, always wanting with regard to itself, filling itself with these lacks for which contentment is promised, satisfying itself already with this impatient process of satisfaction, enjoying its own appetite. There is enjoying of enjoyment before any reflection, but enjoyment does not turn toward enjoyment as sight turns toward the seen. Beyond the multiplication of the visible in images, enjoyment is the singularization of an ego in its coiling back upon itself. Winding of a skein, it is the very movement of egoism. It has to be able to be complacent in itself, as though it exhausted the eidos of sensibility, so that sensibility could, in its passivity, its patience and pain, signify for the other by unwinding its coils. Without egoism, complacent in itself, suffering would not have any sense. It would lose the passivity of patience, if it were not at every moment an overflowing of sense by non-sense. Enjoyment and the singularization of sensibility in an ego take from the supreme passivity of sensibility, from its vulnerability, its exposedness to the other, the anonymousness of the meaningless passivity of the inert. The possibility in suffering of suffering for nothing prevents the passivity in it from reverting into an act. Thus, the for-the-other both thwarts the subject and affects it in its inwardness through pain. Enjoyment in its ability to be complacent in itself, exempt from dialectical tensions, is the condition of the for-the-other involved in sensibility, and in its vulnerability as an exposure to the other.

This sensibility has meaning only as a "taking care of the other's need," of his misfortunes and his faults, that is, as a giving. But giving has meaning only as a tearing from oneself despite oneself, and not only *without* me. And to be torn from oneself despite oneself has meaning only as a being torn from the complacency in oneself characteristic of enjoyment, snatching the bread from one's mouth. Only a subject that eats can be for-the-other, or can signify. Signification, the-one-for-the-other, has meaning only among beings of flesh and blood.

Sensibility can be a vulnerability, an exposedness to the other or a saying only because it is an enjoyment. The passivity of wounds, the "hemorrhage" of the for-the-other, is the tearing away of the mouthful of bread from the mouth that tastes in full enjoyment. This is despite oneself, to be sure, but not as an affection or an indifferent surface. It is an attack made immediately on the plenitude of the complacency in oneself (which is also a complacency of complacency), on the identity in enjoyment (more identical still than any identification of a term in the said), on life in which signification, the for-the-other, is swallowed up, on life living or enjoying life.

The immediacy of the sensible is the immediacy of enjoyment and its frustration. It is the gift painfully torn up, and in the tearing up, immediately spoiling this very enjoyment. It is not a gift of the heart, but of the bread from one's mouth, of one's own mouthful of bread. It is the openness, not only of one's pocketbook, but of the doors of one's home, a "sharing of your bread with the famished," a "welcoming of the wretched into your house" (Isaiah 58). The immediacy of the sensibility is the for-the-other of one's own materiality; it is the immediacy or the proximity of the other. The proximity of the other is the immediate opening up for the other of the immediacy of enjoyment, the immediacy of taste, materialization of matter, altered by the immediacy of contact.[8]

5. VULNERABILITY AND CONTACT

Sensibility is exposedness to the other. Not the passivity of inertia, a persistence in a state of rest or of movement, the capacity to undergo the cause that would bring it out of that state. Exposure as a sensibility is more passive still; it is like an inversion of the *conatus* of *esse*, a having been offered without any holding back, a not finding any protection in any consistency or identity of a state. It is a having been offered without any holding back and not the generosity of offering oneself, which would be an act, and already presupposes the unlimited undergoing of the sensibility. In the having been offered without any holding back the past infinitive form underlines the non-present, the non-commencement, the non-initiative of the sensibility. This non-initiative is older than any present, and is not a passivity contemporaneous with and counterpart of an act. It is the hither side of the free and the non-free, the anarchy of the Good. In the having been offered without any holding back, it is as though the sensibility were precisely what all protection and all absence of protection already presuppose: vulnerability itself.

At the height of its gnoseological adventure everything in sensibility means intuition, theoretical receptivity from a distance (which is that of the look). But as soon as it falls back into contact,[9] it reverts from grasping to being grasped, like in the ambiguity of a kiss. It reverts from the activity of being a hunter of images to the passivity of being prey, from being aim to being wound, from being an intellectual act of apprehension to apprehension as an obsession by another who does not manifest himself. On the hither side of the zero point which marks the absence of protection and cover, sensibility is being affected by a non-phenomenon, a being put in question by the alterity of the other, before the intervention of a cause, before the appearing of the other. It is a pre-original not resting on oneself, the restlessness of someone persecuted — Where to be? How to be? It is a writhing in the tight dimensions of pain, the unsuspected dimensions of the hither side. It is being torn up from oneself, being less than nothing, a rejection into the negative, behind nothingness; it is maternity, gestation of the other in the same. Is not the restlessness of someone persecuted but a modification of maternity, the groaning of the wounded entrails by those it will bear or has borne? In maternity what signifies is a responsibility for others, to the point of substitution for others and suffering both from the effect of persecution and from the persecuting itself in which the persecutor sinks. Maternity, which is bearing par excellence, bears even responsibility for the persecuting by the persecutor.

Rather than a nature, earlier than nature, immediacy is this vulnerability, this maternity, this pre-birth or pre-nature in which the sensibility belongs. This proximity is narrower, more constrictive, than contiguity, older than every past present. The ego repudiates the past present; bent under the charge of an immemorial weight, the inflexible ego, an undeclinable guarantee against any cancellation, supports the other it confronts because it would have committed itself to that weight, or in reminiscence would have assumed, as ancient and essential, commitments it would have taken on unbeknownst to itself. In the proximity of contact arises every committed freedom, which is termed finite by contrast with the freedom of choice of which consciousness is the essential modality. Yet the effort is made to reduce all commitment to freedom. Astonished to find itself implicated in the world of objects — the theme of its free contemplation — consciousness will search in its memory for the forgotten moment in which unbeknownst to itself it allied itself with objects or consented to apperceive itself in union with them. Such a moment, when awakened by memory, would become, after the event, the instant of an alliance made in full freedom. Such a reduction refuses the irreducible anarchy of responsibility for another.

Maternity, vulnerability, responsibility, proximity, contact – sensibility can slip toward touching, palpation, openness upon . . ., consciousness of . . ., pure knowing taking images from the "intact being," informing itself about the palpable quiddity of things.[10]

The doxic thesis, which is dormant in contact, is thematized and comes to the surface to sum up the contact in a knowing concerning the soft, rugged or whatever surface of an object, of things, living bodies or human bodies, and to embed it in the system of significations that figure in the said. But this knowing about the exteriors of things remains in proximity, which is not an "experience of proximity," not a cognition which a subject has of an object. Nor is it the representation of the spatial environment, nor even the "objective" fact of this spatial environment observable by a third party or deducible by me, who am palpating the object, from the fact of this palpation. The non-thematized proximity does not simply belong to the "horizon" of the contact, as a potentiality of this experience. Sensibility — the proximity, immediacy and restlessness which signify in it — is not constituted out of some apperception putting consciousness into relationship with a body. Incarnation is not a transcendental operation of a subject that is situated in the midst of the world it represents to itself; the sensible experience of the body is already and from the start incarnate. The sensible – maternity, vulnerability, apprehension – binds the node of incarnation into a plot larger than the apperception of self. In this plot I am bound to others before being tied to my body. Intentionality, the noesis which the philosophy of consciousness distinguished in sensing, and which it wanted, in a regressive movement, to take hold of again as the origin of the sense ascribed, the sensible intuition, is already in the mode of apprehension and obsession, assailed by the sensed which undoes its noematic appearing in order to command, with a non-thematizable alterity, the very noesis which at the origin should have given it a sense. The Gordean knot of the body, the extremities in which it begins or ends, are forever dissimulated in the knot that cannot be undone, and that commands in the ungraspable noesis its own transcendental origin. Sensible experience as an obsession by the other, or a maternity, is already the corporeality which the philosophy of consciousness wishes to constitute on the basis of it. The corporeality of one's own body signifies, as sensibility itself, a knot or a denouement of being, but it has also to contain a passage to the physico-chemical-physiological meanings of the body. And this latter does devolve from sensibility as proximity, as signification, as one-for-the-other, which signifies in giving, when giving offers not the superfluxion of the superfluous, but the bread taken from one's own mouth. Signification signifies, consequently, in nourishing, clothing, lodging, in maternal relations, in which matter shows itself for the first time in its materiality.

The subject called incarnate does not result from a materialization, an entry into space and into relations of contact and money which would have been realized by a consciousness, that is, a self-consciousness, forewarned against every attack and first non-spatial. It is because subjectivity is sensibility – an exposure to others, a vulnerability and a responsibility in the proximity of the others, the-one-for-the-other, that is, signification – and because matter is the very locus of the for-the-other, the way that signification signifies before showing itself as a said in the system of synchronism, the linguistic system, that a subject is of flesh and blood, a man that is hungry and eats, entrails in a skin, and thus capable of giving the bread out of his mouth, or giving his skin.

Signification is thus conceived on the basis of the-one-for-the-other proper to sensibility, and not on the basis of a system of terms which are simultaneous in a language for the speaker, and which simultaneity is in fact only the situation of the speaker. Never is a multiplicity more co-present in all its elements, more available than in the speaker who states a said, a logos, a thematized sense, an assembling of terms in the amphibology of being and entities.

But the saying extended toward the said received this tension from the other, who forces me to speak before appearing to me. The saying extended toward the said is a being obsessed by the other, a sensibility which the other by vocation calls upon and where no escaping is possible. At least no escape is possible with impunity. The other calls upon that sensibility with a vocation that wounds, calls upon an irrevocable responsibility, and thus the very identity of a subject. Signification is witness or martyrdom. It is intelligibility before the light, before the present of the initiative with which the signification of logos in its present, in its synchrony, signifies being.

To stay with the signification of the said, and of the saying that turns into apophansis, forgetful of the proposition and exposure to the other in which they signify, is to stay with the consciousness-subject, that is, in the last analysis, the subject self-consciousness and origin, arche, to which Western philosophy leads. Whatever be the abyss that separates the psyche of the ancients from the consciousness of the moderns, both belong to a tradition in which intelligibility derives from the assembling of terms united in a system for a locutor that states an apophansis — which is the concrete situation of the assembling into a system. Here the subject is origin, initiative, freedom, present. To move oneself or have self-consciousness is in effect to refer oneself to oneself, to be an origin. Then a subject-origin which is also a subject of flesh and blood becomes problematic. The effort is made to understand it on the basis of an incarnation as an avatar of the representation of oneself, as a deficiency of this representation, the occultation of a translucid and spontaneous consciousness into receptivity and finitude. Whence the necessity of going back to the beginning, or to consciousness, appears as the proper task of philosophy: return to its island to be shut up there in the simultaneity of the eternal instant, approaching the *mens instantanea* of God.

A notion of subjectivity independent of the adventure of cognition, and in which the corporeality of the subject is not separable from its subjectivity, is required if signification signifies otherwise than by the synchrony of being, if intelligibility and being are distinguishable, if essence itself signifies only on the basis of an ascription of meaning that devolves from the-one-for-the-other, the signifyingness of signification. Subjectivity of flesh and blood in matter is not for this subject a "mode of self-certainty." The proximity of beings of flesh and blood is not their presence "in flesh and bone," is not the fact that they take form for a look, present an exterior, quiddities, forms, give images, which the eye absorbs (and whose alterity the hand that touches or holds, suspends easily or lightly, annulling it by the simple grasp, as though no one contested this appropriation.) Nor are material beings reducible to the resistance they oppose to the effort they solicit. Their relationship with a mouth is not an adventure of knowledge or of action. Subjectivity of flesh and blood in matter – the signifyingness of sensibility, the-one-for-the-other itself – is the preoriginal signifyingness that gives sense, because it gives. Not because, as preoriginal, it would be more originary than the origin, but because the diachrony of sensibility, which cannot be assembled in a representational present, refers to an irrecuperable pre-ontological past, that of maternity. It is a plot which cannot be subordinated to the vicissitudes of representation and knowledge, openness upon images, or an exchange of information.

What seems incomprehensible in a humanity of flesh and blood to the Cartesian conception – the animation of a body by thought, which is non-sense according to the intelligibility of a system, in which animation is understood only in terms of union and dovetailing and requires a *deus ex machina* – outlines signification itself: the-one-for-the-other. In the subject it is precisely not an assembling, but an incessant alienation of the ego (isolated as inwardness) by the guest entrusted to it. Hospitality, the-one-for-the-other in the ego, delivers it more passively than any passivity from links in a causal chain. Being torn from oneself for another in giving to the other the bread from one's mouth is being able to give up one's soul for another. The animation of a body by a soul only articulates the-one-for-the-other in subjectivity.[11]

Signifyingness, the for-the-other that marks approach, is to be sure not an "activity" inscribed in the nature of a subject that appears as an entity, nor the subsistence of this entity, its essence, interpretable as a relation. As a sensibility, of flesh and blood, I am on the hither side of the amphibology of being and entities, the non-thematizable, the non-unitable by synthesis. When thematized, synchronized, the one of the-one-for-the-other would be betrayed, even if it showed itself with the stigmata of the betrayal and would then lend itself to reduction. What will show itself in a theme said is the unintelligibility of incarnation, the "I think" separated from extension, the *cogito* separated from the body. But this impossibility of being together is the trace of the diachrony of the-one-for-the-other. That is, it is the trace of *separation* in the form of inwardness, and of the for-the-other in the form of responsibility. Identity here takes form not by a self-confirmation, but, as a signification of the-one-for-the-other, by a deposing of oneself, a deposing which is the incarnation of the subject, or the very possibility of giving, of dealing signifyingness.

Hegel in the *Phenomenology of Mind*, sought to conceive of substance as subject, to reduce the model of an entity or of the in-itself derived from the perceived object to a movement: a mediated recovering of the imme-diate after the negation of this immediate. But in this way a recapture of oneself, a reconquest, a for-oneself still animates the subjectivity caught sight of at the bottom of the substance: essence does not leave its *conatus*. The subjectivity of sensibility, taken as incarnation, is an abandon without return, maternity, a body suffering for another, the body as passivity and renouncement, a pure undergoing. There is indeed an insurmountable ambiguity there: the incarnate ego, the ego of flesh and blood, can lose its signification, be affirmated as an animal in its *conatus* and its joy. It is a dog that recognizes as its own Ulysses coming to take possession of his goods. But this ambiguity is the condition of vulnerability itself, that is, of sensibility as signification. For it is in the measure that sensibility is complacent in itself, is coiled over upon itself, is an ego, that in its benevolence for the other it remains for the other, despite itself, non-act, signification for the other and not for itself.

The signification of the-one-for-the-other in diachrony, the signification of proximity (which will be discussed later) is not purely and simply alongside the signification of systems. It is in the signification of the-one-for-the-other that systems, consciousness, thematization and statement of the true and of being are comprised. To the point that the-one-for-the-other can be expressed as though it were a moment of being. The-one-for-the-other, saying, is on the point of changing into an intentional consciousness, a formulation of truths, a message emitted and received. The doxic thesis is dormant in every relationship in which subjectivity is involved. That is not enough to transform the openness upon being into the sense of subjectivity, and knowing into the prototype of the meaningful. In every vision contact is announced: sight and hearing caress the visible and the audible. Contact is not an openness upon being, but an exposure of being.[12] In this caress proximity signifies as proximity, and not as an experience of proximity.[13]

The pathos of the philosophy of existence directed against the intellectualism of reflexive philosophy was due to the discovery of a psyche irreducible to knowing. Was there in this opposition enough energy to resist the return of the intellectualist models?

In Husserl non-doxic intentionalities harbor an archetypical *doxa*; Heidegger's being-in-the-world is a comprehension: technological activity itself is openness, discovery of Being, even if in the mode of a forgetting of Being. The ontic, which at least involves an opaqueness, everywhere yields before the ontological, before a covered-over luminosity to be disengaged. The *existentiell* reveals its meaning in the existential, which is an articulation of ontology. An entity counts only on the basis of knowing, of appearing, of phenomenology.

But beneath the openness of thematization, beneath the correlation of the saying and the said, in which the logos synchronizes the temporal putting out of phase of the sensible (a putting out of phase by which is produced the appearing to oneself, or essence, and the amphibology of being and entities), beneath the identity of entities, poles of identification, and beneath the verbal character of being being modulated in an apophansis, beneath consciousness which is consciousness of consciousness – sensibility is not reabsorbed in these plays of light and reflections, does not flow like the time susceptible to being remembered of consciousness. It is vulnerability, susceptibility, denuding, circumscribed and concerned by the other, irreducible to the appearing of the other. Self-consciousness is a return path. But the Odyssey has also been an adventure, a history of innumerable encounters. In his native land Ulysses returns dissimulated under false exteriors. The coherent discussions which he knows how to keep up dissimulate an identity that is distinct from them, but whose signifyingness escapes the animal flair.

6. PROXIMITY

a. Proximity and Space

Would proximity be a certain measure of the interval narrowing between two points or two sectors of space, toward a limit of contiguity and even coincidence? But then the term proximity would have a relative meaning and, in the space inhabited by Euclidean geometry, a derivative sense. Its absolute and proper meaning presupposes "humanity." One can even ask if contiguity itself would be comprehensible without proximity – approach, neighborhood, contact – and if the homogeneity of this space would be conceivable without the human signification of justice before all difference, and thus without all the motivations of proximity of which justice is the term.

Space and nature cannot be posited in an initial geometrical and physical impassiveness and then receive from the presence of man, from his desires and passions, a cultural layer that would make them signifying and speaking. If this geometry and physics were at the beginning, the signifying attributes would never have anything but a subjective existence in the heads of men, the customs and writings of peoples. Narcissism would then find in the granite of things but a surface that would refer to men the echos and reflections of their humanity. Never could "psychological" signification draw the infinite spaces out of their silence. The very presence of man in these spaces, alleged source of the signifying attributes, would be, outside of its strictly geometrical or physico-chemical sense, an interior fact of an absurd being cooked in his own juices. In fact, the impassiveness of space refers to the absolute coexistence, to the conjunction of all the points, being together at all points without any privilege, characteristic of the words of a language before the mouth opens. It refers to a universal homogeneity derived from this assembling, from being's nonsubjective essence. But the synchrony of the words of a language before a mouth that opens refers to man that speaks, and to justice, which derives from the first signification. More exactly, it derives from an anarchic signification of proximity, for, as a principle, it would already be a representation and a being. In proximity a subject is implicated in a way not reducible to the spatial sense which proximity takes on when the third party troubles it by demanding justice in the "unity of transcendental consciousness," when a conjuncture is sketched out in a theme which, when said, is garbed with the sense of a contiguity.[14]

To contest the original character of spatial contiguity is then not to affirm that it is always associated with a state of soul and is inseparable from a state of consciousness that reflects this contiguity, or, at least, is inseparable from a state of consciousness in which a term knows the presence of the contiguous term. Not all spirituality is that of theoretical, voluntary or affective representation in an intentional subject. Far from marking a point of departure, the intentional subject refers to the unity of transcendental apperception itself issued from a whole metaphysical tradition. But every spirituality is also not comprehension and truth of Being and openness of a world. As a subject that approaches, I am not in the approach called to play the role of a perceiver that reflects or welcomes, animated with intentionality, the light of the open and the grace and mystery of the world. Proximity is not a state, a repose, but, a restlessness, null site, outside of the place of rest. It overwhelms the calm of the non-ubiquity of a being which becomes a rest in a site. No site then, is ever sufficiently a proximity, like an embrace. Never close enough, proximity does not congeal into a structure, save when represented in the demand for justice as reversible, and reverts into a simple relation. Proximity, as the "closer and closer," becomes the subject. It attains its *superlative* as *my* incessant restlessness, becomes unique, then one, forgets reciprocity, as in a love that does not expect to be shared. Proximity is the subject that approaches and consequently constitutes a relationship in which I participate as a term, but where I am more, or less, than a term. This surplus or this lack throws me outside of the objectivity characteristic of relations. Does relationship here become religion? It is not simply a passage to a subjective point of view. One can no longer say what the ego or I is. From now on one has to speak in the first person. I am a term irreducible to the relation, and yet in a recurrence which empties me of all consistency.

This being thrown outside of objectivity cannot consist in a becoming conscious of this situation, which would annul the non-indifference or fraternity of proximity. Is not a conscious subject one that has no alliance with that of which it is conscious? Does it not feel that any kinship with that of which it is conscious compromises its truth?

The approach is precisely an implication of the approaching one in fraternity. When it becomes conscious, that is, thematized, the indifferent approach destroys this kinship, like a caress surprising itself to be a palpation, or recovering possession of itself. The subjectivity of the approaching subject is then preliminary, anarchic, prior to consciousness, an implication, a being caught up in fraternity. This being caught up in fraternity which proximity is we call signifyingness. It is impossible without the ego (or more exactly without the self) which, instead of representing the signification to itself in it, signifies in signifying itself. The representation of signification is itself born in the signifyingness of proximity in the measure that a third party is alongside the neighbor.

b. Proximity and Subjectivity
Humanity, to which proximity properly so called refers, must then not be first understood as consciousness, that is, as the identity of an ego endowed with knowledge or (what amounts to the same thing) with powers. Proximity does not resolve into the consciousness a being would have of another being that it would judge to be near inasmuch as the other would be under one's eyes or within one's reach, and inasmuch as it would be possible for one to take hold of that being, hold on to it or converse with it, in the reciprocity of handshakes, caresses, struggle, collaboration, commerce, conversation. Consciousness, which is consciousness of a possible, power, freedom, would then have already lost proximity properly so called, now surveyed and thematized, as it would have already repressed in itself a subjectivity older than knowing or power. Proximity is no longer in knowing in which these relations with the neighbor show themselves, but do so already in narration, in the said, as an epos and a teleology. The "three unities" are not exclusively a matter of theatrical action; they command every exposition, assemble into a history, a narration, a tale, the bifid or bifocal relationship with the neighbor. The symbols written double up words, and are still more docile to "assembling"; in the unity of a text they annul the difference between the same and the other. United in the same, assembled into experience, like an effect of any synthesis of multiplicity, proximity has already falsified its extraordinary ambiguity of being a whole broken up by the difference between terms, in which difference is non-indifference and the break is an obsession.

Obsession is not a notion that would be introduced here to express, according to the well-known ritual, proximity as the dialectical unity of unity and difference. Obsession, in which difference shudders as non-indifference, does not simply figure as a relation among all the reciprocal or at least reversible relations that form the system of the intelligibility of being, and in which the ego, even in its uniqueness, is a universal subsuming a multiplicity of unique egos. Consciousness is perhaps the very locus of the reverting of the facticity of individuation into a concept of an individual, and thus into consciousness of its death, in which its singularity is lost in its universality. In consciousness, no supplementary specific difference, no negation of universality can extract the subject out of universality.

The affirmation of such an extraction "says strictly the contrary of what it means."[15] But the obsession by the neighbor is stronger than negativity. It paralyzes with the weight of its very silence the power to assume this weight. The conscious discourse still knows how to tell this impotence without healing the affection that rends consciousness, without extracting through an admission the "seed of folly," the thorn in the flesh of reason, which is the shudder of subjectivity. Even the philosopher that speaks of it, over and beyond the universality in which the subjectivity that is *said* appears, remains a subjectivity obsessed by the neighbor. The saying in which the speaking subject is exposed to the other is not reducible to the objectification of a theme stated. Who then came to wound the subject, so that he should expose his thoughts or expose himself in his saying? He is subject to being affected by the other, and this being affected, by reason of its very irreversibility, does not change into a universal thought. The subject affected by the other cannot think that the affection is reciprocal, for he is still obsessed with the very obsession he could exercise over him that obsesses him. Not to turn into relations that reverse, irreversibility, is the universal subjectness of the subject. The ignorance of it by the subject bears witness not to the naivety of a humanity still incapable of thinking, still shut up in an original identity, prior to all mediation, nor to the everydayness of man, fleeing concepts and death in an original identity prior to all mediation – but to the preoriginary hither side of abnegation. In this nonreciprocity, in this "not thinking of it" is announced, on the hither side of the "state of nature" (from which nature itself arises), the-one-for-the-other, a one-way relationship, not coming back in any form to its point of departure, the *immediacy* of the other, more immediate still than immediate identity in its quietude as a nature – the immediacy of proximity.

Obsession as non-reciprocity itself does not relieve any possibility of suffering in common. It is a one-way irreversible being affected, like the diachrony of time that flows between the fingers of Mnemosyne. It is tied into an ego that states itself in the first person, escaping the concept of an ego in an ipseity – not in an ipseity in general, but in *me*. The knot of subjectivity consists in going to the other without concerning oneself with his movement toward me. Or, more exactly, it consists in approaching in such a way that, over and beyond all the reciprocal relations that do not fail to get set up between me and the neighbor, I have always taken one step more toward him – which is possible only if this step is responsibility. In the responsibility which we have for one another, I have always one response more to give, I have to answer for his very responsibility.

In its refusal of the coincidence and mediation that synchronize (and which issue in writings), the dehiscence of proximity, older than the theme in which it shows itself, is then not the immediacy called abstract and natural. It is *more determinate* than the relations that are ordered into a totality. Signifyingness, the-one-for-the-other, exposedness of self to another, it is immediacy in caresses and in the contact of saying. It is the immediacy of a skin and a face, a skin which is always a modification of a face, a face that is weighted down with a skin.

Neither conjuncture in being, nor reflection of this conjuncture in the unity of transcendental apperception, the proximity of me with the other is in two times, and thus is a transcendence. It temporalizes itself, but with a diachronic temporality, outside, beyond or above, the time recuperable by reminiscence, in which consciousness abides and converses, and in which being and entities show themselves in experience. For subjectivity is not called, in its primary vocation, to take the role and place of the indeclinable transcendental consciousness, which effects syntheses straightway before itself, but is itself excluded from these syntheses, is implicated in them only through the detour of incarnation, which is hardly intelligible in so much indeclinable straightforwardness. It is an irreplaceable oneself. Not strictly speaking an ego set up in the nominative in its identity, but first constrained to . . . . It is set up as it were in the accusative form, from the first responsible and not being able to slip away.[16] If to this subjectivity in the last analysis themes and objects are proposed and given,[17] its being excepted from order does not consist in its assuming the given, representing it, becoming conscious of it (whether in knowledge of objects or self knowledge, or in power exercised over the world or over oneself). The proper signification of subjectivity is proximity, but proximity is the very signifyingness of signification, the very establishing of the-one-for-the-other, the establishing of the sense which every thematized signification reflects in being.

It is then not enough to speak of proximity as a relationship between two terms, and as a relationship assured of the simultaneity of these terms. It is necessary to emphasize the breakup of this synchrony, of this whole, by the difference between the same and the other in the non-indifference of the obsession exercised by the other over the same. The exception of proximity to a rational order, tending in principle toward a system of pure relations, is the hypostasis of the relationship into a subjectivity obsessed, with a non-reciprocatable obsession, by the neighbor. This obsession is not reducible to an intersection of these relations, which would count by virtue of its "universal essence." Subjectivity counts by virtue of hypostasis, showing itself in the said, not, to be sure, under a name, but nonetheless like entities, as a pro-noun. It is both the relation and the term of the relation. But it is as subject to an irreversible relation that the term of the relation becomes a subject.[18] This relation is not a return to oneself: as an incessant exigency, an incessant contraction, a recurrence of remorse, it disengages the *one* as a term, which nothing could rejoin and cover over. Subjectivity is not antecedent to proximity, in which it would later commit itself. On the contrary, it is in proximity, which is a relationship and a term, that every commitment is made. And it is probably starting with proximity that the difficult problem of an incarnate subjectivity has to be broached. One would like a subject to be obstinately free, and yet even an intentional subject gives itself a non-ego in representations, and paradoxically finds itself caught up in its own representations. This paradox is not elucidated by the contradictory notion of finite freedom which philosophers resort to, refusing the excluded middle of "a hither side of freedom and non-freedom."

c. Proximity and Obsession

Proximity is to be described as extending the subject in its very subjectivity, which is both a relationship and a term of this relationship. In the inquiry that goes in this way, there is no slippage of meaning, from the signification of proximity to reflection on the state of soul of the ego which approaches a neighbor. As signification, the-one-for-the-other, proximity is not a configuration produced in the soul. It is an immediacy older than the abstractness of nature. Nor is it fusion; it is contact with the other. To be in contact is neither to invest the other and annul his alterity, nor to suppress myself in the other. In contact itself the touching and the touched separate, as though the touched moved off, was always already other, did not have anything common with me. As though its singularity, thus non-anticipatable and consequently not representable, responded only to designation.

Is it a τόδε τι? But a τόδε τι, even when unique in its genus, is set in its genus, even if that genus has no extension. It still appears through what Husserl calls the "empty horizon of the unknown and the known,"[19] the a priori horizon which already puts the τόδε τι back into a whole, into a conjuncture or a correlation (at least the correlation it forms with the finger that designates it). The neighbor qua other does not have himself be preceded by any precursor who would depict or announce his silhouette. He does not appear. What sort of signalling could he send before me which would not strip him of his exclusive alterity? Absolving himself from all essence, all genus, all resemblance, the neighbor, *the first one on the scene*, concerns me for the first time (even if he is an old acquaintance, an old friend, an old lover, long caught up in the fabric of my social relations) in a contingency that excludes the a priori. Not coming to confirm any signalling made in advance, outside of everything, a priori,[20] the neighbor concerns me with his exclusive singularity without appearing, not even as a τόδε τι. His extreme singularity is precisely his assignation: he assigns me before I designate him as τόδε τι.

The neighbor concerns me before all assumption, all commitment consented to or refused. I am bound to him, him who is, however, the first one on the scene, not signalled, unparalleled; I am bound to him before any liaison contracted. He orders me before being recognized. Here there is a relation of kinship outside of all biology, "against all logic." It is not because the neighbor would be recognized as belonging to the same genus as me that he concerns me. He is precisely *other*. The community with him begins in my obligation to him. The neighbor is a brother. A fraternity that cannot be abrogated, an unimpeachable assignation, proximity is an impossibility to move away without the torsion of a complex, without "alienation" or fault.[21] This insomnia is the psyche.

The neighbor assigns me before I designate him. This is a modality not of a knowing, but of an obsession, a shuddering[22] of the human quite different from cognition. Knowing is always convertible into creation and annihilation; its object lends itself to a concept, is a result. Through the suppression of the singular, through generalization, knowing is idealism. In an approach I am first a servant of a neighbor, already late and guilty for being late. I am as it were ordered from the outside, traumatically commanded, without interiorizing by representation and concepts the authority that commands me. Without asking myself: What then is it to me? Where does he get his right to command? What have I done to be from the start in debt?[23] Consciousness which knows how to multiply its correlates in innumerable images, enriching the world, penetrating into apartments, leaves these correlates intact, unapproached. One makes concepts out of them. Consciousness is not interposed between me and the neighbor; or, at least, it arises only on the ground of this antecedent relationship of obsession, which no consciousness could annul, and of which consciousness itself is a modification.

Obsession is not consciousness, nor a species or a modality of consciousness, even though it overwhelms the consciousness that tends to assume it. It is unassumable like a persecution.[24]

But do we not have to become conscious of this assignation? Does proximity do without representation, ontology, logos? Is not a becoming conscious, a receiving of the given, as Husserl teaches, the precursor of every relation? The extreme urgency of the assignation precisely breaks up the equality or serenity of consciousness, which espouses its visible or conceivable object. The neighbor does not stand in a form, like an object abides in the plasticity of an aspect, a profile or an open series of aspects, which overflows each of them without destroying the adequation of the act of consciousness, since each apparition comes in time, in its own time, and since the series is enveloped by an Idea in the Kantian sense of the term. The extreme urgency of the assignation jostles the "presence of mind" necessary for the reception of a given and the identification of the diverse, in which, as noema of a noesis, a phenomenon appears. Extreme urgency is the modality of obsession – which is known but is not a knowing. I do not have time to face it. Outside of conventions (so many poses of theatrical exposition), no welcome is equal to the measure I have of a neighbor. Adequation is impossible. Obligations are disproportionate to any commitment taken or to be taken or to be kept in a present. In a sense nothing is more burdensome than a neighbor. Is not this desired one the undesirable itself? The neighbor who could not leave me indifferent, the undesirable desired one, has not revealed to desire the ways of access to him, as the maternal milk was able to inscribe the movements of sucking in the instincts of the newly born. To take hold of oneself for a present of welcome is already to take one's distance, and miss the neighbor. In a consciousness that an object affects, the affection reverts into an assumption. Here the blow of the affection makes an impact, traumatically, in a past more profound than all that I can reassemble by memory, by historiography, all that I can dominate by the a priori – in a time before the beginning.[25]

It is not a question of an effect undergoing its cause. The subjective does not only undergo, it suffers. Paining is a distance of "negative extent" behind undergoing. It is a surplus of passivity which is no longer consciousness of . . ., identifying this as that, ascribing a meaning. The neighbor strikes me before striking me, as though I had heard before he spoke. This anachronism attests to a temporality different from that which scans consciousness. It takes apart the recuperable time of history and memory in which representation continues. For if, in every experience, the making of a fact precedes the present of experience, the memory, history, or extra-temporality of the a priori recuperates the divergence and creates a correlation between this past and this present. In proximity is heard a command come as though from an immemorial past, which was never present, began in no freedom. This *way* of the neighbor is a face.

The face of a neighbor signifies for me an unexceptionable responsibility, preceding every free consent, every pact, every contract. It escapes representation; it is the very collapse of phenomenality. Not because it is too brutal to appear, but because in a sense too weak, non-phenomenon because less than a phenomenon. The disclosing of a face is nudity, non-form, abandon of self, ageing, dying, more naked than nudity. It is poverty, skin with wrinkles, which are a trace of itself. My reaction misses a present which is already the past of itself. This past is not *in* the present, but is as a phase retained, the past *of* this present, a lapse already lost which marks ageing, escaping all retention, altering my contemporaneousness with the other. It reclaimed me before I came. The delay is irrecuperable. "I opened . . . he had disappeared."[26] My presence does not respond to the extreme urgency of the assignation. I am accused of having delayed. The common hour marked by the clock is the hour in which the neighbor reveals himself and delivers himself in his image, but it is precisely in his image that he is no longer near. Already he allows me an "as for me," distances, remains commensurable, to the scale of my power and of my present in which I am capable of . . . , capable of accounting for everything by my own identity. The contact is broken. When the other appears to me as an entity in the plastic form of being an image, I am in relationship with the multipliable which, despite the infinity of the reproductions I make of it, remains intact, and I can in his regard be satisfied with words for these images without delivering myself in a saying. The proximity does not enter into the common time of clocks, which makes meetings possible. It is a disturbance.

Proximity as a suppression of distance suppresses the distance of consciousness of . . . The neighbor excludes himself from the thought that seeks him, and this exclusion has a positive side to it: my exposure to him, antecedent to his appearing, my delay behind him, my undergoing, undo the core of what is identity in me. Proximity, suppression of the distance that consciousness of . . . involves, opens the distance of a diachrony without a common present, where difference is the past that cannot be caught up with, an unimaginable future, the non-representable status of the neighbor behind which I am late and obsessed by the neighbor. This difference is my non-indifference to the other. Proximity is a disturbance of the rememberable time.

One can call that apocalyptically the break-up of time. But it is a matter of an effaced but untameable diachrony of non-historical, non-said time, which cannot be synchronized in a present by memory and historiography, where the present is but the trace of an immemorial past. The obligation aroused by the proximity of the neighbor is not to the measure of the images he gives me; it concerns me before or otherwise. Such is the sense of the non-phenomenality of the face.

d. Phenomenon and Face
In the obsession with this nudity and this poverty, this withdrawal or this dying, where synthesis and contemporaneousness are refused, proximity, as though it were an abyss, interrupts being's unrendable essence. A face approached, a contact with a skin – a face weighted down with a skin, and a skin in which, even in obscenity, the altered face breaths[27] – are already absent from themselves, fallen into the past with an unrecuperable lapse. The skin caressed is not the protection of an organism, simply the surface of an entity; it is the divergency between the visible and the invisible, quasi-transparent, thinner than that which would still justify an expression of the

invisible by the visible. This thinness is not an infinitesimal degree of quantity, of thickness. It is a thinness already reduced to the alternating of sense, the ambiguity of a phenomenon and its defect,[28] poverty exposed in the formless, and withdrawn from this absolute exposure in a shame for its poverty. The exorbitance of proximity is distinguished from a conjunction in cognition and intentionality in which subject and object enter. Beyond the disclosure and exhibition of the known alternate, surprised and surprising, an enormous presence and the withdrawal of this presence. The withdrawal is not a negation of presence, nor its pure latency, recuperable in memory or actualization. It is alterity, without common measure with a presence or a past assembling into a synthesis in the synchrony of the correlative. The relation of proximity is disparate just because of that.[29] In a caress, what is there is sought as though it were not there, as though the skin were the trace of its own withdrawal, a languor still seeking, like an absence which, however, could not be more there. The caress is the not coinciding proper to contact, a denuding never naked enough. The neighbor does not satisfy the approach. The tenderness of skin is the very gap between approach and approached, a disparity, a non-intentionality, a non-teleology. Whence the disorder of caresses,[30] the diachrony, a pleasure without present, pity, painfulness. Proximity, immediacy, is to enjoy and to suffer by the other. But I can enjoy and suffer by the other only because I am-for-the-other, am signification, because the contact with skin is still a proximity of a face, a responsibility, an obsession with the other, being-one-for-the-other, which is the very birth of *signification* beyond *being*. In this irreversible diachrony, there is a defecting of the intentional correlation of disclosure, where the other appeared in plastic form as an image, a portrait. Phenomenology defects into a face, even if, in the course of this ever ambiguous defecting of appearing, the obsession itself shows itself in the said.[31] The appearing is broken by the young epiphany, the still essential beauty of a face. But this youth is already past in this youth; the skin is with wrinkles, a trace of itself, the ambiguous form of a supreme presence attending to its appearing, breaking through its plastic form with youth, but already a failing of all presence, less than a phenomenon, already a poverty that hides its wretchedness and calls upon me and orders me. Such is the singular signification of an existence deserting itself, the finition of finitude coming to an end. But it is life that is still not arrested in the absolute immobility of a death mask. The ending up of finitude is not an appearance, which Hegel was able to designate as "a being which *immediately* is its own nothingness." This existence abandoned by all and by itself, a trace of itself, imposed on *me*, assigns me in my last refuge with an incomparable force of assignation, inconvertible into forms. Forms would give me at once a countenance, would accord me a delay for representation, and would put off the urgency of the assignation already missed. I would be diverted by images, with which the neighbor annuls his proximity, pays with empty money and is paid with words. Thus would be established an activity of a subject, a domination of the world, even if the world resists.

A face is a trace of itself, given over to my responsibility, but to which I am wanting and faulty. It is as though I were responsible for his mortality, and guilty for surviving. A face is an anachronous immediacy more tense than that of an image offered in the straightforwardness of an intuitive intention. In proximity the absolutely other, the stranger whom I have "neither conceived nor given birth to," I already have on my arms, already bear, according to the Biblical formula, "in my breast as the nurse bears the nurseling."[32] He has no other place, is not autochthonous, is uprooted, without a country, not an inhabitant, exposed to the cold and the heat of the seasons. To be reduced to having recourse to me is the homelessness or strangeness of the neighbor. It is incumbent on me.

It presses the neighbor up against me. Immediacy is the collapse of the representation into a face, into a "concrete abstraction" torn up from the world, from horizons and conditions,[33] incrusted in the signification without a context of the-one-for-the-other, coming from the emptiness of space, from space signifying emptiness, from the desert and desolate space, as uninhabitable as geometrical homogeneity. Abandoned, but by whom or by what? In this the emptiness of an abandonment, or – equivocation to be demystified! – merely extension, a medium indifferent to the comings and goings of men, penetrable like nothingness, thinkable before all proximity? Or, despite the demystification, is it emptiness again, obsessive as in agoraphobia, the trace of a passage or trace of what could not enter? Is it the trace of the excession, the excessive, of what could not be contained, of the non-content, disproportionate to all measure and all capacity, the trace of the infinite signifying diachronically exactly through these ambiguities? The empty space of what could not be collected there is the trace of a passage which never became present, and which is possibly nothingness. But the surplus over pure nothingness, an infinitesimal difference, is in my non-indifference to the neighbor, where I am obedient as though to an order addressed to me. Such an order throws a "seed of folly" into the universality of the ego. It is given to me who answer before the one for whom I am responsible. The preoriginal here does not have to get its origin in a present of appearing.

The passivity of obsession, where consciousness no longer veils the unassumable assignation which comes from the neighbor, is not another name for naive consciousness, the immediacy prior to philosophy. On the contrary, it is what puts into question the naive spontaneity of the ego. In the most radical way possible. Pure criticism does not lie in the thematization operated by reflection on the self, nor in the simple look of the other that judges me. In thematization, the plastic character of an object, the form, clothes and protects the ego apparently exposed to critique. Apperceiving itself as universal, it has already slipped away from the responsibilities to which I – always contrasting with the ego – am bound, and for which I cannot ask replacements. The ego, in consciousness reflecting on itself, both declinable as an object and protected by its unrendable form of being a universal subject, escapes its own critical eye by its spontaneity, which permits it to take refuge in this very eye that judges it. The negativity in which the ego is detached from itself to look at itself is, from all points of view, a recuperation of the self. Under the eye of another, I remain an unattackable subject in respect. It is the obsession by the other, my neighbor, accusing me of a fault which I have not committed freely, that reduces the ego to a self on the hither side of my identity, prior to all self-consciousness, and denudes me absolutely. Must we call creature status his "hither side," which a being retains no trace of, this hither side older than the plot of egoism woven in the *conatus* of being? To revert to oneself is not to establish oneself at home, even if stripped of all one's acquisitions. It is to be like a stranger, hunted down even in one's home, contested in one's own identity and one's very poverty, which, like a skin still enclosing the self, would set it up in an inwardness, already settled on itself, already a substance. It is always to empty oneself anew of oneself, to absolve oneself, like in a hemophiliac's hemorrhage. It is to be on the hither side of one's own nuclear unity, still identifiable and protected; it is to be emptied even of the quasi-formal identity of a being someone. But it is always to be *coram*, disturbed in oneself to the point of no longer having any intention, exposed over and beyond the act of exposing oneself, answering for this very exposedness, expressing oneself, speaking. It is to be an undeclinable *One*, speaking, that is, exposing one's very exposedness. The act of speaking is the passivity in passivity. The passivity to which the ego is reduced in proximity is the sincerity or veracity which the exchange of information, the interpretation and decoding of signs, already presupposes.

This passivity is the way opposed to the imperialism of consciousness open upon the world. This passivity, this undeclinability due to a responsibility that cannot be declined, this for-the-other, could not be treated in terms of finitude in the prejorative or tragic sense of the term, a congenital and lamentable powerlessness to detach oneself from oneself and reflect totally on oneself. Proximity or fraternity is neither a troubled tranquility in a subject that wants to be absolute and alone, nor the makeshift of an impossible confusion. Is it not, in its restlessness and emptying and diachrony, better than all the rest, all the plenitude of an instant arrested? Everything is successive (even truth), but the diachrony is not only the sadness of the flowing away of things. The word *better*, and the Good it expresses, which turns up here, perhaps makes all our discussion suspect of being "ideology." But the least intoxicated and the most lucid humanity of our time, at the moments most free from the concern "that existence takes for its very existence" has in its clarity no other shadow, in its rest no other disquietude or insomnia than what comes from the destitution of the others. Its insomnia is but the absolute impossibility to slip away and distract oneself.

e. Proximity and Infinity

A trace lost in a trace, less than nothing in the trace of an excessive, but always ambiguously (trace of itself, possibly a mask, in a void, possibly nothingness or "pure form of the sensibility"), the face of the neighbor obsesses me with this destitution. "He is looking at me" – everything in him looks at me; nothing is indifferent to me. Nothing is more imperative than this abandon in the emptiness of space, this trace of infinity which *passes* without being able to enter. In it is hollowed out the face as a trace of an absence, as a skin with wrinkles. In the duplicity of beauty there is the strange trope of a presence which is the shadow of itself, of a being which, anachronously, lurks in its trace.

Does this imperative force which is not a necessity come from this very enigma, this ambiguity of being a trace? In this enigma tends and distends the infinite, the nonoriginal and anarchic as well as infinite, which no present, no historiography, could assemble, and whose passing precedes every memorable past. A gaping open of an abyss in proximity, the infinite which blinks, refusing speculative audacities, is distinguishable from pure and simple nothingness by the committing of the neighbor to my responsibility. But it is also distinguishable from the *Sollen*, for proximity is not a simply asymptotic approach of its "term." Its term is not an end. The more I answer the more I am responsible; the more I approach the neighbor with which I am encharged the further away I am. This debit which increases is infinity as an infinition of the infinite, as glory.[34]

The approach is a non-synchronizable diachrony, which representation and thematization dissimulate by transforming the trace into a *sign* of a departure, and then reducing the ambiguity of the face either to a play of physiognomy or to the indicating of a signified. But thus opens the dangerous way in which a pious thought, or one concerned with order, hastily deduces the existence of God.

A face is not an appearance or sign of some reality, which would be personal like it is, but dissimulated or expressed by the physiognomy, and which would present itself as an invisible theme. The essential of the thesis here expounded is that proximity is not any kind of conjunction of themes, is not a structure formed by their superposition. A face does not function in proximity as a sign of a hidden God who would impose the neighbor on me. It is a trace of itself, a trace in the trace of an abandon, where the equivocation is never dissipated. It obsesses the subject without staying in correlation with him, without equalling me in a consciousness, ordering me before appearing, in the glorious increase of obligation. These are the modalities of signification irreducible to the presents and presences, different from the present, modalities which articulate the very *inordinateness of infinity*. They are not its signs that would await an ontological interpretation, nor some knowing that would be added to its "essence." The approach (which in the last analysis will show itself to be a substitution) cannot be surpassed speculatively; it is the infinition or glory of the infinite. A face as a trace, trace of itself, trace expelled in a trace, does not signify an indeterminate phenomenon; its ambiguity is not an indetermination of a noema, but an invitation to the fine risk of approach qua approach, to the exposure of one to the other, to the exposure of this exposedness, the expression of exposure, saying. In the approach of a face the flesh becomes word, the caress a saying. The thematization of a face undoes the face and undoes the approach. The mode in which a face indicates its own absence in my responsibility requires a description that can be formed only in ethical language.[35]

f. Signification and Existence
Is the question of existence or non-existence the ultimate question? To locate the problem of the existence of God behind the signifyingness of signification and the proximity of a neighbor would, it is said, correspond to the desire to settle things and not let oneself be abused by "nothingness" and words. But that would show the prestige of the totality and of efficacity, to which a philosophy of being would unfailingly return, and from which come the popular certainties. To state the problem of the *existence* of God, despite *signification*, despite the-one-for-the-other, which derogates from the finality of the interestedness of man inhabiting the world, is to hold to the unity of being and the univocity of its *esse*, which, despite the multiplicity of its modalities, would be. verified in efficacity, in action and in the resistance to action, would "enter into account," figure in the calculation that accompanies projects.

Then there sinks away, as illusion or luxurious subtilities of satisfied consciousness, all the differences of dignity, height and distance; there are filled all the abysses of transcendence, all the intervals that cut across "analogical unity." This philosophy of success is itself ensured of success.

One can indeed seek to ensure the human disinterestedness by starting with the supreme efficacity of God; one can seek to seat the religious on a philosophy of the unity and totality of being called Spirit, and to this unity which ensures the efficacity of God in the world, sacrifice transcendence, despite the inversions of the totality into totalitarianism.

All that is possible! The diachronic ambiguity of transcendence lends itself to this choice, to this option for the ultimacy of being. But is this choice the only philosophical one? One can contest the thesis that being signifies behind the-one-for-the-other, and put forth the Platonic word, Good beyond being. It excludes being from the Good, for how could one understand the *conatus* of being in the goodness of the Good? How, in Plotinus, would the One overflow with plenitude and be a source of emanation, if the One persevered in being, if it did not signify from before or beyond being, out of proximity, that is, out of disinterestedness, out of signification, out of the-one-for-the-other? The cordon of totality, a rope neither too short nor worn out, does not prevent the extravagance of transcendence. As a philosopher between the beyond-being and being one can seek a relationship other than the miraculous relationship of epiphany or the intervention in its enigma which is not a mystery, while leaving to faith properly so called hope and beliefs, the solution of the enigma and the symbolic formulas that suggest it. To the faith of the coal-dealer, no doubt. But the coal-dealer today has other certainties, and, after all, his own concerns. Against the denials inflicted by failure, the simplicity of an extreme complexity, and a singularly mature infancy, is needed. That also is the sense of the death of God. Or of his life.

Signification structured as the-one-for-the-other is here set forth independently of ontological finality and of mathematical functionalism, which, in the main tradition of Western philosophy, supply the norms of intelligibility and of sense.

To have a sense is to be the means toward an end, and thus to be inseparable from a will through which the end is an end – whether the will confers finality on the end, or whether it is elicited by this end. The end in itself, divinity, is precisely capable of willing itself. But does the end in itself of theology still have need of means?

One then has to go back, beyond the correlation of end and will, to a system of relations in which the teleological relations themselves constitute but a region, a system of reversible, if not reciprocable relations, which annul the hierarchy of finality in axiological indifference. Beyond teleology, signification would arise out of the configuration which is formed by entities that exhaust in the relations that connect them to one another all the weight of their perseverance in being, like words in a linguistic system. It is not impossible to conceive the totality of the real according to this linguistic model and in the research to approach the substantiality of the beings absorbed in the intersection of relationships, and not retaining any supplementary identity other than that which is due to the reference of each term to all the other terms. Being would be manifested as this qua that, not because its manifestation would be insufficient and reduced to symbolism, but because language and its system would be manifestation itself. The primacy of theoretical reason or the theoretical essence of reason and signification is affirmed in this formalist or mathematical vision of intelligibility. But the finality of the theoretical praxis itself, which is immediately established as a norm of honesty, leads us back to a teleology of cognition.

Husserl's philosophy, before the birth of structuralist science (whose philosophical anticipation occurred in the ideal of the *mathesis universalis* of Descartes and Leibniz), attests as strictly as possible to the invariance of such a teleology behind pure science. By reducing as far as possible the ideology of a subject inhabiting the world as a man to the evidences of a transcendental ego, by excluding also, in conformity with Western rationalism, every sort of transcendence in the structures which the subject uncovers, and whose scope and horizons he fixes, Husserl situates the signifyingness of significations in the "signitive intentions" which fill objects with their "real presence." Despite the extension which phenomenology gives the word *intention*, intentionality bears the trace of the voluntary and the teleological. Signification is signifying out of a lack, a certain negativity, an aspiration which aims emptily, like a hunger, but in a determinate way, at the presence which is to satisfy it. Whether it be an expectation for a representation or a listening for a message, the intuitive fulfillment is the accomplishing of a teleological intention. The meaningful refers to a cognitive subjectivity and to the mathematical configuration of logical structures, as the eidetics of the contents refers to the "spirituality" of the intention conferring a sense on what manifests itself in the openness, by gathering up this sense. In conformity with the whole tradition of the West, knowing, in its thirst and its gratification, remains the norm of the spiritual, and transcendence is excluded both from intelligibility and from philosophy.

The position of the subject in the philosophy issued from Husserl – existence, axiological emotion, practical intentionality, thought of Being and even man as a sign, or man as guardian of Being – preserves, across all the avatars of the interpretation, the theoretical sense of signification insofar as openness, manifestation, phenomenality, appearing remain the proper event, the *Ereignis*, the "appropriating," of *esse*.

What the preceding pages aimed to suggest is a signification where the *for* of the-one-for-the-other, outside of any correlation and any finality, is a *for* of total gratuity, breaking with interest: *for* characteristic of the human fraternity outside of any preestablished system. Spirituality is sense, and sense is not a simple penury of being. Spirituality is no longer to be understood on the basis of knowing. In the splendid indifference of radiant being, there is an overwhelming of this being into sense, into proximity, which does not turn into knowing. It signifies as a difference which is, outside of all knowing, non-indifference. Proximity is signification not because it would be the aim of any theme, the need, fulfilled or on the point of being satisfied, of another being. The-one-for-the-other in proximity does not form an ontological conjunction of satisfaction. The capacity of a being, and of consciousness, its correlate, is insufficient to contain the plot which forms in the face of another, trace of an immemorial past, arousing a responsibility that comes from before and goes beyond what abides in the suspense of an epoque. "Goes beyond" – that is already to make a concession to ontological and theoretical language, as though the *beyond* were still a term, an entity, a mode of being, or the negative counterpart of all that. An approach is not a representation, however detheoreticized its intentionality would be, of a being beyond being. Its diachrony is not an insufficiency of an intuition. The trace of a past in a face is not the absence of a yet non-revealed, but the anarchy of what has never been present, of an infinite which commands in the face of the other, and which, like an excluded middle, could not be aimed at.[36]

CHAPTER IV

SUBSTITUTION[1]

Ich bin du, wenn
ich ich bin.

Paul Célan

1. PRINCIPLE AND ANARCHY

In the relationship with beings, which we call consciousness, we identify beings across the dispersion of silhouettes in which they appear; in self-consciousness we identify ourselves across the multiplicity of temporal phases. It is as though subjective life in the form of consciousness consisted in being itself losing itself and finding itself again so as to *possess itself* by showing itself, proposing itself as a theme, exposing itself in truth. This identification is not the *counterpart* of any image; it is a claim of the mind, proclamation, saying, kerygma. But it is not at all arbitrary, and consequently depends on a mysterious operation of schematism, in language, which can make an ideality correspond to the dispersion of aspects and images, silhouettes or phases. To become conscious of a being is then always for that being to be grasped across an ideality and on the basis of a said. Even an empirical, individual being is broached across the ideality of logos. Subjectivity qua consciousness can thus be interpreted as the articulation of an ontological event, as one of the mysterious ways in which its "act of being" is deployed. Being a theme, being intelligible or open, possessing oneself, the moment of *having* in *being* – all that is articulated in the movement of essence, losing itself and finding itself out of an ideal principle, an ἀρχή, in its thematic exposition, being thus carries on its affair of being. The detour of ideality leads to coinciding with oneself, that is, to certainty, which remains the guide and guarantee of the whole spiritual adventure of being. But this is why this adventure is no adventure. It is never dangerous; it is self-possession, sovereignty, ἀρχή. Anything unknown that can occur to it is in advance disclosed, open, manifest, is cast in the mould of the known, and cannot be a complete surprise.

For the philosophical tradition of the West, all spirituality lies in consciousness, thematic exposition of being, knowing.

In starting with sensibility interpreted not as a knowing but as proximity, in seeking in language contact and sensibility, behind the circulation of information it becomes, we have endeavored to describe subjectivity as irreducible to consciousness and thematization. Proximity appears as the relationship with the other, who cannot be resolved into "images" or be exposed in a theme. It is the relationship with what is not disproportionate to the ἀρχή in thematization, but incommensurable with it, with what does not derive its identity from the kerygmatic logos, and blocks all schematism.

Not able to stay in a theme, not able to appear, this invisibility which becomes contact and obsession is due not to the nonsignifyingness of what is approached, but to a way of signifying quite different from that which connects exposition to sight. Here, beyond visibility there is exposed no signification that would still be thematized in its sign. It is the very transcending characteristic of this beyond that is signification. Signification is the contradictory trope of the-one-for-the-other. The-one-for-the-other is not a lack of intuition, but the surplus of responsibility. My responsibility for the other is the *for* of the relationship, the very signifyingness of signification, which signifies in saying before showing itself in the said. The-one-for-the-other is the very signifyingness of signification! It is not that the "beyond" would be "further" than everything that appears, or "present in absence," or "shown by a symbol"; that would still be to be subject to a principle, to be given in consciousness. Here what is essential is a refusal to allow oneself to be tamed or domesticated by a theme. The movement going "beyond" loses its own signifyingness and becomes an immanence as soon as logos interpellates, invests, presents and exposes it, whereas its adjacency in proximity is an absolute exteriority. Incommensurable with the present, unassemblable in it, it is always "already in the past" behind which the present delays, over and beyond the "now" which this exteriority disturbs or obsesses. This way of passing, disturbing the present without allowing itself to be invested by the ἀρχή of consciousness, striating with its furrows the clarity of the ostensible, is what we have called a trace.[2] Proximity is thus *anarchically* a relationship with a singularity without the mediation of any principle, any ideality. What concretely corresponds to this description is my relationship with my neighbor, a signifyingness which is different from the much-discussed "meaning-endowment," since signification is this very relationship with the other, the-one-for-the-other. This incommensurability with consciousness, which becomes a trace of the *who knows where*, is not the inoffensive relationship of knowing in which everything is equalized, nor the indifference of spatial contiguity; it is an assignation of me by another, a responsibility with regard to men we do not even know. The relationship of proximity cannot be reduced to any modality of distance or geometrical contiguity, nor to the simple "representation" of a neighbor; it is already an assignation, an extremely urgent assignation – an obligation, anachronously prior to any commitment. This anteriority is "older" than the a priori. This formula expresses a way of being affected which can in no way be invested by spontaneity: the subject is affected without the source of the affection becoming a theme of representation. We have called this relationship irreducible to consciousness obsession. The relationship with exteriority is "prior" to the act that would effect it. For this relationship is not an act, not a thematizing, not a position in the Fichtean sense. Not everything that is in consciousness would be posited by consciousness – contrary to the proposition that seemed to Fichte to be fundamental.

Obsession is irreducible to consciousness, even if it overwhelms it. In consciousness it is betrayed, but thematized by a said in which it is manifested. Obsession traverses consciousness countercurrentwise, is inscribed in consciousness as something foreign, a disequilibrium, a delirium. It undoes thematization, and escapes any *principle*, origin, will, or ἀρχή, which are put forth in every ray of consciousness. This movement is, in the original sense of the term, an-archical. Thus obsession can nowise be taken as a hypertrophy of consciousness.

But anarchy is not disorder as opposed to order, as the eclipse of themes is not, as is said, a return to a diffuse "field of consciousness" prior to attention. Disorder is but another order, and what is diffuse is thematizable.[3] Anarchy troubles being over and beyond these alternatives. It brings to a halt the ontological play which, precisely qua play, is consciousness, where being is lost and found again, and thus illuminated. In the form of an ego, anachronously *delayed* behind its present moment, and unable to recuperate this delay – that is, in the form of an ego unable to conceive what is "touching" it,[4] the ascendancy of the other is exercised upon the same to the point of interrupting it, leaving it speechless. Anarchy is persecution. Obsession is a persecution where the persecution does not make up the content of a consciousness gone mad; it designates the form in which the ego is affected, a form which is a defecting from consciousness. This inversion of consciousness is no doubt a passivity – but it is a passivity beneath all passivity. It cannot be defined in terms of intentionality, where undergoing is always also an assuming, that is, an experience always anticipated and consented to, already an origin and ἀρχή. To be sure, the intentionality of consciousness does not designate voluntary intention only. Yet it retains the initiating and incohative pattern of voluntary intention. The given enters into a thought which recognizes in it or invests it with its own project, and thus exercises mastery over it. What affects a consciousness presents itself at a distance from the first, manifests itself a priori from the first, is represented, does not knock without announcing itself, leaves, across the interval of space and time, the leisure necessary for a welcome. What is realized in and by intentional consciousness offers itself to protention and diverges from itself in retention, so as to be, across the divergency, identified and possessed. This play in being is consciousness itself: presence to self through a distance, which is both loss of self and recovery in truth. The *for itself* in consciousness is thus the very power which a being exercises upon itself, its will, its sovereignty. A being is equal to itself and is in possession of itself in this form; domination is in consciousness as such. Hegel thought that the *I* is but consciousness mastering itself in self-equality, in what he calls "the freedom of this infinite equality."

The obsession we have seen in proximity conflicts with this figure of a being possessing itself in an equality, this being άρχή. How can the passivity of obsession find a place in consciousness, which is wholly, or is in the end, freedom? For in consciousness everything is intentionally assumed. Consciousness is wholly equality (equality of self with self, but also equality in that for consciousness responsibility is always strictly measured by freedom, and is thus always limited). How in consciousness can there be an undergoing or a passion whose active source does not, in any way, occur in consciousness? This exteriority has to be emphasized. It is not objective or spatial, recuperable in immanence and thus falling under the orders of – and in the order of – consciousness; it is obsessional, non-thematizable and, in the sense we have just defined, anarchic.

It is in a *responsibility that is justified by no prior commitment*, in the responsibility for another – in an ethical situation – that the me-ontological and metalogical structure of this anarchy takes form, undoing the logos in which the apology by which consciousness always regains its self-control, and commands, is inserted. This passion is absolute in that it takes hold without any a priori. The consciousness is affected, then, before forming an image of what is coming to it, affected in spite of itself. In these traits we recognize a persecution; being called into question prior to questioning, responsibility over and beyond the logos of response. It is as though persecution by another were at the bottom of solidarity with another. How can such a passion[5] take place and have its time in consciousness?

2. RECURRENCE

But consciousness, knowing of oneself by oneself, is not all there is to the notion of subjectivity. It already rests on a "subjective condition," an identity that one calls ego or I. It is true that, when asking about the meaning of this identity, we have the habit either of denouncing in it a reified substance, or of finding in it once again the for-itself of consciousness. In the traditional teaching of idealism, subject and consciousness are equivalent concepts. The *who* or the *me* are not even suspected. This one is a nonrelation, but absolutely a term. Yet this term of an irreversible assignation is perhaps dissimulated, under the outdated notion of the soul. It is a term not reducible to a relation, but yet is in recurrence. The ego is in itself like a sound that would resound in its own echo, the node of a wave which is not once again consciousness.[6] The term in recurrence will be sought here beyond or on the hither side of consciousness and its play, beyond or on the hither side of being which it thematizes, outside of being, and thus in itself as in exile. It will be found under the effect of an expulsion, whose positive meaning has to be explicated. Under the effect of such an expulsion outside of being, it is in itself. There is expulsion in that it assigns me before I show myself, before I set myself up. I am assigned without recourse, without fatherland, already sent back to myself, but without being able to stay there, compelled before commencing. Nothing here resembles self-consciousness. It has meaning only as an upsurge in me of a responsibility prior to commitment, that is, a responsibility for the other. There I am one and irreplaceable, one inasmuch as irreplaceable in responsibility. This is the underside of a fabric woven where there is consciousness and which takes place in being.

Nothing here resembles self-consciousness. The reduction of subjectivity to consciousness dominates philosophical thought, which since Hegel has been trying to overcome the duality of being and thought, by identifying, under different figures, substance and subject. This also amounts to undoing the substantivity of substance, but in relationship with self-consciousness. The successive and progressive disclosure of being to itself would be produced in philosophy. Knowing, the dis-covering, would not be added on to the being of entities, to essence.[7] Being's essence carries on like a vigilance exercised without respite on this very vigilance, like a self-possession. Philosophy which states essence as an ontology, concludes this essence, this lucidity of lucidity, by this logos. Consciousness fulfills the being of entities. For Sartre as for Hegel, the oneself is posited on the basis of the for-itself. The identity of the I would thus be reducible to the turning back of essence upon itself. The I, or the oneself that would seem to be its subject or condition, the oneself taking on the figure of an entity among entities, would in truth be reducible to an abstraction taken from the concrete process of self-consciousness, or from the exposition of being in history or in the stretching out of time, in which, across breaks and recoveries, being shows itself to itself. Time, essence, essence as time, would be the absolute itself in the return to self. The multiplicity of unique subjects, entities immediately, empirically, encountered, would proceed from this universal self-consciousness of the Mind: bits of dust collected by its movement or drops of sweat glistening on its forehead because of the labor of the negative it will have accomplished. They would be forgettable moments of which what counts is only their identities due to their positions in the system, which are reabsorbed into the whole of the system.

The reflection on oneself proper to consciousness, the ego perceiving the self, is not like the antecendent recurrence of the oneself, the oneness without any duality of oneself, from the first backed up against itself, up against a wall, or twisted over itself in its skin, too tight in its skin, in itself already outside of itself. Its restlessness also does not convey dispersion into phases, exterior to one another, in a flux of immanent time in the Husserlian sense, retaining the past and biting on the future. The oneself is not the ideal pole of an identification across the multiciplicity of psychic silhouettes kerygmatically proclaimed to be the same by virtue of a mysterious schematism of discourse.[8] The oneself does not bear its identity as entities, identical in that they are said without being unsaid, and thus are thematized and appear to consciousness. The uncancellable recurrence of the oneself in the subject is prior to any distinction between moments which could present themselves to a synthesizing activity of identification and assemblage to recall or expectation. The recurrence of the oneself is not relaxed and lighted up again, illuminating itself thereby like consciousness which lights up by interrupting itself and finding itself again in the temporal play of retentions and protentions. The oneself does not enter into that play of exposings and dissimulations which we call a phenomenon (or phenomenology, for the appearing of a phenomenon is already a discourse). The oneself takes refuge or is exiled in its own fullness, to the point of explosion or fission, in view of its own reconstitution in the form of an identity identified in the said. Verbs, possessive adjectives and the syntactic figures one would like to use to disarticulate the singular torsion or contraction of the oneself bear already the mark of the oneself, of this torsion, this contraction, this fission. That is perhaps also the meaning of Leibniz' mysterious formula, "the ego is innate to itself." The self involved in maintaining oneself, losing oneself or finding oneself again is not a result, but the very matrix of the relations or events that these pronominal verbs express. The evocation of maternity in this metaphor suggests to us the proper sense of the oneself. The oneself cannot form itself; it is already formed with absolute passivity. In this sense it is the victim of a persecution that paralyzes any assumption that could awaken in it, so that it would posit itself *for* itself. This passivity is that of an attachment that has already been made, as something irreversibly past, prior to all memory and all recall. It was made in an irrecuperable time which the present, represented in recall, does not equal, in a time of birth or creation, of which nature or creation retains a trace, unconvertible into a memory. Recurrence is more past than any rememberable past, any past convertible into a present. The oneself is a creature, but an orphan by birth or an atheist no doubt ignorant of its Creator, for if it knew it it would again be taking up its commencement. The recurrence of the oneself refers to the hither side of the present in which every identity identified in the said is constituted. It is already constituted when the act of constitution first originates. But in order that there be produced in the drawing out of essence, coming out like a colorless thread from the distaff of the Parques, a break in the same, the nostalgia for return, the hunt for the same and the recoveries, and the clarity in which consciousness plays, in order that this divergency from self and this recapture be produced, the retention and protention by which every present is a re-presentation – behind all the articulations of these movements there must be the recurrence of the oneself. The disclosure of being to itself lurks there. Otherwise essence, exonerated by itself, constituted in immanent time, will posit only indiscernible points,[9] which would, to be sure, be together, but which would neither block nor fulfill any fate. Nothing would make itself. The breakup of "eternal rest" by time, in which being becomes consciousness and self-consciousness by equalling itself after the breakup, presuppose the oneself. To present the knot of ipseity in the straight thread of essence according to the model of the intentionality of the for-itself, or as the openness of reflection upon oneself, is to posit a new ipseity behind the ipseity one would like to reduce.

The oneself has not issued from its own initiative, as it claims in the plays and figures of consciousness on the way to the unity of an Idea. In that Idea, coinciding with itself, free inasmuch as it is a totality which leaves nothing outside, and thus, fully reasonable, the oneself posits itself as an always convertible term in a relation, a self-consciousness. But the oneself is hypostasized in another way. It is bound in a knot that cannot be undone in a responsibility for others. This is an anarchic plot, for it is neither the underside of a freedom, a free commitment undertaken in a present or a past that could be remembered, nor slave's alienation, despite the gestation of the other in the same, which this responsibility for the other signifies. In the exposure to wounds and outrages, in the feeling proper to responsibility, the oneself is provoked as irreplaceable, as devoted to the others, without being able to resign, and thus as incarnated in order to offer itself, to suffer and to give. It is thus one and unique, in passivity from the start, having nothing at its disposal that would enable it to not yield to the provocation. It is one, reduced to itself and as it were contracted, expelled into itself outside of being. The exile or refuge in itself is without conditions or support, far from the abundant covers and excuses which the essence exhibited in the said offers. In responsibility as one assigned or elected from the outside, assigned as irreplaceable, the subject is accused in its skin, too tight for its skin. Cutting across every relation, it is an individual unlike an entity that can be designated as τόδε τι. Unless, that is, the said derives from the uniqueness of the oneself assigned in responsibility the ideal unity necessary for identification of the diverse, by which, in the amphibology of being and entities, an entity signifies. The hypostasis is exposed as oneself in the accusative form, before appearing in the said proper to knowing as the bearer of a name. The metaphor of a sound that would be audible only in its echo meant to approach this way of presenting one's passivity as an underside without a right side.

Prior to the return to itself proper to consciousness, this hypostasis, when it shows itself, does so under the borrowed mask of being. The event in which this unity or uniqueness of the hypostasis is brought out is not the grasping of self in consciousness. It is an assignation to answer without evasions, which assigns the self to be a self. Prior to the play of being, before the present, older than the time of consciousness that is accessible in memory, in its "deep yore, never remote enough," the oneself is exposed as a hypostasis, of which the being it is as an entity is but a mask. It bears its name as a borrowed name, a pseudonymn, a pro-noun. In itself, the oneself is the one or the unique separated from being.

The oneself proper to consciousness is then not again a consciousness, but a term in hypostasis. It is by this hypostasis that the person, as an identity unjustifiable by itself and in this sense empirical or contingent, emerges substantively. In its stance it is resistant to the erosion of time and history, that is, struck by a death always violent and premature. An identity prior to the for-itself, it is not the reduced or germinal model of the relationship of oneself with oneself that cognition is. Neither a vision of oneself by oneself, nor a manifestation of oneself to oneself, the oneself does not coincide with the identifying of truth, is not statable in terms of consciousness, discourse and intentionality. The unjustifiable identity of ipseity is expressed in terms such as ego, I, oneself, and, this work aims to show throughout, starting with the soul, sensibility, vulnerability, maternity and materiality, which describe responsibility for others. The "fulcrum" in which this turning of being back upon itself which we call knowing or mind is produced thus designates the singularity par excellence. It can indeed appear in an indirect language, under a proper name, as an entity, and thus put itself on the edge of the generality characteristic of all said, and there refer to essence. But it is first a non-quiddity, no one, clothed with purely borrowed being, which masks its nameless singularity by conferring on it a role. The locus of support for the mind is a personal pronoun. If the return to self proper to cognition, the original truth of being, consciousness, can be realized, it is because a recurrence of ipseity has already been produced. This is an inversion in the process of essence, a withdrawing from the game that being plays in consciousness. It is a withdrawal in-oneself which is an exile in oneself, without a foundation in anything else, a non-condition. This withdrawal excludes all spontaneity, and is thus always already effected, already past. Ipseity is not an abstract point, the center of a rotation, identifiable on the basis of the trajectory traced by this movement of consciousness, but a point already identified from the outside, not having to identify itself in the present nor to state its identity, already older than the time of consciousness.

The identity already realized, the "fact" or the "already done" that the oneself contributes to consciousness and knowing, does not refer mythically to a duration prior to duration, to a fabric that would still be loose enough so as to permit the flexion upon oneself of the for-itself. The for-itself is a torsion irreducible to the beating of self-consciousness, the relaxing and recovering proper to the same. The oneself comes from a past that could not be remembered, not because it is situated very far behind, but because the oneself, incommensurable with consciousness which is always equal to itself, is not "made" for the present. The oneself, an inequality with itself, a deficit in being, a passivity or patience and, in its passivity not offering itself to memory, not affecting retrospective contemplation, is in this sense undeclinable, with an undeclinability which is not that of a pure actuality. It is the identity of the singular, modified only in the erosion of ageing, in the permanence of a loss of self. It is unsayable, and thus unjustifiable. These negative qualifications of the subjectivity of the oneself do not consecrate some ineffable mystery, but confirm the presynthetic, prelogical and in a certain sense atomic, that is, in-dividual, unity of the self, which prevents it from splitting, separating itself from itself so as to contemplate or express itself, and thus show itself, if only under a comic mask, to name itself otherwise than by a pro-noun. This prevention is the positivity of the one. It is in a certain sense atomic, for it is without any rest in itself, "more and more one," to the point of breakup, fission, openness. That this unity be a torsion and a restlessness, irreducible to the function that the oneself exercises in the ontology accomplished by consciousness, which, by the oneself, operates its turning back over itself, presents a problem. It is as though the atomic unity of the subject were exposed outside by breathing, by divesting its ultimate substance even to the mucous membrane of the lungs, continually splitting up.

The oneself does not rest in peace under its identity, and yet its restlessness is not a dialectical scission, nor a process equalizing difference. Its unity is not just added on to some content of ipseity, like the indefinite article which substantifies even verbs, "nominalizing" and thematizing them. Here the unity precedes every article and every process; it is somehow itself the content. Recurrence is but an "outdoing" of unity. As a unity in its form and in its content, the oneself is a singularity, prior to the distinction between the particular and the universal. It is, if one likes, a relationship, but one where there is no disjunction between the terms held in relationship, a relationship that is not reducible to an intentional openness upon oneself, does not purely and simply repeat consciousness in which being is gathered up, as the sea gathers up the waves that wash the shore. The ego is not in itself like matter which, perfectly espoused by its form, is what it is; it is in itself like one is in one's skin, that is, already tight, ill at ease in one's own skin. It is as though the identity of matter resting in itself concealed a dimension in which a retreat to the hither side of immediate coincidence were possible, concealed a materiality more material than all matter – a materiality such that irritability, susceptibility or exposedness to wounds and outrage characterizes its passivity, more passive still than the passivity of effects. Maternity in the complete being "for the other" which characterizes it, which is the very signifyingness of signification, is the ultimate sense of this vulnerability. This hither side of identity is not reducible to the for-itself, where, beyond its immediate identity, being recognizes itself in its difference. We have to formulate what the irremissibility and, in the etymological sense of the term, the anguish of this in-itself of the oneself are. This anguish is not the existential "being-for-death," but the constriction of an "entry inwards," or the "hither side" of all extension. It is not a flight into the void, but a movement into fullness, the anguish of contraction and breakup.[10] This describes the relation in which a subject is immolated without fleeing itself, without entering into ecstasy, without taking a distance from itself, in which it is pursued into itself, to the hither side of rest in itself, of its coincidence with itself. This recurrence, which one can, to be sure, call negativity (but a negativity antecedent to discourse, the unexceptionable homeland of dialectical negativity), this recurrence by contraction, is the self.

It is the negativity characteristic of the *in itself* without the openness of nothingness, penetrating into the plenum – *in itself* in the sense of *an sich* and *in sich*. It lies behind the distinction between rest and movement, between the being at home with oneself (*chez soi*) and wandering, between equality and difference. This negativity reminds us of the formulas of the *Parmenides* concerning the moment in which the One "being in motion . . . . (it) comes to a stand, or being at rest, (. . .) changes to being in motion," and in which it "must not be at any time." (156c). "This strange sort of nature" which "is situated between motion and rest" (156d)[11] is not a cross-section of time at a point that preserves dynamically, in potency, the contradiction between the present and the future or the past. Nor is it an extra-temporal ideality which dominates temporal dispersion, for both points and idealities in their own way presuppose the ontological adventure. This "strange sort of nature" is something on the hither side, without any reference to thematization, without even references to references rising in it, like "itch," without any dialectical germination, quite sterile and pure, completely cut off from adventure and reminiscence. No grounds (*non-lieu*), meanwhile or contra-tempo time (or bad times (*malheur*)), it is on the hither side of being and of the nothingness which is thematizable like being.

The expression "in one's skin" is not a metaphor for the in-itself; it refers to a recurrence in the dead time or the *meanwhile* which separates inspiration and expiration, the diastole and systole of the heart beating dully against the walls of one's skin. The body is not only an image or figure here; it is the distinctive in-oneself of the contraction of ipseity and its breakup.[12] This contraction is not an impossibility to forget oneself, to detach oneself from oneself, in the concern for oneself. It is a recurrence to oneself out of an irrecusable exigency of the other, a duty overflowing my being, a duty becoming a debt and an extreme passivity prior to the tranquillity, still quite relative, in the inertia and materiality of things at rest. It is a restlessness and patience that support prior to action and passion. Here what is due goes beyond having, but makes giving possible. This recurrence is incarnation. In it the body which makes giving possible makes one *other* without alienating. For this other is the heart, and the goodness, of the same, the inspiration or the very psyche in the soul.

The recurrence of ipseity, the incarnation, far from thickening and tumefying the soul, oppresses it and contracts it and exposes it naked to the other to the point of making the subject expose its very exposedness, which might cloak it, to the point of making it an uncovering of self in saying. The concept of the incarnate subject is not a biological concept. The schema that corporeality outlines submits the biological itself to a higher structure; it is dispossession, but not nothingness, for it is a negativity caught up in the impossibility of evading, without any field of initiative. It is, improbably enough, a retreat into the fullness of the punctual, into the inextendedness of the one. Responsibility prior to any free commitment, the oneself outside of all the tropes of essence, would be responsibility for the freedom of the others. The irremissible guilt with regard to the neighbor is like a Nessus tunic my skin would be.

3. THE SELF

Returning now to the theme of the first part of this exposition, we have to ask if this folding back upon oneself proper to ipseity (which does not even have the virtue of being an act of folding itself, but makes the act of consciousness turning back upon itself possible), this passive folding back, does not coincide with the anarchic passivity of an obsession. Is not obsession a relationship with the outside which is prior to the act that would open up this exterior? The total passivity of obsession is more passive still than the passivity of things, for in their "prime matter" things sustain the kerygmatic logos that brings out their outlines in matter. In falling under this saying that ordains, matter takes on meaning, and shows itself to be this or that – a thing. This fall – or, this case – a pure surrender to the logos, without regard for the propositions that will make of the thing a narrative to which the logos belongs, is the essence of the accusative. The logos that informs prime matter in calling it to order is an accusation, or a category. But obsession is anarchical; it accuses me beneath the level of prime matter. For as a category takes hold of matter, it takes as its model still what resistance, impenetrability, or potency remains in that matter, that "being in potency." Prime matter, presented as a being in potency, is still potency, which the form takes into account. It is not by chance that Plato teaches us that matter is eternal, and that for Aristotle matter is a *cause*; such is the truth for the order of *things*. Western philosophy, which perhaps is reification itself, remains faithful to the order of things and does not know the absolute passivity, beneath the level of activity and passivity, which is contributed by the idea of creation.[13] Philosophers have always wished to think of creation in ontological terms, that is, in function of a preexisting and indestructible matter.

In obsession the accusation effected by categories turns into an absolute accusative in which the ego proper to free consciousness is caught up. It is an accusation without foundation, to be sure, prior to any movement of the will, an obsessional and persecuting accusation. It strips the ego of its pride and the dominating imperialism characteristic of it. The subject is in the accusative, without recourse in being, expelled from being, outside of being, like the one in the first hypotheses of *Parmenides*, without a foundation, reduced to itself, and thus without condition. In its own skin. Not at rest under a form, but tight in its skin, encumbered and as it were stuffed with itself, suffocating under itself, insufficiently open, forced to detach itself from itself, to breathe more deeply, all the way, forced to dispossess itself to the point of losing itself. Does this loss have as its term the void, the zero point and the peace of cemeteries, as though the subjectivity of a subject meant nothing? Or do the being encumbered with oneself and the suffering of constriction in one's skin, better than metaphors, follow the exact trope of an alteration of essence, which inverts, or would invert, into a recurrence in which the expulsion of self outside of itself is its substitution for the other? Is not that what the self emptying itself of itself would really mean? This recurrence would be the ultimate secret of the incarnation of the subject; prior to all reflection, prior to every positing, an indebtedness before any loan, not assumed, anarchical, subjectivity of a bottomless passivity, made out of assignation, like the echo of a sound that would precede the resonance of this sound. The active source of this passivity is not thematizable. It is the passivity of a trauma, but one that prevents its own representation, a deafening trauma, cutting the thread of consciousness which should have welcomed it in its present, the passivity of being persecuted. This passivity deserves the epithet of complete or absolute only if the persecuted one is liable to answer for the persecutor. The face of the neighbor in its persecuting hatred can by this very malice obsess as something pitiful. This equivocation or enigma only the persecuted one who does not evade it, but is without any references, any recourse or help (that is its uniqueness or its identity as unique!) is able to endure. To undergo from the other is an absolute patience only if by this from-the-other is already for-the-other. This transfer, other than interested, "otherwise than essence," is subjectivity itself. "To tend the cheek to the smiter and to be filled with shame,"[14] to demand suffering in the suffering undergone (without producing the act that would be the exposing of the other cheek) is not to draw from suffering some kind of magical redemptive virtue. In the trauma of persecution it is to pass from the outrage undergone to the responsibility for the persecutor, and, in this sense from suffering to expiation for the other. Persecution is not something added to the subjectivity of the subject and his vulnerability; it is the very movement of recurrence. The subjectivity as *the other in the same*, as an inspiration, is the putting into question of all affirmation for-oneself, all egoism born again in this very recurrence. (This putting into question is not a preventing!) The subjectivity of a subject is responsibility of being-in-question[15] in the form of the total exposure to offence in the cheek offered to the smiter. This responsibility is prior to dialogue, to the exchange of questions and answers, to the thematization of the said, which is superposed on my being put into question by the other in proximity, and in the saying proper to responsibility is produced as a digression.

The recurrence of persecution in the oneself is thus irreducible to intentionality in which, even in its neutrality as a contemplative movement, the will is affirmed. In it the fabric of the same, self-possession in a present, is never broken. When affected the ego is in the end affected only by itself, freely. Subjectivity taken as intentionality is founded on auto-affection as an auto-revelation, source of an impersonal discourse. The recurrence of the self in responsibility for others, a persecuting obsession, goes against intentionality, such that responsibility for others could never mean altruistic will, instinct of "natural benevolence," or love. It is in the passivity of obsession, or incarnated passivity, that an identity individuates itself as unique, without recourse to any system of references, in the impossibility of evading the assignation of the other without blame. The re-presentation of self grasps it already in its trace. The absolution of the one is neither an evasion,[16] nor an abstraction; it is a concreteness more concrete than the simply coherent in a totality. For under accusation by everyone, the responsibility for everyone goes to the point of substitution. A subject is a hostage.

Obsessed with responsibilities which did not arise in decisions taken by a subject "contemplating freely," consequently accused in its innocence, subjectivity in itself is being thrown back on oneself. This means concretely: accused of what the others do or suffer, or responsible for what they do or suffer. The uniqueness of the self is the very fact of bearing the fault of another. In responsibility for another subjectivity is only this unlimited passivity of an accusative which does not issue out of a declension it would have undergone starting with the nominative. This accusation can be reduced to the passivity of the self only as a persecution, but a persecution that turns into an expiation. Without persecution the ego raises its head and covers over the self. Everything is from the start in the accusative. Such is the exceptional condition or unconditionality of the self, the signification of the pronoun *self* for which our Latin grammars themselves know no nominative form.

The more I return to myself, the more I divest myself, under the traumatic effect of persecution, of my freedom as a constituted, willful, imperialist subject, the more I discover myself to be responsible; the more just I am, the more guilty I am. I am "in myself" through the others. The psyche is the other in the same, without alienating the same.[17] Backed up against itself, in itself because without any recourse in anything, in itself like in its skin, the self in its skin both is exposed to the exterior (which does not happen to things) and obsessed by the others in this naked exposure. Does not the self take on itself, through its very impossibility to evade its own identity, toward which, when persecuted, it withdraws? Does not a beginning rise in this passivity? The undeclinability of the ego is the irremissibility of the accusation, from which it can no longer take a distance, which it cannot evade. This impossibility of taking any distance and of slipping away from the Good is a firmness more firm and more profound than that of the will, which is still a tergiversation.

The inability to decline indicates the anachronism of a debt preceding the loan, of an expenditure overflowing one's resources, as in effort. It would be an exigency with regard to oneself where what is possible is not measured by a reflection on oneself, as in the for-itself. In this exigency with regard to oneself the self answering to the exigency does not show itself in the form of a direct object complement – which would be to suppose an equality between self and self. This exigency with regard to oneself without regard for what is possible, that is, beyond all equity, is produced in the form of an accusation preceding the fault, borne against oneself despite one's innocence. For the order of contemplation it is something simply demented. This extreme accusation excludes the declinability of the self, which would have consisted in measuring the possibles in oneself, so as to accuse oneself of this or that, of something committed even if in the form of original sin. The accusation that weighs on the self as a self is an exigency without consideration for oneself. The infinite passion of responsibility, in its return upon itself goes further than its identity,[18] to the hither side or beyond being and the possible, and puts the being in itself in deficit, making it susceptible of being treated as a negative quantity.

But how does the passivity of the self become a "hold on oneself"? If that is not just a play on words, does it not presuppose an activity behind the absolutely anarchical passivity of obsession, a clandestine and dissimulated freedom? Then what is the object of the exposition developed to this point? We have answered this question in advance with the notion of substitution.

4. SUBSTITUTION

In this exposition of the in itself of the persecuted subjectivity, have we been faithful enough to the anarchy of passivity? In speaking of the recurrence of the ego to the self, have we been sufficiently free from the postulates of ontological thought, where the eternal presence to oneself subtends even its absences in the form of a quest, where eternal being, whose possibles are also powers, always takes up what it undergoes, and whatever be its submission, always arises anew as the principle of what happens to it? It is perhaps here, in this reference to a depth of anarchical passivity, that the thought that names creation differs from ontological thought. It is not here a question of justifying the theological context of ontological thought, for the word creation designates a signification older than the context woven about this name. In this context, this said, is already effaced the absolute diachrony of creation, refractory to assembling into a present and a representation. But in creation, what is called to being answers to a call that could not have reached it since, brought out of nothingness, it obeyed before hearing the order. Thus in the concept of creation *ex nihilo*, if it is not a pure nonsense, there is the concept of a passivity that does not revert into an assumption. The self as a creature is conceived in a passivity more passive still than the passivity of matter, that is, prior to the virtual coinciding of a term with itself. The oneself has to be conceived outside of all substantial coinciding of self with self. Contrary to Western thought which unites subjectivity and substantiality, here coinciding is not the norm that already commands all non-coinciding, in the quest it provokes. Then the recurrence to oneself cannot stop at oneself, but goes to the hither side of oneself; *in* the recurrence to oneself there is a going to the hither side of oneself. A does not, as in identity, return to A, but retreats to the hither side of its point of departure. Is not the signification of responsibility for another, which cannot be assumed by any freedom, stated in this trope? Far from being recognized in the freedom of consciousness, which loses itself and finds itself again, which, as a freedom, relaxes the order of being so as to reintegrate it in a free responsibility, the responsibility for the other, the responsibility in obsession, suggests an absolute passivity of a self that has never been able to diverge from itself, to then enter into its limits, and identify itself by recognizing itself in its past. Its recurrence is the contracting of an ego, going to the hither side of identity, gnawing away at this very identity – identity gnawing away at itself – in a remorse. Responsibility for another is not an accident that happens to a subject, but precedes essence in it, has not awaited freedom, in which a commitment to another would have been made. I have not done anything and I have always been under accusation – persecuted. The ipseity, in the passivity without arche characteristic of identity, is a hostage. The word *I* means *here I am*, answering for everything and for everyone. Responsibility for the others has not been a return to oneself, but an exasperated contracting, which the limits of identity cannot retain. Recurrence becomes identity in breaking up the limits of identity, breaking up the *principle* of being in me, the intolerable rest in itself characteristic of definition. The self is on the hither side of rest; it is the impossibility to come back from all things and concern oneself only with oneself. It is to hold on to oneself while gnawing away at oneself. Responsibility in obsession is a responsibility of the ego for what the ego has not wished, that is, for the others. This anarchy in the recurrence to oneself is beyond the normal play of action and passion in which the identity of a being is maintained, in which it *is*. It is on the hither side of the limits of identity. This passivity undergone in proximity by the force of an alterity in me is the passivity of a recurrence to oneself which is not the alienation of an identity betrayed. What can it be but a substitution of me for the others? It is, however not an alienation, because the other in the same is my substitution for the other through responsibility, for which, I am summoned as someone irreplaceable. I exist through the other and for the other, but without this being alienation: I am inspired. This inspiration is the psyche. The psyche can signify this alterity in the same without alienation in the form of incarnation, as being-in-one's-skin, having-the-other-in-one's-skin.

In this substitution, in which identity is inverted, this passivity more passive still than the passivity conjoined with action, beyond the inert passivity of the designated, the self is absolved of itself. Is this freedom? It is a different freedom from that of an initiative. Through substitution for others, the oneself escapes relations. At the limit of passivity, the oneself escapes passivity or the inevitable limitation that the terms within relation undergo. In the incomparable relationship of responsibility, the other no longer limits the same, it is supported by what it limits. Here the overdetermination of the ontological categories is visible, which transforms them into ethical terms. In this most passive passivity, the self liberates itself ethically from every other and from itself. Its responsibility for the other, the proximity of the neighbor, does not signify a submission to the non-ego; it means an openness in which being's essence is surpassed in inspiration. It is an openness of which respiration is a modality or a foretaste, or, more exactly, of which it retains the aftertaste. Outside of any mysticism, in this respiration, the possibility of every sacrifice for the other, activity and passivity coincide.

For the venerable tradition to which Hegel refers, the ego is an equality with itself, and consequently the return of being to itself is a concrete universality, being having separated itself from itself in the universality of the concept and death. But viewed out of the obsession of passivity, of itself anarchical, there is brought out, behind the equality of consciousness, an inequality. This inequality does not signify an inadequation of the apparent being with the profound or sublime being, nor a return to an original innocence (such as the inequality of the ego itself in Nabert, who is perhaps faithful to the tradition in which non-coincidence is only privation). It signifies an inequality in the oneself due to substitution, an effort to escape concepts without any future but attempted anew the next day. It signifies a uniqueness, under assignation, of responsibility, and because of this assignation not finding any rest in itself. The self without a concept, unequal in identity, signifies itself in the first person, setting forth the plane of saying, pro-ducing itself in saying as an ego or as me, that is, utterly different from any other ego, that is, having a meaning despite death. Contrary to the ontology of death this self opens an order in which death can be not recognized. An identity in diastasis, where coinciding is wanting. I am a self in the identifying recurrence in which I find myself cast back to the hither side of my point of departure! This self is out of phase with itself, forgetful of itself, forgetful in biting in upon itself, in the reference to itself which is the gnawing away at oneself of remorse. These are not events that happen to an empirical ego, that is, to an ego already posited and fully identified, as a trial that would lead it to being more conscious of itself, and make it more apt to put itself in the place of others. What we are here calling oneself, or the other in the same, where inspiration arouses respiration, the very pneuma of the psyche, precedes this empirical order, which is a part of being, of the universe, of the State, and is already conditioned in a system. Here we are trying to express the unconditionality of a subject, which does not have the status of a principle. This unconditionality confers meaning on being itself, and welcomes its gravity. It is as resting on a self, supporting the whole of being, that being is assembled into a unity of the universe and essence is assembled into an event. The self is a *sub-jectum*; it is under the weight of the universe, responsible for everything. The unity of the universe is not what my gaze embraces in its unity of apperception, but what is incumbent on me from all sides, regards me in the two senses of the term, accuses me, is my affair. In this sense, the idea that I am sought out in the intersideral spaces is not science-fiction fiction, but expresses my passivity as a self.

The self is what inverts the upright imperturbable work, without exemptions, in which being's essence unfolds. To be in-oneself, backed up against oneself, to the extent of substituting oneself for all that pushes one into this null-place, is for the I to be in itself, lying in itself beyond essence. The reclusion of the ego in itself, on the hither side of its identity, in the other, the expiation supporting the weight of the non-ego, is neither a triumph nor a failure. Failing already presupposes a freedom and the imperialism of a political or ecclesiastical ego, that is, a history of constituted and free egos. The self as an expiation is prior to activity and passivity.

In opposition to the vision of thinkers such as Eugen Fink or Jeanne Delhomme, who require, among the conditions of the world, a freedom without responsibility, a freedom of play, we discern in obsession a responsibility that rests on no free commitment, a responsibility whose entry into being could be effected only without any choice. To be without a choice can seem to be violence only to an abusive or hasty and imprudent reflection, for it precedes the freedom non-freedom couple, but thereby sets up a vocation that goes beyond the limited and egoist fate of him who is only for-himself, and washes his hands of the faults and misfortunes that do not begin in his own freedom or in his present. It is the setting up of a being that is not for itself, but is for all, is both being and disinterestedness. The for itself signifies self-consciousness; the for all, responsibility for the others, support of the universe. Responsibility for the other, this way of answering without a prior commitment, is human fraternity itself, and it is prior to freedom. The face of the other in proximity, which is more than representation, is an unrepresentable trace, the way of the infinite. It is not because among beings there exists an ego, a being pursuing ends, that being takes on signification and becomes a universe. It is because in an approach, there is inscribed or written the trace of infinity, the trace of a departure, but trace of what is inordinate, does not enter into the present, and inverts the *arche* into anarchy, that there is forsakeness of the other, obsession by him, responsibility and a self.[19] The non-interchangeable par excellence, the I, the unique one, substitutes itself for others. Nothing is a game. Thus being is transcended.

The ego is not just a being endowed with certain qualities called moral which it would bear as a substance bears attributes, or which it would take on as accidents in its becoming. Its exceptional uniqueness in the passivity or the passion of the self is the incessant event of subjection to everything, of substitution. It is a being divesting itself, emptying itself of its being, turning itself inside out, and if it can be put thus, the fact of "otherwise than being." This subjection is neither nothingness, nor a product of a transcendental imagination. In this analysis we do not mean to reduce an entity that would be the ego to the act of substituting itself that would be the being of this entity. Substitution is not an act; it is a passivity inconvertible into an act, the hither side of the act-passivity alternative, the exception that cannot be fitted into the grammatical categories of noun or verb, save in the said that thematizes them. This recurrence can be stated only as an in-itself, as the underside of being or as otherwise than being.[20] To be oneself, otherwise than being, to be dis-interested, is to bear the wretchedness and bankruptcy of the other, and even the responsibility that the other can have for me. To be oneself, the state of being a hostage, is always to`have one degree of responsibility more, the responsibility for the responsibility of the other.[21]

Why does the other concern me? What is Hecuba to me? Am I my brother's keeper? These questions have meaning only if one has already supposed that the ego is concerned only with itself, is only a concern for itself. In this hypothesis it indeed remains incomprehensible that the absolute outside-of-me, the other, would concern me. But in the "prehistory" of the ego posited for itself speaks a responsibility. The self is through and through a hostage, older than the ego, prior to principles. What is at stake for the self, in its being, is not to be. Beyond egoism and altruism it is the religiosity of the self.

It is through the condition of being hostage that there can be in the world pity, compassion, pardon and proximity – even the little there is, even the simple "After you, sir." The unconditionality of being hostage is not the limit case of solidarity, but the condition for all solidarity. Every accusation and persecution, as all interpersonal praise, recompense, and punishment presuppose the subjectivity of the ego, substitution, the possibility of putting oneself in the place of the other, which refers to the transference from the "by the other" into a "for the other," and in persecution from the outrage inflicted by the other to the expiation for his fault by me. But the absolute accusation, prior to freedom, constitutes freedom which, allied to the Good, situates beyond and outside of all essence.

All the transfers of feeling, with which the theorists of original war and egoism explain the birth of generosity (it is, however, not certain that war was at the beginning, before the altars), would not succeed in being fixed in the ego if it were not with its whole being, or rather with its whole disinterestedness, subjected not, like matter, to a category, but to the unlimited accusative of persecution. The self, a hostage, is already substituted for the others. "I am an other," but this is not the alienation Rimbaud refers to. I am outside of any place, in myself, on the hither side of the autonomy of auto-affection and identity resting on itself. Impassively undergoing the weight of the other, thereby called to uniqueness, subjectivity no longer belongs to the order where the alternative of activity and passivity retains its meaning. We have to speak here of expiation as uniting identity and alterity. The ego is not an entity "capable" of expiating for the others: it is this original expiation. This expiation is voluntary, for it is prior to the will's initiative (prior to the origin). It is as though the unity and uniqueness of the ego were already the hold on itself of the gravity of the other. In this sense the self is goodness, or under the exigency for an abandon of all having, of all *one's own* and all *for oneself*, to the point of substitution. Goodness is, we have said, the sole attribute which does not introduce multiplicity into the One that a subject is, for it is distinct from the One. If it showed itself to the one, it would no longer be a goodness in it. Goodness invests me in my obedience to the hidden Good.

The individuation or superindividuation of the ego consists in being in itself, in its skin, without sharing the *conatus essendi* of all beings which are beings in themselves. It consists in my being faced with everything that is only because I am by regard for all that is. It is an expiating for being. The self is the very fact of being exposed under the accusation that cannot be assumed, where the ego supports the others, unlike the certainty of the ego that rejoins itself in freedom.

5. COMMUNICATION

It is with subjectivity understood as self, with the exciding and dispossession, the contraction, in which the ego does not appear, but immolates itself, that the relationship with the other can be communication and transcendence, and not always another way of seeking certainty, or the coinciding with oneself. Paradoxically enough, thinkers claim to derive communication out of self-coinciding.[22] They do not take seriously the radical reversal, from cognition to solidarity, that communication represents with respect to inward dialogue, to cognition of oneself, taken as the trope of spirituality. They seek for communication a full coverage insurance, and do not ask if inward dialogue is not beholden to the solidarity that sustains communication. In expiation, the responsibility for the others, the relationship with the non-ego, precedes any relationship of the ego with itself. The relationship with the other precedes the auto-affection of certainty, to which one always tries to reduce communication.

But communication would be impossible if it should have to begin in the ego, a free subject, to whom every other would be only a limitation that invites war, domination, precaution and information. To communicate is indeed to open oneself, but the openness is not complete if it is on the watch for recognition. It is complete not in opening to the spectacle of or the recognition of the other, but in becoming a responsibility for him. The overemphasis of openness is responsibility for the other to the point of substitution, where the for-the-other proper to disclosure, to monstration to the other, turns into the for-the-other proper to responsibility. This is the thesis of the present work. The openness of communication is not a simple change of place, so as to situate a truth outside instead of keeping it in oneself. What is surprising is the idea or the folly of situating it outside. Would communication be something added on? Or is not the ego a substitution in its solidarity as something identical, a solidarity that begins by bearing witness of itself to the other? Is it not then first of all a communicating of communication, a sign of the giving of signs, and not a transmission of something in an openness? It is to singularly displace the question to ask if what shows itself in this openness is as it shows itself, if its appearing is not an appearance. The problem of communication reduced to the problem of the truth of this communication for him that receives it amounts to the problem of certainty, of the coinciding of self with self, as though coinciding were the ultimate secret of communication, and as though truth were only disclosure. The idea that truth can signify a witness given of the infinite[23] is not even suggested. In this preeminence of certainty, the identity of a substance is taken on for the ego, is said to be a monad, and is henceforth incapable of communication, save by a miracle. One is then led to look for a theory, from Cassirer to Binswanger, according to which a prior dialogue sustains the ego which states it, rather than the ego holding forth a conversation.

Those who wish to found on dialogue and on an original *we* the upsurge of egos, refer to an original communication behind the *de facto* communication (but without giving this original communication any sense other than the empirical sense of a dialogue or a *manifestation* of one to the other – which is to presuppose that *we* that is to be founded), and reduce the problem of communication to the problem of its certainty. In opposition to that, we suppose that there is in the transcendence involved in language a relationship that is not an empirical speech, but responsibility. This relationship is also a resignation (prior to any decision, in passivity) at the risk of misunderstanding (like in love, where, unless one does not love with love, one has to resign oneself to not being loved), at the risk of lack of and refusal of communication. The ego that thematizes is also founded in this responsibility and substitution. Regarding communication and transcendence one can indeed only speak of their uncertainty. Communication is an adventure of a subjectivity, different from that which is dominated by the concern to recover itself, different from that of coinciding in consciousness; it will involve uncertainty. It is by virtue of its eidos possible only in sacrifice, which is the approach of him for which one is responsible. Communication with the other can be transcendent only as a dangerous life, a fine risk to be run. These words take on their strong sense when, instead of only designating the lack of certainty, they express the gratuity of sacrifice. In a fine risk to be run, the word "fine" has not been thought about enough. It is as antithetical to certainty, and indeed to consciousness, that these terms take on their positive meaning, and are not the expression of a makeshift.

It is only in this way that the absolutely exterior other is near to the point of obsession. Here there is proximity and not truth about proximity, not certainty about the presence of the other, but responsibility for him without deliberation, and without the compulsion of truths in which commitments arise, without certainty. This responsibility commits me, and does so before any truth and any certainty, making the question of trust and norms an *idle* question, for in its uprightness a consciousness is not only naivety and opinion.[24]

The ethical language we have resorted to does not arise out of a special moral experience, independent of the description hitherto elaborated. The ethical situation of responsibility is not comprehensible on the basis of ethics. It does indeed arise from what Alphonse de Waelhens called non-philosophical experiences, which are ethically independent. The constraint that does not presuppose the will, nor even the core of being from which the will arises (or which it breaks up), and that we have described starting with persecution, has its place between the necessity of "what cannot be otherwise" (Aristotle, *Metaphysics*, E), of what today we call eidetic necessity, and the constraint imposed on a will by the situation in which it finds itself, or by other wills and desires, or by the wills and desires of others. The tropes of ethical language are found to be adequate for certain structures of the description: for the sense of the approach in its contrast with knowing, the face in its contrast with a phenomenon.

Phenomenology can follow out the reverting of thematization into anarchy in the description of the approach. Then ethical language succeeds in expressing the paradox in which phenomenology finds itself abruptly thrown. For ethics, beyond politics, is found at the level of this reverting. Starting with the approach, the description finds the neighbor bearing the trace of a withdrawal that orders it as a face. This trace is significant for behavior, and one would be wrong to forget its anarchic insinuation by confusing it with an indication, with the monstration of the signified in the signifier. For that is the itinerary by which theological and edifying thought too quickly deduces the truths of faith. Then obsession is subordinated to a principle that is stated in a theme, which annuls the very anarchy of its movement.[25] The trace in which a face is ordered is not reducible to a sign: a sign and its relationship with the signified are synchronic in a theme. The approach is not the thematization of any relationship, but is this very relationship, which resists thematization as anarchic. To thematize this relation is already to lose it, to leave the absolute passivity of the self. The passivity prior to the passivity-activity alternative, more passive than any inertia, is described by the ethical terms accusation, persecution, and responsibility for the others. The persecuted one is expelled from his place and has only himself to himself, has nothing in the world on which to rest his head. He is pulled out of every game and every war. Beyond auto-affection, which is still an activity, even if it is strictly contemporaneous with its passivity, the self is denuded in persecution, from which an accusation is inseparable, in the absolute passivity of being a creature, of substitution. In divesting the ego of its imperialism, the hetero-affection establishes a new undeclinability: the self, subjected to an absolute accusative, as though this accusation which it does not even have to assume came from it. The self involved in the *gnawing away at oneself* in responsibility, which is also incarnation, is not an objectification of the self by the ego. The self, the persecuted one, is accused beyond his fault before freedom, and thus in an unavowable innocence. One must not conceive it to be in the state of original sin; it is, on the contrary, the original goodness of creation. The persecuted one cannot defend himself by language, for the persecution is a disqualification of the apology. Persecution is the precise moment in which the subject is reached or touched with the mediation of the logos.[26]

6. "FINITE FREEDOM"

The views that have been expounded can then not be reproached for the imprudence of affirming that the first word of the "mind," that which makes all the others possible, and even the words "negativity" and "consciousness," would be naive unconditioned "Yes" of submission, negating truth, and all the highest values! The unconditionality of this *yes* is not that of an infantile spontaneity. It is the very exposure to critique, the exposure prior to consent, more ancient than any naive spontaneity. We have been accustomed to reason in the name of the freedom of the ego – as though I had witnessed the creation of the world, and as though I could only have been in charge of a world that would have issued out of my free will. These are presumptions of philosophers, presumptions of idealists! Or evasions of irresponsible ones. That is what Scripture reproaches Job for. He would have known how to explain his miseries if they could have devolved from his faults! But he never wished evil! His false friends think like he does: in a meaningful world one cannot be held to answer when one has not done anything. Job then must have forgotten his faults! But the subjectivity of a subject come late into a world which has not issued from his projects does not consist in projecting, or in treating this world as one's project. The "lateness" is not insignificant. The limits it imposes on the freedom of subjectivity is not reducible to pure privation. To be responsible over and beyond one's freedom is certainly not to remain a pure result of the world. To support the universe is a crushing charge, but a divine discomfort. It is better than the merits and faults and sanctions proportionate to the freedom of one's choices. If ethical terms arise in our discourse, before the terms freedom and non-freedom, it is because before the bipolarity of good and evil presented to choice, the subject finds himself committed to the Good in the very passivity of supporting. The distinction between free and non-free would not be the ultimate distinction between humanity and inhumanity, nor the ultimate mark of sense and nonsense. To understand intelligibility does not consist in going back to the beginning. There was a time irreducible to presence, an absolute unrepresentable past. Has not the Good chosen the subject with an election recognizable in the responsibility of being hostage, to which the subject is destined, which he cannot evade without denying himself, and by virtue of which he is unique? A philosopher can give to this election only the signification circumscribed by responsibility for the other. This antecedence of responsibility to freedom would signify the Goodness of the Good: the necessity that the Good choose me first before I can be in a position to choose, that is, welcome its choice. That is my pre-originary *susceptiveness*. It is a passivity prior to all receptivity, it is transcendent. It is an antecendence prior to all representable antecendence: immemorial. The Good is before being. There is diachrony: an unbridgeable difference between the Good and me, without simultaneity, odd terms. But also a non-indifference in this difference. The Good assigns the subject, according to a susception that cannot be assumed, to approach the other, the neighbor. This is an assignation to a non-erotic proximity,[27] to a desire of the non-desirable, to a desire of the stranger in the neighbor. It is outside of concupiscence, which for its part does not cease to seduce by the appearance of the Good. In a Luciferian way it takes on this appearance and thus claims to belong to the Good, gives itself out to be its equal, but in this very pretention which is an admission it remains subordinated. But this desire for the non-desirable, this responsibility for the neighbor, this substitution as a hostage, is the subjectivity and uniqueness of a subject.

From the Good to me, there is assignation: a relation that survives the "death of God." The death of God perhaps signifies only the possibility to reduce every value arousing an impulse to an impulse arousing a value. The fact that in its goodness the Good declines the desire it arouses while inclining it toward responsibility for the neighbor, preserves *difference* in the non-indifference of the Good, which chooses me before I welcome it. It preserves its *illeity* to the point of letting it be excluded from the analysis, save for the trace it leaves in words or the "objective reality" in thoughts, according to the unimpeachable witness of the Descartes' Third Meditation. That in the responsibility for another, the ego, already a self, already obsessed by the neighbor, would be unique and irreplaceable is what confirms its election. For the condition for, or the unconditionality of, the self does not begin in the auto-affection of a sovereign ego that would be, after the event, "compassionate" for another. Quite the contrary: the uniqueness of the responsible ego is possible only *in* being obsessed by another, in the trauma suffered prior to any auto-identification, in an unrepresentable *before*. The one affected by the other is an anarchic trauma, or an inspiration of the one by the other, and not a causality striking mechanically a matter subject to its energy.[28] In this trauma the Good reabsorbs, or redeems, the violence of non-freedom. Responsibility is what first enables one to catch sight of and conceive of value.

What of the notion of finite freedom? No doubt the idea of a responsibility prior to freedom, and the compossibility of freedom and the other such as it shows itself in responsibility for another, enables us to confer an irreducible meaning to this notion, without attacking the dignity of freedom which is thus conceived in finitude. What else can finite freedom mean? How can a will be partially free? How can the Fichtean free ego undergo the suffering that would come to it from the non-ego? Does the finitude of freedom signify the necessity by which a will to will finds itself in a given situation which limits the arbitrariness of the will? That does not cut into the infinity of freedom beyond what the situation determines. In finite freedom, there can then be disengaged an element of pure freedom, which limitation does not affect, in one's will. Thus the notion of finite freedom rather poses than resolves the problem of a limitation of the freedom of the will.

The responsibility for another, an unlimited responsibility which the strict book-keeping of the free and non-free does not measure, requires subjectivity as an irreplaceable hostage. This subjectivity it denudes under the ego in a passivity of persecution, repression and expulsion outside of essence, into oneself. In this self, outside of essence, one is in a deathlike passivity! But in responsibility for the other for life and death, the adjectives unconditional, undeclinable, absolute take on meaning. They serve to qualify freedom, but wear away the substrate, from which the free act arises in essence. In the accusative form, which is a modification of no nominative form, in which I approach the neighbor for whom, without having wished it, I have to answer, the irreplaceable one is brought out (*s'accuse*). This finite freedom is not primary, is not initial; but it lies in an infinite responsibility where the other is not other because he strikes up against and limits my freedom, but where he can accuse me to the point of persecution, because the other, absolutely other, is another one (*autrui*). That is why finite freedom is not simply an infinite freedom operating in a limited field. The will which it animates wills in a passivity it does not assume. And the proximity of the neighbor in its trauma does not only strike up against me, but exalts and elevates me, and, in the literal sense of the term, inspires me. Inspiration, heteronomy, is the very pneuma of the psyche. Freedom is borne by the responsibility it could not shoulder, an elevation and inspiration without complacency. The for-the-other characteristic of the subject can be interpreted neither as a guilt complex (which presupposes an *initial* freedom), nor as a natural benevolence or divine "instinct," nor as some love or some tendency to sacrifice. This is quite the opposite of the Fichtean conception, where all suffering due to the action of the non-ego is first a positing of this action of the non-ego by the ego.

But in the irreplaceable subject, unique and chosen as a responsibility and a substitution, a mode of freedom, ontologically impossible, breaks the unrendable essence. Substitution frees the subject from ennui, that is, from the enchainment to itself, where the ego suffocates in itself due to the tautological way of identity, and ceaselessly seeks after the distraction of games and sleep in a movement that never wears out. This liberation is not an action, a commencement, nor any vicissitude of essence and of ontology, where the equality with oneself would be established in the form of self-consciousness. An anarchic liberation, it emerges, without being assumed, without turning into a beginning, in inequality with oneself. It is brought out without being assumed, in the undergoing by sensibility beyond its capacity to undergo. This describes the suffering and vulnerability of the sensible as *the other in me*. The other is in me and in the midst of my very identification. The ipseity has become at odds with itself in its return to itself. The self-accusation of remorse gnaws away at the closed and firm core of consciousness, opening it, fissioning it. In consciousness equality and equilibrium between the trauma and the act is always reestablished. Or at least this equilibrium is sought in reflection and its *figures*, although the possibility of total reflection and of the unity of Mind, beyond the multiplicity of souls, is not effectively ensured. But is not that the way an other can of itself be in the same without alienating it, and without the emancipation of the same from itself turning into a slavery to anyone? This way is possible because, since an "immemorial time," anarchically, in subjectivity the by-the-other is also the for-the-other. In suffering by the fault of the other dawns suffering for the fault of others, supporting. The for-the-other keeps all the patience of undergoing imposed by the other. There is substitution for another, expiation for another. Remorse is the trope of the literal sense of the sensibility. In its passivity is effaced the distinction between being accused and accusing oneself.

The recurrence in the subject is thus neither freedom of possession of self by self in reflection, nor the freedom of play where I take myself for this or that, traversing avatars under the carnival masks of history. It is a matter of an exigency coming from the other, beyond what is available in my powers, to open an unlimited "deficit," in which the self spends itself without counting, freely. All the suffering and cruelty of essence weighs on a point that supports and expiates for it.

Essence, in its seriousness as *persistence in essence*, fills every interval of nothingness that would interrupt it. It is a strict book-keeping where nothing is lost nor created. Freedom is compromised in this balance of accounts in an order where responsibilities correspond exactly to liberties taken, where they compensate for them, where time relaxes and then is tightened again after having allowed a decision in the interval opened up. Freedom in the genuine sense can be only a contestation of this book-keeping by a gratuity. This gratuity could be the absolute *distraction* of a play without consequences, without traces or memories, of a pure pardon. Or, it could be responsibility for another and expiation.

In expiation, on a point of the essence there weighs the rest of the essence, to the point of expelling it. The self, the subjection or subjectivity of the subject, is the very over-emphasis of a responsibility for creation. Responsibility for the other, for what has not begun in me is responsibility in the innocence of being a hostage. My substitution for another is the trope of a sense that does not belong to the empirical order of psychological events, an *Einfühlung* or a compassion which signify by virtue of this sense.

My substitution – it is as *my own* that substitution for the neighbor is produced. The Mind is a multiplicity of individuals. It is in me – in me and not in another, in me and not in an individuation of the concept Ego – that communication opens. It is I who am integrally or absolutely ego, and the absolute is my business. No one can substitute himself for me, who substitutes myself for all. Or, if one means to remain with the hierarchy of formal logic – genus, species, individual – it is in the course of the individuation of the ego in me that is realized the elevation in which the ego is for the neighbor, summoned to answer for him. When this relation is really thought through, it signifies the wound that cannot heal over of the self in the ego accused by the other to the point of persecution, and responsible for its persecutor. Subjection and elevation arise in patience above non-freedom. It is the subjection of the allegiance to the Good.

The disinterestedness of the subject is a descent or elevation of the ego to me. This movement is not reducible to the formalism of the logical operation of generalization or specification. Philosophy, which is consigned in the said, converts disinterestedness and its signification into essence and, by an abuse of language, to be sure, says that of which it is but a servant, but of which it makes itself master by saying it, and then reduces its pretensions in a new said. The subject posited as deposed is me; I universalize myself. And that is also my truth, my truth of being mortal, belonging to generation and corruption, which the negativity of the universalization presupposes. But the concept of the ego can correspond to me only inasmuch as it can signify responsibility, which summons me as irreplaceable. That is, in my flight out of concepts, which is not the naivety or blindness of non-thought, for positively it is responsibility for my neighbor. (It is time the abusive confusion of foolishness with morality were denounced.) Thus there is true movement between the conceptuality of the ego and the patience of a refusal of concepts, between universality and individuation, between mortality and responsibility. The very diachrony of truth is in this alternation. This ambiguity puts concepts into question inasmuch as it shakes the very idea of truth as a result, truth abiding in the present with an as it were monosyllabic sense. The ego involved in responsibility is me and no one else, me with whom one would have liked to pair up a sister soul, from whom one would require substitution and sacrifice. But to say that the other has to sacrifice himself to the others would be to preach human sacrifice! "Me" is not an inimitable nuance of *Jemeinigkeit* that would be added on to a being belonging to the genus "soul" or "man" or "individual," and would thus be common to several souls, men and individuals, making reciprocity possible among them from the first. The uniqueness of the ego, overwhelmed by the other in proximity, is the other in the same, the psyche. But is it I, I and no one else, who am a hostage for the others. In substitution my being that belongs to me and not to another is undone, and it is through this substitution that I am not "another," but me. The self in a being is exactly the not-being-able-to-slip-away-from an assignation that does not aim at any generality. There is no ipseity common to me and the others; "me" is the exclusion from this possibility of comparison, as soon as comparison is set up. The ipseity is then a privilege or an unjustifiable election that chooses me and not the ego. I am unique and chosen; the election is in the subjection. The conceptualization of this last refusal of conceptualization is not contemporaneous with this refusal; it transcends this conceptualization. This transcendence separating itself from the consideration that conceptualizes it, the diachrony of subjectivity, is my entry into the proximity of the neighbor.

Subjectivity is being hostage. This notion reverses the position where the presence of the ego to itself appears as the beginning or as the conclusion of philosophy.[29] This coinciding in the same, where I would be an origin, or, through memory, a covering over of the origin, this presence, is, from the start, undone by the other. The subject resting on itself is confounded by wordless accusation. For in discourse it would have already lost its traumatic violence. The accusation is in this sense persecuting; the persecuted one can no longer answer it. More exactly, it is accusation which I cannot answer, but for which I cannot decline responsibility. Already the position of the subject is a deposition, not a *conatus essendi*. It is from the first a substitution by a hostage expiating for the violence of the persecution itself. We have to conceive in such terms the de-substantiation of the subject, its de-reification, its disinterestedness, its subjection, its subjectivity. It is a pure self, in the accusative, responsible before there is freedom. Whatever be the ways that lead to the superstructure of society, in justice the dissymmetry that holds me at odds with regard to the other will find again law, autonomy, equality.

To say that the ego is a substitution is then not to state the universality of a principle, the quiddity of an ego, but, quite the contrary, it is to restore to the soul its egoity which supports no generalization. The way by which, from this situation, the logos arises to the concept of the ego passes through the third party.[30] The subject as an ego is not an entity provided with egoity as an eidetic structure, which should make it possible to form a concept of it, and make the singular entity be its realization.

Modern antihumanism, which denies the primacy that the human person, free and for itself, would have for the signification of being, is true over and beyond the reasons it gives itself. It clears the place for subjectivity positing itself in abnegation, in sacrifice, in a substitution which precedes the will. Its inspired intuition is to have abandoned the idea of person, goal and origin of itself, in which the ego is still a thing because it is still a being. Strictly speaking, the other is the end; I am a hostage, a responsibility and a substitution supporting the world in the passivity of assignation, even in an accusing persecution, which is undeclinable. Humanism has to be denounced only because it is not sufficiently human.

Will it be said that the world weighs with all its suffering and all its fault on the ego because this ego is a free consciousness, capable of sympathy and compassion? Will it be said that only a free being is sensitive to the weight of the world that weighs on it? Let us admit for a moment a free ego, capable of deciding for solidarity with others. At least it will be recognized that this freedom has no time to assume this urgent weight, and that consequently it is as checked or undone under the suffering. It is impossible to evade the appeal of the neighbor, to move away. One approaches the other perhaps in contingency, but henceforth one is not free to move away from him. The assumption of the suffering and the fault of another nowise goes beyond the passivity: it is a passion. This condition or unconditionality of being a hostage will then at least be an essential modality of freedom, the first, and not an empirical accident of the freedom, proud in itself, of the ego.

To be sure – but this is another theme – my responsibility for all can and has to manifest itself also in limiting itself. The ego can, in the name of this unlimited responsibility, be called upon to concern itself also with itself. The fact that the other, my neighbor, is also a third party with respect to another, who is also a neighbor, is the birth of thought, consciousness, justice and philosophy. The unlimited initial responsibility, which justifies this concern for justice, for oneself, and for philosophy can be forgotten. In this forgetting consciousness is a pure egoism. But egoism is neither first nor last. The impossibility of escaping God, the adventure of Jonas, indicates that God is at least here not a value among values. (I pronounce the word God without suppressing the intermediaries that lead me to this word, and, if I can say so, the anarchy of his entry into discourse, just as phenomenology states concepts without ever destroying the scaffoldings that permit one to climb up to them.) The impossibility of escaping God lies in the depths of myself as a self, as an absolute passivity. This passivity is not only the possibility of death in being, the possibility of impossibility. It is an impossibility prior to that possibility, the impossibility of slipping away, absolute susceptibility, gravity without any frivolity. It is the birth of a meaning in the obtuseness of being, of a "being able to die" subject to sacrifice.

The self inasmuch as, in an approach, it abrogates the egoism of perseverance in being, which is the imperialism of the ego, introduces meaning into being. There could be no meaning in being which could not be measured to being. Mortality renders senseless any concern that the ego would have for its existence and its destiny. It would be but an evasion in a world without issue, and always ridiculous. No doubt nothing is more comical than the concern that a being has for an existence it could not save from its destruction, as in Tolstoi's tale where an order for enough boots for 25 years is sent by one that will die the very evening he gives his order. That is indeed as absurd as questioning, in view of action, the stars whose verdict would be without appeal. But through this image one sees that the comical is also tragic, and that it belongs to the same man to be a tragic and a comical personage.

The approach, inasmuch as it is a sacrifice, confers a sense on death. In it the absolute singularity of the responsible one encompasses the generality or generalization of death. In it life is no longer measured by being, and death can no longer introduce the absurd into it. Death gives lie to pleasure, in which for the space of an instant the tragi-comedy is forgotten, and which would be defined by this forgetting. But despite all its adversity, it is accorded with the for-the-other of approach. No one is so hypocritical as to claim that he has taken from death its sting, not even the promisers of religions. But we can have responsibilities and attachments through which death takes on a meaning. That is because, from the start, the other affects us despite ourselves.

If one had the right to retain one trait from a philosophical system and neglect all the details of its architecture (even though there are no details in architecture, according to Valery's profound dictum, which is eminently valid for philosophical construction, where the details alone prevent collapse), we would think here of Kantism, which finds a meaning to the human without measuring it by ontology and outside of the question "What is there here...?" that one would like to take to be preliminary, outside of the immortality and death which ontologies run up against. The fact that immortality and theology could not determine the categorical imperative signifies the novelty of the Copernican revolution: a sense that is not measured by being or not being; but being on the contrary is determined on the basis of sense.

CHAPTER V

SUBJECTIVITY AND INFINITY

I. SIGNIFICATION AND THE OBJECTIVE RELATION

a. The Subject Absorbed by Being

The implication of the subject in signification, shown in proximity, is equivalent neither to the shifting of signification over to the objective side, spreading out its terms on a common ground through their apparition in being and through the very appearing of being – nor to its reduction to what is called a subjective lived experience. But we should first recall the way being carries on on the objective side, absorbing the subject which is correlative with an object, and triumphing, in the truth of its "move," both over the primacy of the subjective and over the subject-object correlation.

That one could think being means, indeed, that the appearing of being belongs to its very movement of being, that its phenomenality is essential, and that being cannot do without consciousness, to which manifestation is made. But then being's *essence* which manifests itself in truth and the very truth of the true, the appearing of essence, are nowise inscribed in the form of properties of the disclosed terms or in the quiddity of these terms, nor in the particularity of the system that assembles these terms. The truth of the true, its being uncovered or the nudity of the disclosed, does not receive, on the other hand, any false or true semblance, any imaginary character, that would come from the consciousness that welcomes the presentation of the discovered or disclosed being. And that is so to the extent that the manifestation itself, as we have just affirmed, would be a false semblance if it did not belong to the movement, or the play, that being carries on qua being. What is more, objectivity, being's essence revealed in truth, somehow protects the unfolding of being against the projection of subjective phantasms which would trouble the process or procession of essence. Objectivity concerns the being of entities that bears it; it signifies the indifference of what appears to its own appearing. The phenomenality of essence and of the terms that are true is at the same time as it were the epiphenomenality of this phenomenality. There is indifference, a purely negative reference, of the system to what comes to pass outside the system. In fact outside the system there takes place the extraordinary event of knowing, which could not affect the system it thematizes. Subjectivity qua knowing is thus subordinated to the sense of objectivity.

Phenomenality, the exhibition of being's essence in truth, is a permanent presupposition of the philosophical tradition of the West. Being's *esse*, through which an entity is an entity, is a matter of thought, gives something to thought, stands from the first in the open. In that there is indeed a kind of indigence in being, constrained to an other than itself, to a subject called upon to welcome the manifestation. It has recourse to a receptivity necessary to its sort of life, if we can put it that way. There is a finitude of essence.[1] It also follows that, outside of the part subjectivity plays in the disclosure of being, every game that consciousness would play for its own account would be but a veiling or an obscuring of being's essence, a lie or an ideology, whose status is difficult to establish without ambiguity. For that lie or ideology can be interpreted both as a pure effect of the finitude of being and as the effect of a ruse: the Ulysses of Plato's Petit Hippias was born in the "emptiness" of the subject effacing itself before the true, played tricks with the true, was smarter than the wisdom of the subject, smart to the point of malice, of industry.

b. The Subject at the Service of the System

But the disclosure of truth is not a simple optical phenomenon. If in the quiddity of the beings that show themselves their visibility and their being is not inscribed in the form of an attribute, it is their grouping, their co-presence, that is – and this is new! – the position of the one with regard to the other, the relativity in which the one makes a sign to the other, the reciprocal signifyingness of the one with respect to the other, that is equivalent to the coming to light of qualified quiddities themselves. The regrouping of all these significations or structures into a system, intelligibility, is the disclosure itself. The intelligibility or systematic structure of the totality would allow the totality to appear and would protect it against any alteration that could come to it from the look. And this indifference to the subjective look is not ensured in the same way for the terms, the structures, and the system. For a shadow veils the terms taken outside of the relationship in which they are implicated, the relations and the structures taken or surprised outside of the system that locks them in at the moment, when, still isolated or already abstract, they have to search for or rejoin their place in the conjuncture, when the structures still have to be packed into a system. An order manifested in which the terms of the structures or the elements of a system hold together as an abstraction is still obscure and, despite its thematization, offers resistance to the light, that is, is not fully objective. A structure is precisely an intelligibility, a rationality or a signification whose terms by themselves do not have signification (except through the already kerygmatic ideality of language). In the relationship the terms receive a weightlessness, a grace, and something like transparency for the look, and get weighted down and occulted as soon as they separate from it. We can then indeed observe a divergence between the separated simply thematized intelligibles – if it is true that a phenomenon is possible without the kerygmatic logos, without a phenomenology – and the state of intelligibility of a system; we can speak of a passage from a simple exposition of a theme to its intelligibility. We can distinguish in the movement from one to the other a hesitation, a time, the need for an effort, for good or bad luck, for the structures to be packed in. It is through this event, this becoming open, in the intelligible itself that we can understand the subjectivity that would here still be wholly conceived out of the intelligibility of being. The intelligibility of being is always high noon without shadows, where the subject intervenes without even projecting the silhouette of its own density. Dissolving into this intelligibility of structures, it continually sees itself to be at the service of this intelligibility, equivalent to the very appearing of being. This is rational theoretical consciousness in its purity, when the clarity of appearing in truth is equivalent to intelligibility, as in the good Cartesian tradition, where the clear and distinct ideas still receive light from the Plato's intelligible sun. But the clarity comes from a certain arrangement which orders the entities or the moments and the *esse ipsum* of these entities into a system, assembling them. Being's appearing cannot be separated from a certain conjunction of elements in a structure, a lining up of structures in which being carries on – from their simultaneity, that is, their copresence. The present is the privileged time of truth and being, of being in truth; it is contemporaneousness itself, and the manifestation of being is a re-presentation. A subject would then be a power for re-presentation in the quasi-active sense of the word: it would draw up the temporal disparity into a present, into a simultaneousness. At the service of being, it unites the temporal phases into a present by retention and protention. It thus acts in the midst of the time that disperses; it acts like a subject endowed with memory and as a historian, author of books in which the lost elements of the past or the elements still hoped for and feared receive simultaneity in a volume. An isolated element or an isolated structure cannot be exhibited without being obscured by its nonsignifyingness.

It is because the assembling of nonsignifying elements into a structure and the arrangement of structures into systems or into a totality involves chances or delays, and something like good or bad luck, because the finitude of being is not only due to the fate that destines the way it carries on to manifestation, but also to the vicissitudes and risks of a packing in of its manifested aspects, that subjectivity in retention, memory and history,

intervenes to hasten the assembling, to confer more chances for the packing in, to unite the elements into a present, to re-present them. Kant (B102-
103) describes this spontaneity of the subject which called for the pure
exhibition of being in intuition *Hinzuthun* and *Sammeln*. Through them
the *Begreifen* is obtained, the conception through which intuition ceases to
be blind.

The thinking subject, called up to search for this intelligible arrangement, is then, despite the activity of its searching, despite its spontaneity,
to be interpreted as a detour that being's essence takes to get arranged and
thus to truly appear, to appear in truth. Intelligibility or signifyingness is
part of the very exercise of being, of the *ipsum esse*. Everything is then on
the same side, on the side of being. This ability to absorb the subject to
which the essence is entrusted is what is proper to essence. Everything is
enclosed in it. The subjectivity of the subject would always consist in effacing itself before being, letting it be by assembling structures into a signification, a global proposition in a said, a great present of synopsis in which
being shines with all its radiance.

It is true that the role that is incumbent on the subject in the manifestation of being makes the subject part of the way being carries on. Then, as a
participant in the event of being, the subject also manifests itself. The function of disclosing being is disclosed in its turn. That would be the self-
consciousness of consciousness. As a moment of being, subjectivity shows
itself to itself, and presents itself as an object to human sciences. As
mortal, the ego is conceptualized. But as other than the true being, as
different from the being that shows itself, subjectivity is nothing. Despite
or because of its finiteness, being has an encompassing, absorbing, enclosing essence. The veracity of the subject would have no other signification
than this effacing before presence, this representation.

c. The Subject as a Speaking that is Absorbed in the Said
Nor would it have another signification if one attends to the communication of essence manifested to the other, if one takes the saying as a pure
communication of a said. The manifestation to the other and the interhu-
man, intersubjective understanding concerning the being that manifests
itself can in turn play its part in this manifestation and this being. The
veracity of the subject would be the virtue of a saying in which the emission of signs, insignificant in their own figures, would be subordinate to the
signified, the said, which in turn would be conformed to the being that
shows itself. The subject would not be the source of any signification independently of the truth of the essence which it serves. A lie would be only
the price that being's finitude costs it. A science would be able to totalize
being at all levels of its *esse* by fixing the ontological structures that articu-

late being. Subjectivity, the ego and the others would be the signifiers and signified in which the subjective representation of being is realized.

The said can indeed be understood to be prior to communication and the intersubjective representation of being. Being would have a signification, that is, would manifest itself as already invoked in silent and nonhuman language, by the voices of silence, in the *Geläut der Stille*, the language that speaks before men and harbors the *esse ipsum*, the language which poetry puts into human words. A phenomenon itself, in this still new sense, would be a phenomenology. But saying the truth or lying would be in this hypothesis read in the said, as when speech, according to the traditional philosophy of language, would express the inward experience of a subject. To make the evocation of being, which makes a poem possible resound in a poem would be to make a said resound. Signification, intelligibility and mind would reside in the manifestation and in contemporaneousness, in synopsis, presence, in essence which is a phenomenon, that is, a signification whose very movement involves thematization, visibility and the said. Any radical non assemblable diachrony would be excluded from meaning.

The psyche in the subject then consists in representation in its gift for synchronizing, commencing, that of, its gift of freedom, a freedom, however, that is absorbed in the said, and free inasmuch as not opposing anything. The psyche would be consciousness excluding any trauma, since being is in fact what shows itself before striking, what amortizes its violence in knowledge.

d. The Responsible Subject that is not Absorbed in Being

The conjuncture in which a man is responsible for other men, the ethical relationship, which is habitually considered as belonging to a derivative or founded order, has been throughout this work approached as irreducible. It is structured as the-one-for-the-other. It signifies outside of all finality and every system, where finality is but one of the principles of systematization possible. This responsibility appears as a plot without a beginning, anarchic. No freedom, no commitment undertaken in a present, a present among others, recuperable, is the obverse of which this responsibility would be the reverse, but no slavery is included in the alienation of the same who is "for the other." In responsibility the same, the ego, is me, summoned, provoked, as irreplaceable, and thus accused as unique in the supreme passivity of one that cannot slip away without fault.[2] The models of being and the subject-object correlation, which are justifiable but derivative, do not depict signification, the-one-for-the-other. It indeed shows itself in the said, but does so only after the event, betrayed, foreign to the said of being; it shows itself in it as a contradiction – which incites Plato to parricide. To understand that A could be B, nothingness has to be a sort of being. Matrix of every thematizable relation, the-one-for-the-other, signification, sense or intelligibility, does not rest in being. Its restlessness must not be put in terms of rest. It guides discourse beyond being. By the implication of the *one* in the-one-for-the-other, by the substitution of the one for the other, the foundations of being are shaken or ensured. But this undermining or this ensuring do not in any way belong to being's deed, contrary to the mythologies in which the origin of things and beings is already the effect of a history that happens to things and beings called gods, or cast in an imposing format. The signifyingness of signification is not brought about as a mode of representation, nor as the symbolic evocation of an absence, that is, a makeshift or a failing of presence. Nor as an outdoing of presence, as idealism conceives of subjectivity, where presence rejoins and confirms itself and becomes a coinciding. There is indeed an outdoing in signification: the implication of the one in the-one-for-the-other in responsibility goes beyond the representable unity of the identical, not by a surplus or lack of presence, but by the uniqueness of the ego, my uniqueness as a respondent, a hostage, for whom no one else could be substituted without transforming responsibility into a theatrical role. The play of being and nothingness does not reduce this signification to non-sense. The condition of being hostage is not chosen; if there had been a choice, the subject would have kept his as-for-me, and the exits found in inner life. But this subjectivity, his very psyche, is for the other, his very bearing independence consists in supporting the other, expiating for him.

The implication of the one in the-one-for-the-other is then not reducible to the way a term is implicated in a relationship, an element in a structure, a structure in a system, which Western thought in all its forms sought for as a sure harbor, or a place of retreat which the soul should enter.

e. The-One-for-the-Other is not a Commitment
The-one-for-the-other is the foundation of theory, for it makes possible relationship, and the point outside of being, the point of disinterestedness, necessary for a truth that does not wish to be pure ideology. But it is not what one means by "committed subjectivity." Commitment already presupposes a theoretical consciousness, as a possibility to assume, before or after the event, a taking up that goes beyond the susceptiveness of passivity. Without this assumption, would not commitment amount to a pure and simple capture of an element in a mechanical or logical determinism, like a finger can be caught in a gear system? As the result of a decision freely taken or consented to, the result of a reverting of susceptiveness into a project, commitment refers – is there need to repeat this again? – to an intentional thought, an assumption, a subject open upon a present, repre-

sentation, a logos. A committed consciousness, if it does not appear in the interference of the series in which it is thrown, is in situation. What is imposed on it is already measured, forms a condition and a site, in which, by dwelling, the obstacle of the incarnation of consciousness is inverted into freedom and origin – and its weight into past. Consciousness in situation, with all that is taken from its choice, forms a conjuncture whose terms are synchronic or synchronizable, assembled by memory and prevision into a horizon of past and future. The *beyond* has meaning only negatively, by its non-sense.

It is in a way very different from commitment that the one is implicated in the-one-for-the-other. It is not a question of a forsakenness in a world, a situation which is from the first its own reversal, in which I can settle and build myself a place, a situation that is produced and reverses into the representation of a diversity put in conjunction. It is a question of a signification in which the meaning of establishment and representation are indeed justified, but this signification signifies *prior to any world*, signifies the proximity of the same and the other, in which the implication of the one in the other signifies the assignation of the one by the other. This assignation is the very signifyingness of signification, or the psyche of the same. Through the psyche proximity is my approaching of the other, the fact that the proximity of the same and the other is never close enough. The summoned one is the ego – me. I repel and send away the neighbor through my very identity, my occupying the arena of being; I then have always to reestablish peace. What in this signifying, in this the-one-for-the-other, can and must lead to knowing, to questioning, to the "what is this about . . . ," the explicit formulation of a familiarity with being as though it had been antecedent and implicit – what in this signifying leads to ontology and thus to presence, to the shadowless high noon manifestation of truth, to reckoning, thought, settling down, institution – we will no doubt have to show. But neither this familiarity nor the ontological movements found the approach. The antecedent familiarity with being is not prior to the approach. The sense of the approach is goodness, without knowledge or blindness, beyond essence. Goodness will indeed show itself in ontology metamorphosed into essence, and to be reduced; but essence cannot contain it.

All the analysis conducted up to now would justify the refusal to consider proximity as a vicissitude of the thematizing intentionality, openness, ontology, that is, of the event in which indeed everything shows itself, even if it is betrayed by the manifestation, the event which alone is recognized by the main tradition of Western philosophy as an articulation of meaning, that is, as an adventure of mind. But proximity, conceived independently of this spiritualism of consciousness and recognized as signification or goodness, allows us to understand goodness in another way than as an altruistic inclination to be satisfied. For signification, the-one-for-the-other, is never an *enough*, and the movement of signification does not return. This is also not to conceive of it as a decision of the will, an act of consciousness beginning in the present of a choice, having an origin in consciousness, or in the present of a choice conditioned by inhabitation (which is the context of every origin!). Goodness in the subject is anarchy itself. As a responsibility for the freedom of the other, it is prior to any freedom in me, but it also precedes violence in me, which would be the contrary of freedom. For if no one is good voluntarily, no one is a slave of the Good. The plot of goodness and of the Good, outside of consciousness, outside of essence, is the exceptional plot of substitution, which the said in its dissimulated truths betrays, and conveys, before us. The I approached in responsibility is for-the-other, is a denuding, an exposure to being affected, a pure susceptiveness. It does not posit itself, possessing itself and recognizing itself; it is consumed and delivered over, dis-locates itself, loses its place, is exiled, relegates itself into itself, but as though its very skin were still a way to shelter itself in being, exposed to wounds and outrage, emptying itself in a no-grounds, to the point of substituting itself for the other, holding on to itself only as it were in the trace of its exile. What verbs like "to deliver itself," "consume itself," "exile itself" (*se* livrer, *se* consumer, *s'*exiler), suggest by their pronominal form is not an act of reflection on oneself, of concern for oneself; it is not an act at all, but a modality of passivity which in substitution is beyond even passivity. To be oneself as in the trace of one's exile is to be as a pure withdrawal from oneself,[3] and as such, an inwardness. Inwardness is not at all like a way of disposing of private matters. This inwardness without secrets is a pure witness to the inordinateness which already commands me, to give to the other taking the bread out of my own mouth, and making a gift of my own skin.

It is not commitment that describes signification; it is signification, the-one-for-the-other characteristic of proximity, which justifies all commitment.

In the non-indifference to a neighbor, where proximity is never close enough, the difference between me and the other, and the undeclinability of the subject are not effaced, as they are in the situation in which the relationship of the one with the other is understood to be reciprocal. The non-indifference to the other as other and as neighbor in which I exist is something beyond any commitment in the voluntary sense of the term, for it extends into my very bearing as an entity, to the point of substitution. It is at the same time prior to commitments, for it disengages in this extreme passivity an undeclinable and unique subject. Responsibility, the signification which is non-indifference, goes one way, from me to the other. In the saying of responsibility, which is an exposure to an obligation for which no one could replace me, I am unique. Peace with the other is first of all my business. The non-indifference, the saying, the responsibility, the approach, is the disengaging of the unique one responsible, me. The way I appear is a summons. I am put in the passivity of an undeclinable assignation, in the accusative, a self. Not as a particular case of the universal, an ego belonging to the concept of ego, but as I, said in the first person – I, unique in my genus. It is indeed true that this I has already become a universal in the present exposition itself. But I am capable of conceiving of a break with this universal, and the apparition of the unique I which always precedes the reflection which comes again (with an alternating which we find in the refutation and rebirth of skepticism) to include me in the concept – which I again evade or am torn up from. The uniqueness of this ego, this I, is not due to a unique trait of its nature or its character; nothing is unique, that is, refractory to concepts, except the I involved in responsibility. In signification I am disengaged as unique. In the saying in responsibility, the one is not concealed in itself, but denudes itself in recurrence, substituting itself for another on the hither side of its own identity for another. This is the only way for it to be not multiplied in this relationship, but for its unity to be brought out in it. The "never enough" of proximity, the restlessness of this peace, is the acute uniqueness of subjectivity. The subject arising in the passivity of unconditionality, in the expulsion outside of its bing at home with itself, is undeclinable. This undeclinability is not that of transcendental subjectivity, is not an intentionality or openness upon the world, not even a world that overflows me, and in which the alleged ecstatic subjectivity is only dissimulated.

Proximity, difference which is non-indifference, is responsibility. It is a response without a question, the immediacy of peace that is incumbent on me. It is the signification of signs. It is the humanity of man not understood on the basis of transcendental subjectivity. It is the passivity of exposure, a passivity itself exposed. Saying does not occur in consciousness nor in a commitment understood in terms of consciousness or memory; it does not form a conjuncture and a synchrony. Proximity is fraternity before essence and before death, having a meaning despite being and nothingness, despite concepts.

Signification as proximity is thus the latent birth of the subject. Latent birth, for prior to an origin, an initiative, a present designatable and assumable, even if by memory. It is an anachronous birth, prior to its own present, a non-beginning, an anarchy. As a latent birth, it is never a presence, excluding the present of coinciding with oneself, for it is *in contact*, in sensibility, in vulnerability, in exposure to the outrages of the other. The subject is the more responsible the more it answers for, as though the distance between it and the other increased in the measure that proximity was increased. The latent birth of the subject occurs in an obligation where no commitment was made. It is a fraternity or complicity for nothing, but the more demanding that it constrains without finality and without end. The subject is born in the beginninglessness of an anarchy and in the endlessness of obligation, gloriously augmenting as though infinity came to pass in it. In the absolute assignation of the subject the Infinite is enigmatically heard: before and beyond. The extent and accent of the voice in which the Infinite is thus heard will have to be made clear.

We have several times indicated that a way leads from the proximity of the other to the appearing of being, and we will come back to this. Subjectivity is described as a substituting for the other, as disinterestedness, or a break with essence; it leads us to contest the thesis about the ultimacy or the priority of the ontological problem.[4] But does it conjure away the essence it nonetheless arouses? As an impersonal going on, an incessant splashing, a mute murmuring, as *there is*, does not essence swallow up the signification that will give light to it? Is not the insistence of this impersonal noise the threat of an end of the world felt in our days? One runs the risk of, or persists in taking the signification of the-one-for-the-other to be a limited or particular phenomenon, the "ethical aspect of being." But it is necessary to ask if in it there is not heard a voice coming from horizons at least as vast as those in which ontology is situated.

2. THE GLORY OF THE INFINITE

a. Inspiration

The assembling of being in the present, its synchronization by retention, memory and history, reminiscence, is representation; it does not integrate the responsibility for the separated entity. Representation does not integrate the responsibility for the other inscribed in human fraternity; human fraternity does not arise out of any commitment, any principle, that is, any recallable present. The order that orders me to the other does not show itself to me, save through the trace of its reclusion, as a face of a neighbor. There is the trace of a withdrawal which no actuality had preceded, and which becomes present only in my own voice, already obedient in the harsh present of offerings and gifts. Before this anarchy, this beginninglessness, the assembling of being fails. Its essence is undone in signification, in saying beyond being and its time, in the diachrony of transcendence. This transcendence is not convertible into immanence. What is beyond reminiscence, separated by the night of an interval from every present, is a time that does not enter into the unity of transcendental apperception.

This book has exposed the signification of subjectivity in the extraordinary everydayness of my responsibility for other men, the extraordinary forgetting of death or the being without regard for death. The signification of my responsibility for what escapes my freedom is the defeat or defecting of the unity of transcendental apperception, the originary actuality of every act, source of the spontaneity of the subject or of the subject as a spontaneity. This book has exposed my passivity, passivity as the-one-for-the-other; it transcends essence understood as potency and as act. It is as such that my passivity is signification. The-one-for-the-other goes to the extent of the-one-being-hostage-for-the-other. In its identity invoked the one is irreplaceable, and does not return to itself; in its bearing of itself, it is an expiation for the other, in its "essence" an ex-ception to essence, or a substitution. The-one-for-the-other is not the one trans-substantified into another, but for-the-other, in the discontinuity or diachrony of signification not yet set up in a theme, in which as a said it does indeed manifest itself, but seems immediately trapped in the theme, in synchrony and essence. The theme is not adequate for signification which is nonetheless spread out in it to show itself. Yet we must not take it as a "lived signification." Responsibility for the other is extraordinary, and is not prevented from floating over the waters of ontology. We do not have to find for it at all costs a status in the transcendental unity of apperception, in the actual and thus active unity of a synthesis. The one and the other separated by the interval of difference, or by the *meanwhile* which the non-indifference of responsibility does not nullify, are not bound to rejoin one another in the synchrony of a structure, or be compressed into a "state of soul."

Responsibility for the other, going against intentionality and the will, which intentionality does not succeed in dissimulating, signifies not the disclosure of a given and its reception, but the exposure of me to the other, prior to every decision. There is a claim laid on the same by the other in the core of myself, the extreme tension of the command exercised by the other in me over me, a traumatic hold of the other on the same, which does not give the same time to await the other. Through this alteration the soul animates the object; it is the very pneuma of the psyche. The psyche signifies the claiming of the same by the other, or inspiration, beyond the logic of the same and the other, of their insurmountable adversity. It is an undoing of the substantial nucleus of the ego that is formed in the same, a fission of the mysterious nucleus of inwardness of the subject by this assignation to respond, which does not leave any place of refuge, any chance to slip away, and is thus despite the ego, or, more exactly, despite me. Quite the contrary of nonsense, it is an alteration without alienation or election. The subject in responsibility is alienated in the depths of its identity with an alienation that does not empty the same of its identity, but constrains it to it, with an unimpeachable assignation, constrains it to it as no one else, where no one could eplace it. The psyche, a uniqueness outside of concepts, is a seed of folly, already a psychosis. It is not an ego, but me under assignation. There is an assignation to an identity for the response of responsibility, where one cannot have oneself be replaced without fault. To this command continually put forth only a "here I am" (*me voici*) can answer, where the pronoun "I" is in the accusative, declined before any declension, possessed by the other, sick,[5] identical. Here I am – is saying with inspiration, which is not a gift for fine words or songs. There is constraint to give with full hands, and thus a constraint to corporeality.

For Descartes the union of the soul and the body would presuppose a miraculous intervention, for Descartes looks for it, according to the rationality of representations, as an assembling and a simultaneity of distinct terms. He understands the soul to be a thematizing thought. But approached in responsibility for the other man, the psyche in the subject, the-one-for-the-other, would be signification or intelligibility, or signifyingness itself. It is the subjectivity of a man of flesh and blood, more passive in its extradition to the other than the passivity of effects in a causal chain, for it is beyond the unity of apperception of the *I think*, which is actuality itself. It is a being torn up from oneself for another in the giving to the other of the bread out of one's own mouth. This is not an anodyne formal relation, but all the gravity of the body extirpated from its *conatus essendi* in the possibility of giving. The identity of the subject is here brought out, not by a rest on itself, but by a restlessness that drives me outside of the nucleus of my substantiality.

b. Inspiration and Witness

But does not this exposure, this exile, this interdiction to remain in oneself revert into a position, and in pain itself, into complacency puffing itself up with substance and pride? This reverting signifies a residue of activity that cannot be absorbed into the subjective passivity, an ultimate substantiality of the ego even in the very vulnerability of sensibility, and at the same time, or in turn, ambiguously, the infinite path of the approach. The path does not remain simply asymptotic of the neighbor. Beyond the bad infinity of the *Sollen* it increases infinitely, living infinity, an obligation more and more strict in the measure that obedience progresses and the distance to be crossed untraversable in the measure that one approaches. The giving then shows itself to be a parcimony, the exposure a reserve, and holiness guilt. It is life without death, the life of the Infinite or its glory, a life outside of essence and nothingness.

For subjectivity to signify unreservedly, it would then be necessary that the passivity of its exposure to the other not be immediately inverted into activity, but expose itself in its turn; a passivity of passivity is necessary, and in the glory of the Infinite ashes from which an act could not be born anew. Saying is this passivity of passivity and this dedication to the other, this sincerity. Not the communication of a said, which would immediately cover over and extinguish or absorb the said, but saying holding open its openness, without excuses, evasions or alibis, delivering itself without saying anything said. Saying saying saying itself, without thematizing it, but exposing it again. Saying is thus to make signs of this very signifyingness of the exposure; it is to expose the exposure instead of remaining in it as an act of exposing. It is to exhaust oneself in exposing oneself, to make signs by making oneself a sign, without resting in one's every figure as a sign. In the passivity of the obsidional extradition this very extradition is delivered over to the other, before it could be established. This is the pre-reflexive iteration of the saying of this very saying, a statement of the "here I am" which is identified with nothing but the very voice that states and delivers itself, the voice that signifies. But to thus make signs to the point of making oneself a sign is not a babbling language, like the expression of a mute, or the discourse of a stranger shut up in his maternal language. It is the extreme tension of language, the for-the-other of proximity, which closes in on me from all sides and concerns me even in my identity. The logos of monologue or of dialogue will have already relaxed its potential, by scattering into possibilities of being, playing between the couples: conscious-unconscious, explicit-implicit.[6] A sign given to the other and already a sign of this giving of signs, pure signification, proximity is not a confusion with another, which would be a way of resting in an avatar, but incessant signification, a restlessness for the other. The response is put forth for the other, without any "taking up of attitudes." This responsibility is like a cellular irritability; it is the impossibility of being silent, the scandal of sincerity.[7]

Sincerity is not an attribute of saying; it is saying that realizes sincerity. It is inseparable from giving, for it opens reserves[8] from which the hand that gives draws without being able to dissimulate anything. Sincerity undoes the alienation which saying undergoes in the said, where, under the cover of words, in verbal indifference, information is exchanged, pious wishes are put out, and responsibilities are fled. No said equals the sincerity of the saying, is adequate to the veracity that is prior to the true, the veracity of the approach, of proximity, beyond presence. Sincerity would then be saying without the said, apparently a "speaking so as to say nothing," a sign I make to another of this giving of signs, "as simple as 'hello,'" but ipso facto the pure transparency of an admission, the recognition of a debt. Does saying as the admission of a debt precede all the other forms of saying? Is not a salutation the giving of a sign signifying this very giving, this recognition of a debt? Sincerity in which signification signifies, in which one is exposed without holding back to the other, in which the one approaches the other, is not exhausted in invocation, in the salutation that does not cost anything, understood as a pure vocative. The vocative indicates a meaning, but does not suffice for the sense of proximity and sincerity which signifies it. A fission of the ultimate substantiality of the ego, sincerity is not reducible to anything ontic, or anything ontological, and leads as it were beyond or on this side of everything positive, every position. It is not an act or a movement, or any sort of cultural gesture; they presuppose the absolute breakthrough of oneself.[9]

c. Sincerity and the Glory of the Infinite
Does not the sense of sincerity refer to the glory of infinity, which calls for sincerity as for a saying? This glory could not appear, for appearing and presence would belie it by circumscribing it as a theme, by assigning it a beginning in the present of representation, whereas, as infinition of infinity, it comes from a past more distant than that which is within the reach of memory, and is lined up on the present. It comes from a past that has never been represented, has never been present, and which consequently has not let a beginning germinate. Glory could not become a phenomenon without entering into conjunction with the very subject to which it would appear, without closing itself up in finitude and immanence. But without a principle, without a beginning, and anarchy, glory breaks up themes and, prior to the logos, signifies positively the extraditing of the subject that rests on itself, to what it has never assumed. For, out of an unrepresentable past, the subject has been sensitive to the provocation that has never presented itself, but has struck traumatically. Glory is but the other face of the passivity of the subject. Substituting itself for the other, a responsibility ordered to the first one on the scene, a responsibility for the neighbor, inspired by the other, I, the same, am torn up from my beginning in myself, my equality with myself. The glory of the Infinite is glorified in this responsibility. It leaves to the subject no refuge in its secrecy that would protect it against being obsessed by the other, and cover over its evasion. Glory is glorified by the subject's coming out of the dark corners of the "as-for-me," which, like the thickets of Paradise in which Adam hid himself upon hearing the voice of the eternal God traversing the garden from the side from which the day comes, offered a hiding-place from the assignation, in which the position of the ego at the beginning, and the very possibility of origin, is shaken. The glory of the Infinite is the anarchic identity of the subject flushed out without being able to slip away. It is the ego led to sincerity, making signs to the other, for whom and before whom I am responsible, of this very giving of signs, that is, of this responsibility:

"here I am." The saying prior to anything said bears witness to glory. This witness is true, but with a truth irreducible to the truth of disclosure, and does not narrate anything that shows itself. Saying is without noematic correlation in the pure obedience to glory that orders. It is without dialogue, in the passivity from the first subordinate to the "here I am." The distance that is enlarged in the measure that proximity narrows, the glory of infinity, is the inequality between the same and the other, the difference that is also the non-indifference of the same for the other and the substitution which, in its turn, is a nonequality with oneself, a non-recovering of self by self, a dispossession of self, the self leaving the clandestinity of its identification. It is already a sign made to another, a sign of this giving of signs, that is, of this non-indifference, a sign of this impossibility of slipping away and being replaced, of this identity, this uniqueness: here I am.[10] The identity aroused thus behind identification is an identity by pure election. Election traverses the concept of the ego to summon me as me through the inordinateness of the other. It extracts me from the concept in which I continually take refuge, for I find in it the measure of an obligation which is not defined in the election. Obligation calls for a unique response not inscribed in universal thought, the unforseeable response of the chosen one.

This identity is pre-original, anarchic, older than every beginning. It is not self-consciousness attaining itself in the present, but the extreme exposure to the assignation by the other, already realized behind consciousness and freedom. The assignation is entry into me by burglary, that is, without showing itself, speaking in the saying of the assigned one. I have always been exposed to assignation in responsibility, as though put under a leaden sun without protecting shadows, where every residue of mystery vanishes, every mental reservation through which evasion would be possible. This exposure without anything held back at the very spot where the trauma is produced, a cheek offered already to the smiter, is sincerity as saying, witnessing to the glory of the Infinite. It breaks the secret of Gyges, the subject that sees without being seen, without exposing himself, the secret of the inward subject.

d. Witness and Language
Subjectivity is from the first substitution offered in place of another, but before the distinction between freedom and nonfreedom. Not a victim offering itself in his place, which would suppose there is a reserved region of subjective will behind the subjectivity of substitution. It is the null-place in which inspiration by the other is also expiation for the other, the psyche by which consciousness itself would come to signify. The psyche is not grafted on to a substance, but alters the substantiality of this substance

which supports all things. It alters it with an alteration in which identity is brought out. Substitution is not the psychological event of compassion or intropathy in general, but makes possible the paradoxical psychological possibilities of putting oneself in the place of another. The subjectivity of the subject, as being subject to everything, is a pre-originary susceptibility, before all freedom and outside of every present. It is accused in uneasiness or the unconditionality of the accusative, in the "here I am" (*me voici*) which is obedience to the glory of the Infinite that orders me to the other.[11] "Each of us is guilty before everyone for everyone, and I more than the others," writes Dostoyevsky in *Brothers Karamazov*.[12] The subjectivity of the subject is persecution and martyrdom. It is a recurrence which is not self-consciousness, in which the subject would still be maintained distant from itself in non-indifference, would still remain somehow in itself and be able to veil its face. This recurrence is not self-coinciding, rest, sleep or materiality. It is a recurrence on this side of oneself, prior to indifference to itself. It is a substitution for another. In the interval, it is *one* without attributes, and not even the unity of the one doubles it up as an essential attribute. It is one absolved from every relationship, every game, literally without a situation, without a dwelling place, expelled from everywhere and from itself, one saying to the other "I" or "here I am."[13] The ego stripped by the trauma of persecution of its scornful and imperialist subjectivity, is reduced to the "here I am," in a transparency without opaqueness, without heavy zones propitious for evasion. "Here I am" as a witness of the Infinite, but a witness that does not thematize what it bears witness of, and whose truth is not the truth of representation, is not evidence. There is witness, a unique structure, an exception to the rule of being, irreducible to representation, only of the Infinite. The Infinite does not appear to him that bears witness to it. On the contrary the witness belongs to the glory of the Infinite. It is by the voice of the witness that the glory of the Infinite is glorified.

No theme, no present, has a capacity for the Infinite. The subject in which the other is in the same, inasmuch as the same is for the other, bears witness to it. The difference of proximity is absorbed in the measure that proximity becomes closer, and by this very absorption is brought out gloriously, and accuses me always more. The same in its bearing as same is more and more extended to the other, to the point of substitution as a hostage. Expiation coincides in the last analysis with the extraordinary and diachronic reversal of the same into the other, in inspiration and the psyche.

The idea of the Infinite, which in Descartes is lodged in a thought that cannot contain it, expresses the disproportion between glory and the present, which is inspiration itself. Under the weight that exceeds my capacity, a passivity more passive than all passivity correlative with acts, my own passivity breaks out in a saying. The exteriority of the Infinite becomes somehow an inwardness in the sincerity of a witness borne. Glory, which does not affect me as a representation or as an interlocutor before which and before whom I put myself, is glorified in my saying, commanding me by my own mouth. Inwardness is not a secret place somewhere in me; it is that reverting in which the eminently exterior, precisely in virtue of this eminent exteriority, this impossibility of being contained and consequently entering into a theme, forms, as infinity, an exception to essence, concerns me and circumscribes me and orders me by my own voice. The command is stated by the mouth of him it commands. The infinitely exterior becomes an "inward" voice, but a voice bearing witness to the fission of the inward secrecy that makes signs to another, signs of this very giving of signs. The way is crooked. Claudel chose as an epigraph for his *Satin Slipper* a Portuguese proverb that can be understood in a sense we have just put forth: "God writes straight with crooked lines."

Witness, this way for a command to sound in the mouth of the one that obeys, of being revealed before all appearing, before all presentation before a subject, is not a psychological wonder, but the modality in which the anarchic Infinite passes its command. Not an industrious recourse to man to reveal itself, and to his psalms to be glorified, but the very way the Infinite in its glory passes the finite, or the way it passes itself, not entering by the signification of the-one-for-the-other into the being of a theme, but signifying and thus excluding itself from nothingness. The saying in the said of the witness born signifies in a plot other than that which is spread out in a theme, other than that which attaches a noesis to a noema, a cause to an effect, the memorable past to the present. This plot connects to what detaches itself absolutely, to the Absolute. The detachment of the Infinite from the thought that seeks to thematize it and the language that tries to hold it in the said is what we have called *illeity*. One is tempted to call this plot religious; it is not stated in terms of certainty or uncertainty, and does not rest on any positive theology.

The Infinite passes in saying. This is what could be understood, when we see that saying is irreducible to an act, a psychological attitude, a state of soul, a thought among others, or a moment of being's essence, through which, one knows not why, man would double up his essence. Of itself saying is witness, whatever be the ulterior destiny into which it enters through the said in a system of words. The saying from which this system derives is not the babbling infancy of this system and of the circulation of the information in which it functions. For one can show how this new destiny is inscribed in the witness borne.[14] But saying without the said, a sign given to the other, a witness in which the subject quits his clandestineness as a subject, by which the Infinite passes, is not something added on as an information, expression, repercussion or symptom, to some experience of the Infinite or of its glory, as though there could be an experience of the Infinite, and something else than glorification, that is, responsibility for the neighbor. This saying is not from the first held in the structures of subject-object, signifier-signified, saying-said correlation. A sign given to the other, it is sincerity or veracity, with which glory is glorified. The Infinite then has glory only through subjectivity, in the human adventure of the approach of the other, through the substitution for the other, by the expiation for the other. The subject is inspired by the Infinite, which, as *illeity*, does not appear, is not present, has always already past. is neither theme, telos nor interlocutor. It is glorified in the glory that manifests a subject, is glorified already in the glorification of its glory by the subject, thus undoing all the structures of correlation. Glorification is saying, that is, a sign given to the other, peace announced to the other, responsibility for the other, to the extent of substitution.[15]

That the way the Infinite passes the finite and passes itself has an ethical meaning is not something that results from a project to construct the "transcendental foundation" of "ethical experience." The ethical is the field outlined by the paradox of an Infinite in relationship with the finite without being belied in this relationship. Ethics is the breakup of the originary unity of transcendental apperception, that is, it is the beyond of experience. Witnessed, and not thematized, in the sign given to the other, the Infinite signifies out of responsibility for the other, out of the-one-for-the-other, a subject supporting everything, subject to everything, that is, suffering for everyone, but charged with everything, without having had to decide for this taking charge, which is gloriously amplified in the measure that it is imposed. Obedience precedes any hearing of the command. The possibility of finding, anachronously, the order in the obedience itself, and of receiving the order out of oneself, this reverting of heteronomy into autonomy, is the very way the Infinite passes itself. The metaphor of the inscription of the law in consciousness expresses this in a remarkable way, reconciling autonomy and heteronomy. It does so in an ambivalence, whose diachrony is the signification itself, an ambivalence which, in the present, is an ambiguity. The inscription of the order in the for-the-other of obedience is an anarchic being affected, which slips into me "like a thief" through the outstretched nets of consciousness. This trauma has surprised me completely; the order has never been represented, for it has never been presented, not even in the past coming in memory, to the point that it is I that only says, and after the event, this unheard-of obligation. This ambivalence is the exception and subjectivity of the subject, its very psyche, a possibility of inspiration. It is the possibility of being the author of what had been breathed in unbeknownst to me, of having received, one knows not from where, that of which I am author. In the responsibility for the other we are at the heart of the ambiguity of inspiration. The unheard-of saying is enigmatically in the anarchic response, in my responsibility for the other. The trace of infinity is this ambiguity in the subject, in turns beginning and makeshift, a diachronic ambivalence which ethics makes possible.

e. Witness and Prophecy

We call prophecy this reverting in which the perception of an order coincides with the signification of this order given to him that obeys it. Prophecy would thus be the very psyche in the soul: the other in the same, and all of man's spirituality would be prophetic. Infinity is not announced in the witness given as a theme. In the sign given to the other, by which I find myself torn up from the secrecy of Gyges, "taken by the hair"[16] from the bottom of my obscurity in the saying without the said of sincerity, in my "here I am," from the first present in the accusative, I bear witness to the Infinite. The Infinite is not in front of its witness, but as it were outside, or on the "other side" of presence, already past, out of reach, a thought behind thoughts which is too lofty to push itself up front. "Here I am, in the name of God," without referring myself directly to his presence. "Here I am," just that! The word God is still absent from the phrase in which God is for the first time involved in words. It does not at all state "I believe in God." To bear witness God is precisely not to state this extraordinary word, as though glory would be lodged in a theme and be posited as a thesis, or become being's essence. As a sign given to the other of this very signification, the "here I am" signifies me in the name of God, at the service of men that look at me,[17] without having anything to identify myself with, but the sound of my voice or the figure of my gesture — the saying itself. This recurrence is quite the opposite of return upon oneself, self-consciousness. It is sincerity, effusion of oneself, "extraditing" of the self to the neighbor. Witness is humility and admission; it is made before all theology; it is kergyma and prayer, glorification and recognition. But what is proper to all the relations that are thus unfolded – and what a deception for the friends of truth that thematizes being, and of the subject that effaces itself before Being! – is the fact that the return is sketched out in the going, the appeal is understood in the response, the "provocation" coming from God is in my invocation, gratitude is already gratitude for this state of gratitude, which is at the same time or in turn a gift and a gratitude. The transcendence of the revelation lies in the fact that the "epiphany" comes in the saying of him that received it. The order that orders me does not leave me any possibility of setting things right side up again with impunity, of going back from the exteriority of the Infinite, as when before a theme one goes back from the signifier to the signified, or as when in a dialogue one finds in "you" a being. It is in prophecy that the Infinite escapes the objectification of thematization and of dialogue, and signifies as *illeity*, in the third person. This "thirdness" is different from that of the third man, it is the third party that interrupts the face to face of a welcome of the other man, interrupts the proximity or approach of the neighbor, it is the third man with which justice begins.[18]

The Infinite orders to me the neighbor as a face, without being exposed to me, and does so the more imperiously that proximity narrows. The order has not been the cause of my response, nor even a question that would have preceded it in a dialogue. I find the order in my response itself, which, as a sign given to the neighbor, as a "here I am," brings me out of invisibility, out of the shadow in which my responsibility could have been evaded. This saying belongs to the very glory of which it bears witness. This way for the order to come from I know not where, this coming that is not a recalling, is not the return of a present modified or aged into a past, this non-phenomenality of the order which, beyond representation affects me unbeknownst to myself, "slipping into me like a thief,"[19] we have called *illeity*.[20] It is the coming of the order to which I am subjected before hearing it, or which I hear in my own saying. It is an august command, but one that does not constrain or dominate and leaves me outside of any correlation with its source. No *structure* is set up with a correlate. Thus the saying that comes to me is my own word. Authority is not somewhere, where a look could go seek it, like an idol, or assume it like a logos.[21] It is not only outside of all intuition, but outside of all thematization, even that of symbolism. It is the pure trace of a "wandering cause," inscribed in me.

An obedience preceding the hearing of the order, the anachronism of inspiration or of prophecy is, for the recuperable time of reminiscence, more paradoxical than the prediction of the future by an oracle. "Before they call, I will answer,"[22] the formula is to be understood literally. In approaching the other I am always late for the meeting. But this singular obedience to the order to go, without understanding the order, this obedience prior to all representation, this allegiance before any oath, this responsibility prior to commitment, is precisely the other in the same, inspiration and prophecy, the *passing itself* of the Infinite.

That the glory of the Infinite is glorified only by the signification of the-one-for-the-other, as sincerity, that in my sincerity the Infinite passes the finite, that the Infinite comes to pass there, is what makes the plot of ethics primary, and what makes language irreducible to an act among acts. Before putting itself at the service of life as an exchange of information through a linguistic system, saying is witness; it is saying without the said, a sign given to the other. Sign of what? Of complicity? Of a complicity for nothing, a fraternity, a proximity that is possible only as an openness of self, an imprudent exposure to the other, a passivity without reserve, to the point of substitution. It is thus exposing of the exposure, saying, saying that does not say a word, that signifies, that, as responsibility, is signification itself, the-one-for-the-other. It is the subjectivity of the subject that makes itself a sign, which one would be wrong to take as a babbling utterance of a word, for it bears witness to the glory of the Infinite.

This witness is not reducible to the relationship that leads from an index to the indicated. That would make it a disclosure and a thematization. It is the bottomless passivity of responsibility, and thus, sincerity. It is the meaning of language, before language scatters into words, into themes equal to the words and dissimulating in the said the openness of the saying exposed like a bleeding wound. But the trace of the witness given, the sincerity or glory, is not effaced even in its said.

I can indeed state the meaning borne witness to as a said. It is an extraordinarry word, the only one that does not extinguish or absorb its saying, but it cannot remain a simple word. The word God is an overwhelming semantic event that subdues the subversion worked by illeity. The glory of the Infinite shuts itself up in a word and becomes a being. But it already undoes its dwelling and unsays itself without vanishing into nothingness. It invests being in the very copula with which it receives attributes. (It is receiving them at this very moment, when this semantic adventure is here being thematized.) A said unique of its kind, it does not narrowly espouse grammatical categories like a noun (neither proper nor common noun), and does not incline exactly to logical rules, like a meaning (being an excluded middle between being and nothingness). This said gets its meaning from the witness borne, which thematization does betray in theology which introduces it into the system of a language, in the order of the said. But this abusive statement is at once forbidden. The limits of the present in which infinity betrays itself break up. Infinity is beyond the scope of the unity of transcendental apperception, cannot be assembled into a present, and refuses being recollected. This negation of the present and of representation finds its positive form in proximity, responsibility and substitution. This makes it different from the propositions of negative theology. The refusal of presence is converted into my presence as present, that is, as a hostage delivered over as a gift to the other. In proximity, in signification, in my giving of signs, already the Infinite speaks through the witness I bear of it, in my sincerity, in my saying without said, preoriginary saying which is said in the mouth of the very one that receives the witness. Its signification has let itself be betrayed in the logos only to convey itself before us. It is a word already stated as a kerygma in prayer or blasphemy. It thus retains in its statement the trace of the excession of transcendence, of the beyond.

Thematization is then inevitable, so that signification itself show itself, but does so in the sophism with which philosophy begins, in the betrayal which philosophy is called upon to reduce. This reduction always has to be attempted, because of the trace of sincerity which the words themselves bear and which they owe to saying as witness, even when the said dissimulates the saying in the correlation set up between the saying and the said. Saying always seeks to unsay that dissimulation, and this is its very veracity. In the play activating the cultural keyboard of language, sincerity or witness signifies by the very ambiguity of every said, where, in the midst of the information communicated to another there signifies also the sign that is given to him of this giving of signs. That is the resonance of every language "in the name of God," the inspiration or prophecy of all language.

By reason of these ambiguities, prophecy is not the makeshift of a clumsy revelation. They belong to the glory of the Infinite. That prophecy could take on the appearances of information circulating among others, issued from the subject or from influences undergone by the subject, starting with those that would come from its own physiology, or from its wounds or its triumphs – that is the enigma, the ambiguity, but also the order of transcendence, of the Infinite. The Infinite would be belied in the proof that the finite would like to give of its transcendence; entering into conjunction with the subject that would make it appear, it would lose its glory. Transcendence owes it to itself to interrupt its own demonstration. Its voice has to be silent as soon as one listens for its message. It is necessary that its pretension be exposed to derision and refutation, to the point of suspecting in the "here I am" that attests to it a cry or a slip of a sick subjectivity. But of a subjectivity responsible for the other! There is an enigmatic ambivalence, and an alternating of meaning in it. In its saying, the said and being are stated, but also a witness, an inspiration of the same by the other, beyond essence, an overflowing of the said itself by a rhetoric which is not only a linguistic mirage, but a surplus of meaning of which consciousness all by itself would be incapable. Here there is a possibility both of ideology and of sacred delirium: ideology to be circumvented by linguistics, sociology and psychology, delirium to be reduced by philosophy, to be reduced to signification, the-one-for-the-other, a mission toward another in the glory of the Infinite. Transcendence, the beyond essence which is also being-in-the-world, requires ambiguity, a blinking of meaning which is not only a chance certainty, but a frontier both ineffaceable and finer than the tracing of an ideal line. It needs the diachrony that breaks the unity of transcendental apperception, which does not succeed in assembling the time of modern humanity, in turn passing from prophecy to philology and transcending philology toward prophetic signification. For it is incapable of denying the fraternity of men.

3. FROM SAYING TO THE SAID, OR THE WISDOM OF DESIRE

Not includable in the present, refractory to thematization and representation, the alterity of the neighbor calls for the irreplaceable singularity that lies in me, by accusing this ego, reducing it, in the accusative, to itself. But the self is not in a state, is not in position, is not at rest in itself, ensured in itself as by a condition. Through the obsession with the other, accusing, persecuting, the uniqueness of oneself is also the defection of the identity that identifies itself in the same. In the coinciding with oneself, this identity would still be protected, would not be exposed enough, would not be passive enough. The defection of identity is a for-the-other in the midst of identity; it is the inversion of being into a sign, the subversion of essence that begins to signify before being, the disinterestedness of essence. The sign is not posited for itself. not even in the figure that is proper to it, such as it is exposed in a theme. In subjectivity, subjected to everything, a sign gives over its plasticity and its function of being sign to the other, repeating, always anew, the exposure of what the exposure can outline as essence. This iteration of exposure is expression, sincerity, saying. To not be reabsorbed into meaning, the patience of passivity must be always at the limit, exceeded by a demented suffering, "for nothing," a suffering of pure misery. Saying prolongs this extreme passivity, despite its apparent activity.

Is it apparent? How does saying differ from an act commencing in a conquering and voluntary ego, whose signifying is an act being converted into being, and whose "for the other" takes root in identity? The for-the-other of responsibility for the other does not proceed from any free commitment, any present, in which its origin would germinate, or in which an identity identifying itself would catch its breath. That is so, but then there is a new dilemma. Responsibility without a prior commitment, without a present, without an origin, anarchic, is thus an infinite responsibility of the one for the other who is abandoned to me without anyone being able to take my place as the one responsible for him. Does this confer upon me a new identity, that of being the unique chosen one? Or does this exclusive election, as signification of the Infinite, reduce me to the status of an articulation in its divine economy? Are we reduced to humanity as an extreme possibility in being, where the substantiality of "supporting oneself" is desubstantified in a "supporting the other," "substituting oneself for him"? Or through this ipseity reduced to being irreplaceable hostage, is the self equivalent to the entry of the subject into the play or designs of the Infinite?

But is not this dilemma rather an ambivalence, and the alternative an enigma? The enigma of a God speaking in man and of man not counting on any god? It is a dilemma or an alternative if one sticks to the phenomena, to the said, where one passes, successively, without being able to stop, from the affirmation of the Infinite to its negation in me. But the question mark in this said, which, contrary to the univocal logos of the theologians, is alternating, is the very pivot of revelation, of its blinking light. It is experienced precisely by incessently running up against it, and crossing over its own contestation. There is a dilemma in the said, but an ambivalence in the signification of saying, in subjectivity, the entity expelled outside of being into itself; saying enigmatically and diachronically signifies transcendence or the Infinite, the otherwise than being and the disinterestedness from essence.

The enigma of the Infinite, whose saying in me, a responsibility where no one assists me, becomes a contestation of the Infinite. By this contestation eveything is incumbent on me, and there is produced my entry into the designs of the Infinite. The enigma séparates the Infinite from all phenomenality, from appearing, thematization and essence. In re-presentation, the Infinite would be belied without ambiguity, as though it were an infinite object which subjectivity tries to approach, but misses. The plot of the Infinite is not elaborated according to the scenario of being and consciousness. The extraordinary illeity, in its diachrony of which the present is incapable, is not an extrapolation of the finite, is not the invisible taken to be behind the visible. The refusal that the infinity opposes to assembling by reminiscence does not come to pass in the form of a veiling and does not exhaust its meaning in terms of consciousness: clarity and obscurity, or distinctness and confusion, known and unknown. The not-known and the unknowable would still refer to a present, would form a structure in it, would belong to order. Diachrony is not a difference amounting to relations between the known and the unknown, where the dissimulated and the knowable would already share the thematizable plane of essence. The transcendence of the Infinite is an irreversible divergency from the present, like that of a past that was never present. A difference of the irrecuperable, it is not a "further" than the given, belonging still to the order of the given. A face is not a presence announcing a "non-said," which will be said from behind it. Substitution, responsibility without recallable commitment, without beginning, infinite approach in the proximity of another – is not an attitude taken in regard to a being, close in its face.

And yet as a destitution, a trace or shadow of itself and an accusation, a face makes itself an apparition and an epiphany; it shows itself to a cognition as though the plane of the known were all the same ultimate, and cognition all-inclusive. Does a face abide both in representation and in proximity; is it community and difference? What meaning can community take on in difference without reducing difference? When, in the description of proximity, we have named enigma the hesitation between knowing and responsibility, between being and substituting oneself for, the point where the positivity of essence turns into involuntary debt, into a bankruptcy beyond duty, have we not expressed ourselves in terms of appearing, as though knowing recuperated everything that diverges from it? Have we eliminated from signification the idea of lack and want of presence? Have we removed from the idea of enigma, where infinity comes to pass, the idea of uncertainty? Have we overcome the primacy of the theoretical plane, of essence and the said?

That would be the case, unless the said bearing the theme and the essence appearing in truth extended *behind* the essence it bears, and unless the assembling that is produced in it remained *sine fundamento in re*, having assembled the unassemblable. The apophansis, the said, more formal still than the formal, is not in any way a statement of being, not even an onto-logical statement of formal ontology. It is irreducible to essence, but like it by the exhibition, the indiscretion it makes possible. It is already a hypostasis of the *eon*, and the source of a subreption that limits what is thought to essence and reminiscence (that is, to synchronic time and representation) rather than the source of an illusion leading from being (or from the world) to God, the source of a tyranny exercised by the totality. What shows itself thematically in the synchrony of the said in fact lets itself be unsaid as a difference of what cannot be assembled, signifying as the-one-for-the-other, from me to the other. The very exhibition of the difference goes diachronically from the said to the unsaid. The very discussion which we are at this moment elaborating about signification, diachrony and the transcendence of the approach beyond being, a discussion that means to be philosophy, is a thematizing, a synchronizing of terms, a recourse to system-atic language, a constant use of the verb being, a bringing back into the bosom of being all signification allegedly conceived beyond being. But are we being duped by this subreption? The objections are facile, like those that, since the birth of philosophy, are thrown at skepticism. What about our discussion, narrating, as though they were fixed in themes, the anarchy and the non-finality of the subject in which the Infinite would pass? They are thus found to answer in the end not with responsibility, but in the form of theoretical propositions, to the question "What about . . . ?" They do not answer the proximity of the neighbor. The discussion thus remains onto-logical, as though the comprehension of being ordered all thought and thinking itself. By the very fact of formulating statements, is not the uni-versality of the thematized, that is, of being, confirmed by the project of the present discussion, which ventures to question this universality? Does this discourse remain then coherent and philosophical? These are familiar objections!

But does the coherence that would be lacking in this discussion consist in the immobility of the instant of truth, in its possibility of synchrony? The objection would then presuppose what is in question: the reference of all signification to essence. But our whole purpose was to ask if subjectivity, despite its foreignness to the said, is not stated by an abuse of language through which in the indiscretion of the said everything is shown. Everything is shown by indeed betraying its meaning, but philosophy is called upon to reduce that betrayal, by an abuse that justifies proximity itself in which the Infinite comes to pass. But this remains to be shown.

That the ontological form of the said could not alter the signification of the beyond being which shows itself in this said devolves from the very contestation of this signification. How would the contestation of the pretension beyond being have meaning if this pretention were not heard? Is there a negation in which the sense of which the negation is a negation is not conserved? The contradiction which the signification of the beyond being – which evidently is not – should compromise is inoperative without a second time, without *reflection* on the condition of the statement that states this signification. In this reflection, that is, only after the event, contradiction appears: it does not break out between two simultaneous statements, but between a statement and its conditions, as though they were in the same time. The statement of the beyond being, of the name of God, does not allow itself to be walled up in the conditions of its enunciation. It benefits from an ambiguity or an enigma, which is not the effect of an inattention, a relaxation of thought, but of an extreme proximity of the neighbor, where the Infinite comes to pass. The Infinite does not enter into a theme like a being to be given in it, and thus belie its beyond being. Its transcendence, an exteriority, more exterior, more other than any exteriority of being, does not come to pass save through the subject that confesses or contests it. Here there is an inversion of order: the revelation is made by him that receives it, by the inspired subject whose inspiration, alterity in the same, is the subjectivity or psyche of the subject. The revelation of the beyond being is perhaps indeed but a word, but this "perhaps" belongs to an ambiguity in which the anarchy of the Infinite resists the univocity of an originary or a principle. It belongs to an ambiguity or an ambivalence and an inversion which is stated in the word God, the *apex* of vocabulary, admission of the stronger than me in me and of the "less than nothing," nothing but an abusive word, a beyond themes in a thought that does not yet think or thinks more than it thinks.

But it is time to show the place that this purely apophantic synthesis, source of the subreption which confers onto ontology the locus of the ultimate questioning, this synthesis more formal than the formal, occupies in thought thinking beyond being. It is not by chance, through foolishness or through usurpation that the order of truth and essence, which the present exposition itself claims to hold to, is at the first rank in Western philosophy. Why would proximity, the pure signification of saying, the anarchic one-for-the-other of beyond being, revert to being or fall into being, into a conjunction of entities, into essence showing itself in the said? Why have we gone to seek essence on its empyrean? Why know? Why is there a problem? Why philosophy?

We then have to follow in signification or proximity or saying the latent birth of cognition and essence, of the said, the latent birth of a question, in responsibility. Proximity becoming knowing would signify as an enigma, the dawn of a light which proximity changes into, without the other, the neighbor, being absorbed in the theme in which he shows himself. We have to follow down the latent birth of knowing in proximity. Proximity can remain the signification of the very knowing in which it shows itself.

If proximity ordered to me only the other alone, there would have not been any problem, in even the most general sense of the term. A question would not have been born, nor consciousness, nor self-consciousness. The responsibility for the other is an immediacy antecedent to questions, it is proximity. It is troubled and becomes a problem when a third party enters.

The third party is other than the neighbor, but also another neighbor, and also a neighbor of the other, and not simply his fellow. What then are the other and the third party for one another? What have they done to one another? Which passes before the other? The other stands in a relationship with the third party, for whom I cannot entirely answer, even if I alone answer, before any question, for my neighbor. The other and the third party, my neighbors, contemporaries of one another, put distance between me and the other and the third party. "Peace, peace to the neighbor and the one far-off" (Isaiah 57: 19) – we now understand the point of this apparent rhetoric. The third party introduces a contradiction in the saying whose signification before the other until then went in one direction. It is of itself the limit of responsibility and the birth of the question: What do I have to do with justice? A question of consciousness. Justice is necessary, that is, comparison, coexistence, contemporaneousness, assembling, order, thematization, the visibility of faces, and thus intentionality and the intellect, and in intentionality and the intellect, the intelligibility of a system, and thence also a copresence c n an equal footing as before a court of justice. Essence as synchrony is togetherness in a place. Proximity takes on a new meaning in the space of contiguity. But pure contiguity is not a "simple nature." It already presupposes both thematizing thought and a locus and the cutting up of the continuity of space into discrete terms and the whole – out of justice.

Thus one would understand, in proximity, in the saying without problems, in responsibility, the reason for the intelligibility of systems. The entry of a third party is the very fact of consciousness, assembling into being, and at the same time, in a being, the hour of the suspension of being in possibility, the finitude of essence accessible to the abstraction of concepts, to the memory that assembles in presence, the reduction of a being to the possible and the reckoning of possibles, the comparison of incomparables. It is the thematization of the same on the basis of the relationship with the other, starting with proximity and the immediacy of saying prior to problems, whereas the identification of knowing by itself absorbs every other.

It is not that the entry of a third party would be an empirical fact, and that my responsibility for the other finds itself constrained to a calculus by the "force of things." In the proximity of the other, all the others than the other obsess me, and already this obsession cries out for justice, demands measure and knowing, is consciousness. A face obsesses and shows itself, between transcendence and visibility/invisibility. Signification signifies in justice, but also, more ancient than itself and than the equality implied by it, justice passes by justice in my responsibility for the other, in my inequality with respect to him for whom I am a hostage. The other is from the first the brother of all the other men.[23] The neighbor that obsesses me is already a face, both comparable and incomparable, a unique face and in relationship with faces, which are visible in the concern for justice.

In proximity the other obsesses me according to the absolute asymetry of signification, of the-one-for-the-other: I substitute myself for him, whereas no one can replace me, and the substitution of the one for the other does not signify the substitution of the other for the one. The relationship with the third party is an incessant correction of the assymetry of proximity in which the face is looked at. There is weighing, thought, objectification, and thus a decree in which my anarchic relationship with illeity is betrayed,[24] but in which it is conveyed before us. There is betrayal of my anarchic relation with illeity, but also a new relationship with it: it is only thanks to God that, as a subject incomparable with the other, I am approached as an other by the others, that is, "for myself." "Thanks to God" I am another for the others. God is not involved as an alleged interlocutor: the reciprocal relationship binds me to the other man in the trace of transcendence, in illeity. The passing of God, of whom I can speak only by reference to this aid or this grace, is precisely the reverting of the incomparable subject into a member of society.

In the comparison of the incomparable there would be the latent birth of representation, logos, consciousness, work, the neutral notion *being*. Everything is together, one can go from the one to the other and from the other to the one, put into relationship, judge, know, ask "what about . . . ?", transform matter. Out of representation is produced the order of justice moderating or measuring the substitution of me for the other, and giving the self over to calculus. Justice requires contemporaneousness of representation. It is thus that the neighbor becomes visible, and, looked at, presents himself, and there is also justice for me. The saying is fixed in a said, is written, becomes a book, law and science.

All the others that obsess me in the other do not affect me as examples of the same genus united with my neighbor by resemblance or common nature, individuations of the human race, or chips of the same block, like the stones metamorphosed into men by Deucalion, who, behind his back, had to collect into cities with their hearts of stone. The others concern me from the first. Here fraternity precedes the commonness of a genus. My relationship with the other as neighbor gives meaning to my relations with all the others. All human relations as human proceed from disinterestedness. The one for the other of proximity is not a deforming abstraction. In it justice is shown from the first, it is thus born from the signifyingness of signification, the-one-for-the-other, signification. This means concretely or empirically that justice is not a legality regulating human masses, from which a technique of social equilibrium is drawn, harmonizing antagonistic forces. That would be a justification of the State delivered over to its own necessities. Justice is impossible without the one that renders it finding himself in proximity. His function is not limited to the "function of judgment," the subsuming of particular cases under a general rule. The judge is not outside the conflict, but the law is in the midst of proximity. Justice, society, the State and its institutions, exchanges and work are comprehensible out of proximity. This means that nothing is outside of the control of the responsibility of the one for the other. It is important to recover all these forms beginning with proximity, in which being, totality, the State, politics, techniques, work are at every moment on the point of having their center of gravitation in themselves, and weighing on their own account.

In no way is justice a degradation of obsession, a degeneration of the for-the-other, a diminution, a limitation of anarchic responsibility, a neutralization of the glory of the Infinite, a degeneration that would be produced in the measure that for empirical reasons the initial duo would become a trio. But the contemporaneousness of the multiple is tied about the diachrony of two: justice remains justice only, in a society where there is no distinction between those close and those far off, but in which there also remains the impossibility of passing by the closest. The equality of all is borne by my inequality, the surplus of my duties over my rights. The forgetting of self moves justice. It is then not without importance to know if the egalitarian and just State in which man is fulfilled (and which is to be set up, and especially to be maintained) proceeds from a war of all against all, or from the irreducible responsibility of the one for all, and if it can do without

160

friendships and faces. It is not without importance to know that war does not become the insaturation of a war in good conscience. It is also not without importance to know, as far as philosophy is concerned, if the rational necessity that coherent discourse transforms into sciences, and whose principle philosophy wishes to grasp, has thus the status of an origin, that is, origin of self, of a present, a contemporaneousness of the sucessive (the work of deduction), the manifestation of being – or if this necessity presupposes a hither side, a pre-original, a non-presentable, an invisible, and consequently a hither side not presupposed like a principle is presupposed by the consequence of which it is synchronous. This anarchic hither side is borne witness to, enigmatically, to be sure, in responsibility for the others. Responsibility for the others or communication is the adventure that bears all the discourse of science and philosophy. Thus this responsibility would be the very rationality of reason or its universality, a rationality of peace.

Consciousness is born as the presence of a third party. It is in the measure that it proceeds from it that it is still disinterestedness. It is the entry of the third party, a permanent entry, into the intimacy of the face to face. The concern for justice, for the thematizing, the kerygmatic discourse bearing on the said, from the bottom of the saying without the said, the saying as contact, is the spirit in society. And it is because the third party does not come empirically to trouble proximity, but the face is both the neighbor and the face of faces, visage and visible, that, between the order of being and of proximity the bond is unexceptionable. Order, appearing, phenomenality, being are produced in signification, in proximity, starting with the third party. The apparition of a third party is the very origin of appearing, that is, the very origin of an origin.

The foundation of consciousness is justice. Not that justice makes a preexisting meditation intervene. An event like meditation – synchronization, comparison, thematization – is the work of justice, an entry of the diachrony of proximity, of the signifyingness of saying into the synchrony of the said, a "fundamental historicity" in the sense of Merleau-Ponty. It is the necessary interruption of the Infinite being fixed in structures, community and totality.[25] Synchronization is the act of consciousness which, through representation and the said, institutes "with the help of God," the original locus of justice, a terrain common to me and the others where I am counted among them, that is, where subjectivity is a citizen with all the duties and rights measured and measurable which the equilibrated ego involves, or equilibrating itself by the concourse of duties and the concurrence of rights. But justice can be established only if I, always evaded from the concept of the ego, always desituated and divested of being, always in non-reciprocatable relationship with the other, always for the other, can become an other like the others. Is not the Infinite which enigmatically commands me, commanding and not commanding, from the other, also the turning of the I into "like the others," for which it is important to concern oneself and take care? My lot is important. But it is still out of my responsibility that my salvation has meaning, despite the danger in which it puts this responsibility, which it may encompass and swallow up, just as the State issued from the proximity of the neighbor is always on the verge of integrating him into a we, which congeals both me and the neighbor. The act of consciousness would thus be political simultaneousness, but also in reference to God, to a God always subject to repudiation and in permanent danger of turning into a protector of all the egoisms.

The pre-original, anarchic saying is proximity, contact, duty without end, a saying still indifferent to the said and saying itself without giving the said, the-one-for-the-other, a substitution. It requires the signification of the thematizable, states the idealized said, weighs and judges in justice. Judgments and propositions are born in justice, which is putting together, assembling, the being of entities. Here with a problem begins the concern for truth, for the disclosure of being. But it is for justice that everything shows itself, and to the extravagance of substitution is superimposed, through the exigencies for responsibility itself which substitution is, a rational order, the ancillary or angelic order of justice, and the very fact of seeing, seeing everywhere clearly and recounting everything.

The way leads from responsibility to problems. A problem is posited by proximity itself, which, as the immediate itself, is without problems. The extraordinary commitment of the other to the third party calls for control, a search for justice, society and the State, comparison and possession, thought and science, commerce and philosophy, and outside of anarchy, the search for a principle. Philosophy is this measure brought to the infinity of the being-for-the-other of proximity, and is like the wisdom of love.

But, come out of signification, a modality of proximity, justice, society and truth itself which they require, must not be taken for an anonymous law of the "human forces" governing an impersonal totality.

It is through its ambivalence which always remains an enigma that infinity or the transcendent does not let itself be assembled. Removing itself from every memorable present, a past that was never present, it leaves a trace of its impossible incarnation and its inordinateness in my proximity with the neighbor, where I state, in the autonomy of the voice of conscience, a responsibility, which could not have begun in me, for freedom, which is not my freedom. The fleeting trace effacing itself and reappearing is like a question mark put before the scintillation of the ambiguity: an infinite responsibility of the one for the other, or the signification of the Infinite in responsibility. There is an ambiguity of the order that orders to me the neighbor who obsesses me, for whom and before whom I answer by my ego, in which being is inverted into a substitution, into the very possibility of gift – and of an infinite illeity, glorious in the human plot hatched in proximity, the subversion of essence into substitution. In it I could not arise soon enough to be there on time, nor approach without the extraordinary distance to be crossed augmenting before every effort to assemble it into an itinerary. Illeity overflows both cognition and the enigma through which the Infinite leaves a trace in cognition. Its distance from a theme, its reclusion, its holiness, is not its way to effect its being (since its past is anachronous and anarchic, leaving a trace which is not the trace of any presence), but is its glory, quite different from being and knowing. It makes the word God be pronounced, without letting "divinity" be said. That would have been absurd, as though God were an essence (that is, as though he admitted the amphibology of being and entities), as though he were a process, or as though he admitted a plurality in the unity of a genus. Does God, a proper and unique noun not entering into any grammatical category, enter without difficulties into the vocative? It is non-thematizable, and even here is a theme only because in a said everything is conveyed before us, even the ineffable, at the price of a betrayal which philosophy is called upon to reduce. Philosophy is called upon to conceive ambivalence, to conceive it in several times. Even if it is called to thought by justice, it still synchronizes in the said the diachrony of the difference between the one and the other, and remains the servant of the saying that signifies the difference between the one and the other as the one for the other, as non-indifference to the other. Philosophy is the wisdom of love at the service of love.

4. SENSE AND THE *THERE IS*

From signification proceed justice and consciousness: the terms of the-one-for-the-other appear in a theme, in the said, are compared and judged in the neutrality of essence. Being qua being is a function of justice. Substitution shows itself there as a coexistence and a correlation, proximity a historical world, that is, simultaneous in a book. Diachrony, through the diastasis or dephasing of the instant and the recuperation of the divergency by retention, shows itself as a continuous and indefinite time in memory and in history, that is, a time that can be assembled in a present. Subjectivity then shows itself as an ego, capable of a present, capable of beginning, an act of intelligence and of freedom going back to a principle and a beginning, a subject opposed to an object – an ego which, for Fichte is an origin of itself. It is an absolute, thinkable as such in the forgetting of the saying, in appearing or in the order of themes that can be assembled and the said.

But everything shows itself for justice. Being's essence, and consciousness before being and after having been, signify. Neither realism nor idealism, twin brothers, have the birth-right. It is justice signified by signification, by the-one-for-the-other that requires phenomenality, that is, the equivalence or simultaneity between consciousness acceding to being and being open to consciousness.

Everything shows itself and is said in being for justice, and receives the structures of the thematized and the said – even signification and justice. The diachrony of the-one-for-the-other itself refers to the indefinite time of essence, the neutrality of its historical flow; it shows itself in this time. But the imperturbable essence, equal and indifferent to all responsibility which it henceforth encompasses, turns, as in insomnia, from this neutrality and equality into monotony, anonymity, insignificance, into an incessant buzzing that nothing can now stop and which absorbs all signification, even that of which this bustling about is a modality. Essence stretching on indefinitely, without any possible halt or interruption, the equality of essence not justifying, in all equity, any instant's halt, without respite, without any possible suspension, is the horrifying *there is* behind all finality proper to the thematizing ego, which cannot sink into the essence it thematizes. It is inasmuch as the signification of the-one-for-the-other is thematized and assembled, and through the simultaneity of essence, that the one is posited as an ego, that is, as a present or as a beginning or as free, as a subject facing an object. But it is also posited as belonging to essence, which when assembled cannot leave anything outside, has no outside, cannot be worn away. This way for the subject to find itself again in essence, whereas essence, as assembled, should have made possible the present and freedom, is not a harmonious and inoffensive participation. It is the incessant buzzing that fills each silence, where the subject detaches itself from essence and posits itself as a subject in face of its objectivity. A rumbling intolerable to a subject that faces itself as a subject, and assembles essence before itself as an object. But its own subtraction is unjustifiable in an equal woven fabric, of absolute equity. The rumbling of the *there is* is the nonsense in which essence turns, and in which thus turns the justice issued out of signification. There is ambiguity of sense and non-sense in being, sense turning into non-sense. It cannot be taken lightly. With that right does the idealist extract the ego from being and confer upon it a transcendental status, when the subject returns to being in the very stability of its status? But the forgetting of ambiguity would be as little philosophical. It is in its ex-ception and ex-pulsion as a responsible one that a subject outside of being can be conceived. In signification, in the-one-for-the-other, the self is not a being provisionally transcendental and awaiting a place in the being it constitutes. Nor is it the absolute being of which phenomena would express only the coherent dream. The one in the-one-for-the-other is not a being outside of being, but signification, evacuation of Being's essence for the other. The self is a substitution for the other, subjectivity as a subjection to everything, as a supporting everything and supporting the whole. The incessant murmur of the *there is* strikes with absurdity the active transcendental ego, beginning and present.

But the absurdity of the *there is*, as a modality of the-one-for-the-other, signifies. The insignificance of its objective insistence, recommencing behind every negation, overwhelms me like the fate of a subjection to all the other to which I am subject, is the surplus of nonsense over sense, through which for the self expiation is possible, an expiation which the oneself indeed signifies. The *there is* is all the weight that alterity weighs supported by a subjectivity that does not found it. But one must not say that the *there is* results from a "subjective impression." In this overflowing of sense by nonsense, the sensibility, the self, is first brought out, in its bottomless passivity, as pure sensible point, a dis-interestedness, or subversion of essence. Behind the anonymous rustling of the *there is* subjectivity reaches passivity without any assumption. Assumption would already put in a correlation with an act this passivity of the *otherwise than being*, this substitution prior to the opposition of the active and the passive, the subjective and the objective, being and becoming. In the subjectivity of the self, substitution is the ultimate retraction of passivity, the opposite of the assumption in which the receptivity which the finitude of a transcendental *I think* describes is completed, or which it presupposes. The identity of the chosen one, that is, the assigned one, which signifies before being, would get a foothold and be affirmed in essence, which negativity itself determines. To support without compensation, the excessive or disheartening hubbub and encumberment of the *there is* is needed. Signification, the for-the-other, will not be an act of free assumption, will not be a for-itself that denies its own resignation, nor ludic gratuity in which the gravity of alterity goes off in smoke in cheerfulness and ecstasy (of him who only hides himself) as a "nothing at all" in the equivalence of everything and nothing. Signification is the ethical deliverance of the self through substitution for the other. It is consumed as an expiation for the other. The self before any initiative, before any beginning, signifies anarchically, before any present. There is deliverance into itself of an ego awakened from its imperialist dream, its transcendental imperialism, awakened to itself, a patience as a subjection to everything. In this spirituality infinity comes to pass, more ancient than the time of remembering, a diachrony without memory and thus out of season. The expiation for the other indeed shows itself only in themes and as a mode of being, but is proposed to philosophical reduction.

The non-simultaneity of exhibition is the diachrony of what shows itself to be the ambiguity of subjectivity, the enigma of sense and being. Philosophy serves justice by thematizing the difference and reducing the thematized to difference. It brings equity into the abnegation of the one for the other, justice into responsibility. Philosophy, in its very diachrony, is the consciousness of the breakup of consciousness. In an alternating movement, like that which leads from skepticism to the refutation that reduces it to ashes, and from its ashes to its rebirth, philosophy justifies and criticizes the laws of being and of the city, and finds again the signification that consists in detaching from the absolute one-for-the-other both the one and the other.

5. SKEPTICISM AND REASON

Reason is sought in the relationship between terms, between the one and the other showing themselves in a theme. Reason consists in ensuring the coexistence of these terms, the coherence of the one and the other despite their difference, in the unity of a theme; it ensures the agreement of the different terms without breaking up the present in which the theme is held. This coexistence or accord between different terms in the unity of a theme is called a system: the one with the other are present in it as one signifying the other, the one as a sign of the other, the one as renouncing its figure to trespass over to the other. The-one-for-the-other constitutes signification or intelligibility. But the present of the theme, where the one and the other enter into signification or become significations, is correlative with a subject which is a consciousness. Its subjectivity consists in rendering present, that is, in not being struck without being forewarned by the manifestation of what strikes, in not being disturbed from beyond the visible and the thematizable. The flow of time does not break up this presence and this presentation: through retention, memory or historical reconstruction, through reminiscence. consciousness is a re-presentation, understood in an almost active sense, as in the act of rendering present anew and of collecting the dispersion into a presence, and in this sense being always at the beginning or free. Reason, in which the different terms are present, that is, are contemporaneous in a system, is also the fact that they are present to consciousness inasmuch as consciousness is representation, beginning, freedom.

But the problem is that one can ask if a beginning is at the beginning, if the beginning as an act of consciousness is not already preceded by what could not be synchronized, that is, by what could not be present, the unrepresentable, if an anarchy is not more ancient than the beginning and freedom.

The signification of the relation thematized, the-one-for-the-other of signifyingness, was nonetheless unintelligible for Plato, and had to lead him to commit a parricide on his father Parmenides. Was it not guided by the structure of the-one-for-the-other inscribed in human fraternity, in the one keeper of his brother, the one responsible for the other, which would be the-one-for-the-other par excellence? One can call it utopian, yet it is the exact situation of men, at least in our time, when intellectuals feel themselves to be hostages for destitute masses unconscious of their wretchedness. Intellectuals are today mistrustful of a philosophy of the one keeper of his brother, the-one-for-the-other set forth as significations par excellence; they would scornfully call it humanist and even hagiographical. In these significations is overturned the whole context in which we have described the other intelligibility, intelligibility as a relation between terms collected into a present and a presence, presented in a theme, the intelligibility of the correlation between this relationship and the subject to which it is present.

The other as other, as a neighbor, is in his presence never equal to his proximity. Is not his presence for me already supported in proximity, and never supported patiently enough? Between the one I am and the other for whom I am responsible there gapes open a difference, without a basis in community. The unity of the human race is in fact posterior to fraternity. Proximity is a difference, a non-coinciding, an arrythmia in time, a diachrony refractory to thematization, refractory to the reminiscence that synchronizes the phases of a past. The unnarratable other loses his face as a neighbor in narration. The relationship with him is indescribable in the literal sense of the term, unconvertible into a history, irreducible to the simultaneousness of writing, the eternal present of a writing that records or presents results.

This difference in proximity between the one and the other, between me and a neighbor, turns into non-indifference, precisely into my responsibility. Non-indifference, humanity, the-one-for-the-other is the very signifyingness of signification, the intelligibility of the intelligible, and thus reason. The non-indifference of responsibility to the point of substitution for the neighbor is the source of all compassion. It is responsibility for the very outrage that the other, who qua other excludes me, inflicts on me, for the persecution with which, before any intention, he persecutes me. Proximity thus signifies a reason before the thematization of signification by a thinking subject, before the assembling of terms in a present, a pre-original reason that does not proceed from any initiative of the subject, an anarchic reason. It is a reason before the beginning, before any present, for my responsibility for the other commands me before any decision, any deliberation. Proximity is communication, agreement, understanding, or peace. Peace is incumbent on me in proximity, the neighbor cannot relieve me of it. Peace then is under my responsibility. I am a hostage, for I am alone to wage it, running a fine risk, dangerously. This danger will appear to knowing as an uncertainty, but it is transcendence itself, before certainty and uncertainty, which arise only in knowledge. To require that a communication be sure of being heard is to confuse communication and knowledge, to efface the difference, to fail to recognize the signifyingness of the-one-for-the-other in me. I am extracted from the concept of the ego, and am not measured by being and death, that is, escape the totality and structures. I am reduced to myself in responsibility, outside of the fundamental historicity Merleau-Ponty speaks of. Reason is the one-for-the-other! One is immediately inclined to call such a signification lived, as though the bipolarity of the lived and the thematized, to which Husserl's phenomenology has habituated us, did not already express a certain way of interpreting all meaning in function of being and consciousness. As though the responsibility of the-one-for-the-other could express only the naivety of lived experience that is unreflected but promised to thematization. As though the-one-for-the-other of responsibility, the signification of fraternity, could not "float above the waters" of ontology in its irreducible diachrony. As though the interval or the difference that separates the one from the other, which the non-indifference of the-one-for-the-other did not annul, could only be gathered up in a theme or be compressed into a state of soul. To intelligibility as an impersonal logos is opposed intelligibility as proximity. But does the reason characteristic of justice, the State, thematization, synchronization, re-presentation, the logos and being succeed in absorbing into its coherence the intelligibility of proximity in which it unfolds? Does not the latter have to be subordinated to the former, since the very discussion which we are pursuing at this moment counts by its said, since in thematizating we are synchronizing the terms, forming a system among them, using the verb to be, placing in being all signification that allegedly signifies beyond being? Or must we reinvoke alternation and diachrony as the time of philosophy?

If the preoriginal reason of difference, non-indifference, responsibility, a fine risk, conserves its signification, the couple *skepticism* and *refutation of skepticism* has to make its appearance alongside of the reason in representation, knowing, and deduction, served by logic and synchronizing the successive.

The periodic return of skepticism and of its refutation signify a temporality in which the instants refuse memory which recuperates and represents. Skepticism, which traverses the rationality or logic of knowledge, is a refusal to synchronize the implicit affirmation contained in saying and the negation which this affirmation states in the said. The contradiction is visible to reflection, which refutes it, but skepticism is insensitive to the refutation, as though the affirmation and negation did not resound in the same time. Skepticism then contests the thesis that between the saying and the said the relationship that connects in synchrony a condition with the conditioned is repeated. It is as though skepticism were sensitive to the difference between my exposure without reserve to the other, which is saying, and the exposition or statement of the said in its equilibrium and justice.

Philosophy is not separable from skepticism, which follows it like a shadow it drives off by refuting it again at once on its footsteps. Does not the last word belong to philosophy? Yes, in a certain sense, since for Western philosophy the saying is exhausted in things said. But skepticism in fact makes a difference, and puts an interval between saying and the said. Skepticism is refutable, but it returns.

The truth of skepticism is put on the same level as the truths whose interruption and failure its discourse states, as though the negation of the possibility of the true were ranked in the order restored by this negation, as though every difference were incontestably reabsorbed into the same order. But to contest the possibility of truth is precisely to contest this uniqueness of order and level.

The skeptical discourse, which states the rupture, failure, impotence or impossibility of disclosure, would be self-contradictory if the saying and the said were only correlative, if the signifyingness of proximity and the signification known and said could enter into a common order, if the saying reached a full contemporaneousness with the said, if the saying entered into essence without betraying the diachrony of proximity, if the saying could remain saying by showing itself to be knowledge, that is, if thematization entered into the theme in the form of a memory. But the skeptical saying undone by philosophy in fact recalls the breakup of synchronizable, that is, the recallable, time. Then, the trace of saying, which has never been present, obliges me; the responsibility for the other, never assumed, binds me; a command never heard is obeyed. This trace does not belong to the assembling of essence. Philosophy underestimates the extent of the negation in this "not appearing," which exceeds the logical scope of negation and affirmation. It is the trace of a relationship with illeity that no unity of apperception grasps, ordering me to responsibility. This relationship is religion, exceeding the psychology of faith and of the loss of faith. It orders me in an anarchic way, without ever becoming or being made into a presence or a disclosure of a principle.

The philosophical speaking that betrays in its said the proximity it conveys before us still remains, as a saying, a proximity and a responsibility. Philosophy circumscribes the life of the approach and it measures obligations before the third party with justice and knowledge, with wisdom; it does not undo this life. It says to the other who is outside of themes. This return of the diachrony refusing the present makes up the invincible force of skepticism.

Western philosophy and the State, which have issued out of proximity, nonetheless refute it in discourse absorbed in the said and in being, in ontology: the history of Western philosophy has not been the refutation of skepticism as much as the refutation of transcendence. The logos said has the last word dominating all meaning, the word of the end, the very possibility of the ultimate and the result. Nothing can interrupt it. Every contestation and interruption of this power of discourse is at once related and invested by discourse. It thus recommences as soon as one interrupts it. In the logos said, and written, it survives the death of the interlocutors that state it, and assures the continuity of culture. But does it not die with the end of civilizations, which recognize themselves to be mortal? The question can be raised. But the philosophical discourse of the West knows how to find again, under the ruins or in the hieroglyphs, the interrupted discourses of every civilization and of the prehistory of civilizations that were set up as separated. This discourse will affirm itself to be coherent and one. In relating the interruption of the discourse or my being ravished into discourse I connect its thread. The discourse is ready to say all the ruptures in itself, and consume them as silent origin or as eschatology. If the philosophical discourse is broken, withdraws from speech and murmurs, is spoken, it nonetheless speaks of that, and speaks of the discourse which a moment ago it was speaking and to which it returns to say its provisional retreat. Are we not·at this very moment in the process of barring the issue that our whole essay attempts, and of encircling our position from all sides? The exceptional words by which the trace of the past and the extravagance of the approach are said – One, God – become terms, reenter into the vocabulary and are put at the disposition of philologists, instead of confounding philosophical language. Their very explosions are recounted.

But this account is itself without end and without continuity, that is, goes from the one to the other, is a tradition. It thereby renews itself. New meanings arise in its meaning, and their exegesis is an unfolding, or history before all historiography. Thus the ladder-proof equivocation that language weaves signifies. Is it then not an aberration or a distortion of being which is thematized in it, a twisting of identity? An impossible simultaneousness of meaning, the non-assemblable but also inseparable one-for-the-other, is an excluded middle signifying as an equivocation or an enigma. And yet can not this very beyond become a notion, while undoing itself? Language would exceed the limits of what is thought, by suggesting, letting be understood without ever making understandable, an implication of a meaning distinct from that which comes to signs from the simultaneity of systems or the logical definition of concepts. This possibility is laid bare in the poetic said, and the interpretation it calls for ad infinitum. It is shown in the prophetic said, scorning its conditions in a sort of levitation. It is by the approach, the-one-for-the-other of saying, related by the said, that the said remains an insurmountable equivocation, where meaning refuses simultaneity, does not enter into being, does not compose a whole. The approach, or saying, is a relationship with what is not understood in the together, the out-of-the-series. A subversion of essence, it overflows the theme it states, the "all together," the "everything included" of the said. Language is already skepticism. Does not the coherent discourse, wholly absorbed in the said, owe its coherence to the State, which, violently excludes subversive discourse? Coherence thus dissimulates a transcendence, a movement from the one to the other, a latent diachrony, uncertainty and a fine risk.

Are the rendings of the logical text mended by logic alone? It is in the association of philosophy with the State and with medicine that the breakup of discourse is surmounted. The interlocutor that does not yield to logic is threatened with prison or the asylum or undergoes the prestige of the master and the medication of the doctor: violence or reasons of State or an approach ensures to the rationalism of logic a universality and to law its subject matter. The discourse then recuperates its meaning by repression or mediation, by just violences, on the verge of the possible injustice where repressive justice is exercised. It is through the State that reason and knowledge are force and efficacity. But the State does not irrevocably discount folly, not even the intervals of folly. It does not untie the knots, but cuts them. The said thematizes the interrupted dialogue or the dialogue delayed by silences, failure or delirium, but the intervals are not recuperated. Does not the discourse that suppresses the interruptions of discourse by relating them maintain the discontinuity under the knots with which the thread is tied again?

The interruptions of the discourse found again and recounted in the immanence of the said are conserved like knots in a thread tied again, the trace of a diachrony that does not enter into the present, that refuses simultaneity.

And I still interrupt the ultimate discourse in which all the discourses are stated, in saying it to one that listens to it, and who is situated outside the said that the discourse says, outside all it includes. That is true of the discussion I am elaborating at this very moment. This reference to an interlocutor permanently breaks through the text that the discourse claims to weave in thematizing and enveloping all things. In totalizing being, discourse qua discourse thus belies the very claim to totalize. This reversion is like that which the refutation of skepticism brings out. In the writing the saying does indeed become a pure said, a simultaneousness of the saying and of its conditions. A book is interrupted discourse catching up with its own breaks. But books have their fate; they belong to a world they do not include, but recognize by being written and printed, and by being prefaced and getting themselves preceded with forewords. They are interrupted, and call for other books and in the end are interpreted in a saying distinct from the said.

The reflection of discourse on itself does not include it in itself. The totality that includes all eschatology and every interruption could have been closed if it were silence, if silent discourse were possible, if a writing could remain written for ever, if it could, without losing its meaning, renounce all the tradition that bears it and interprets it. Is silent discourse with oneself really possible? The self is non-indifference to the others, a sign given to the others. Every discourse, even when said inwardly, is in proximity and does not include the totality. The permanent return of skepticism does not so much signify the possible breakup of structures as the fact that they are not the ultimate framework of meaning, that for their accord repression can already be necessary. It reminds us of the, in a very broad sense, political character of all logical rationalism, the alliance of logic with politics.

The return of skepticism, despite the refutation that puts its thesis into contradiction with the conditions for any thesis, would be pure nonsense if everything in time were recallable, that is, able to form a structure with the present, if the saying were rigorously contemporaneous with the said, if everything in the past could be evoked and shown, if time were but a succession of instants and a pure form of being, the a priori form of being's essence, of the *esse* of entities, and if in the last analysis the indirect discourse about the anarchic diachrony contributed a truth true in the same sense that the truth bearing on the thematized being is true, if the truth about the diachrony could be collected in a theme without thereby refuting itself.

The periodic rebirth of skepticism and its invincible and evanescent force to be sure does not permit us to confer any privilege on its said over against the implicit presuppositions of its saying. But that the contradiction that opposes one to the other does not strangle the speaker, also recalls the fault which, upon the critical examination of this returner, shows itself in the totality of representation, in the universal simultaneity that knowledge requires qua reason. It recalls the breakup of the unity of the transcendental apperception, without which one could not *otherwise than be.*

IN OTHER WORDS

OUTSIDE

The concept being, purged of all the content which determines it, is, according to Hegel, not distinguishable from pure nothingness. But already the intellectual power to strip of all content, the boldness of the abstraction and the universalization are sanctioned by this nothingness which undermines being, the decomposition that exhausts being's *esse*, the finitude of essence. Without the generalization and the corruption that wear it down, there would not be produced the procession of the concept of the individual through negation, whatever could have been the efforts of purely logical generalization. The concept emanates from essence. The nothingness that wearies it mortally perpetuates the truth of idealisms, the privilege of thematization and the interpretation of the being of entities by the objectivity of objects. Without this erosion of essence accomplished by its very *esse*, nothing would ever have shown itself. For does not the object of perception traverse an indefinite multiplicity of silhouettes to be identified with identity, distinct from any concrete similitude between images? Science which is science of the universal, play of essence playing at being and at nothingness, would never have been born. Essence would never have had to be revealed through a detour, passing through humanity. The energy of its movement in the efficacity of praxis in which the abstract and as it were asthenic concept takes hold of the immediate to fashion it according to its own idea by institutions and laws. Essence, cognition and action are bound to death. It is as though the Platonic Ideas themselves owed their eternity and their purity as universals only to the perishing of the perishable, before requiring a republic so as to come out of their bad idealism and be efficacious.

The human subject, the conscious, cognitive and active ego, is then interpreted as the pivot of this return of the concept, this event of finitude. It is as an entity subject to the concept which from all sides envelops its singularity and absorbs it into the universal and into death. One can then wonder if the *Phaedo* is not part of Socratic irony, which the full wisdom of lucid resignation can allow itself, answering with a smile of understanding and complicity the irony of essence itself. The subject aroused for the play of essence is "the space of a morning" for itself, but then it refuses death, through which, however, it gains access to the concept, and, as universal, puts into act the very essence that would have invested it. This refusal of death in fact measures the depth of its inwardness in essence, or its interest. The belongingness to being is in fact not a rest in a harbor of peace; the dialectic of being and nothingness within essence is an anxiety over nothingness and struggle for existence. From the irony of essence probably come comedy, tragedy and the eschatological consolations which mark the spiritual history of the West, in which to the ultimacy of the concept and of the death of the subject is opposed the hope of escaping the end.

Does not the subject then find itself shut up in an alternative? A term is constituted by the understanding of the irony of essence, and by the possibility of being confused with the universal at the moment that thought, which embraces the whole and is engulfed in it, thinks of "nothing less than death." This is an admission of the ultimacy of essence, of the immanence without exit of its play that encloses, the Stoic wisdom in its variations from Zeno to Spinoza and Hegel, a wisdom of resignation and sublimation. The other term of the alternative would likewise lie within this closure and these walls, but it would consist in letting itself be tempted by the labyrinths that open in the instant extracted from its retentions and its protentions – in the pleasure which is still not enough of a "cross section of time" in the instant, is still a dream running along the edge of nightmares and symbolisms, and seeks another time and a "second state" in intoxication and drugs, which are the far off outcomes or prolongations of the Epicurean innocence and purity. In it nonetheless pleasure was separated from the responsibility for another, and already love separated from law, and eroticism seeped in. An illusory solution, it is also inside essence and its play, without finding in essence itself a sense in a new or older signification. The dilemma is without a resolution; essence has no exits: to the death anxiety is added horror of fatality, of the incessant bustling of the *there is*, the horrible eternity at the bottom of essence.

The present study puts into question this reference of subjectivity to essence which dominates the two terms of the alternative brought out. It asks if all meaning proceeds from essence. Does subjectivity draw its own meaning from it? Is it brought out as a struggle for existence, to let itself be seduced by the power of powers, in the violences of nationalism, even when it hypocritically pretends to be only at the service of essence and not to will will? The true problem for us Westerners is not so much to refuse violence as to question ourselves about a struggle against violence which, without blanching in non-resistance to evil, could avoid the institution of violence out of this very struggle. Does not the war perpetuate that which it is called to make disappear, and consecrate war and its virile virtues in good conscience? One has to reconsider the meaning of a certain human weakness, and no longer see in patience only the reverse side of the ontological finitude of the human. But for that one has to be patient oneself without asking patience of the others – and for that one has to admit a difference between oneself and the others. One has to find for man another kinship than that which ties him to being, one that will perhaps enable us to conceive of this difference between me and the other, this inequality, in a sense absolutely opposed to oppression.

Such a reconsideration is hardly conceivable in a world where infidelity to Nietzsche, even conceived outside of all National-Socialist contaminations, is (despite "the death of God") taken as blasphemy. But does the subject escape the concept and essence, anxiety over death and horror of the *there is*, only in resignation and illusion, against which at the hour of truth or of the inevitable awakening essence is stronger? Can one not understand the subjectivity of the subject beyond essence, as on the basis of a leaving the concept, a forgetting of being and non-being? Not of an "unregulated" forgetting, which still lies within the bipolarity of essence, between being and nothingness. But a forgetting that would be an ignorance in the sense that nobility ignores what is not noble, and in the sense that certain monotheists do not recognize, while knowing, what is not the highest. Such ignorance is beyond consciousness; it is an open-eyed ignorance. It is not in the interest in which mystics sought their salvation, and in which there still is both diversion and hope for eternal life (which are countersensical in essence) but is at the source of all meaning. It is not in all that is structured as need, that is, as an insinuation of essence through its own interstices, in which the plenitude lost is already there, already rediscovered, in appetition and the taste for the search. It is not like that aspiration to the other which still stays in the midst of essence, and is thus complacent in aspiring, erotic. There is ignorance of the concept in the openness of the subject beyond this struggle for oneself and this complacency in oneself. This is a non-erotic openness, and it is not again the openness of a look fixing a theme. But this openness would not be illusion: the play of being and nothingness itself would acquire its meaning in it. The openness would not be a modality of this play, even if it shows itself to the philosopher only thanks to this game. It defies myth in which tales about the origin of the world are fixed, tales which already unfold in the world and among its inhabitants. It is an ignorance of being and death which could be not an evasion, a cowardice, or a fall into the everyday, or the courage for suicide, still interest, in which the subject, through fear of dying or horror of the *there is* would fall the more surely under their domination. This ignorance and openness, an indifference to essence, is designated in the title of this book by the barbarous expression "otherwise than being"; it has to measure all the scope of disinterestedness and, as ontological indifference, is the terrain necessary for the distinction between truth and ideology. This indifference is not purely negative, for in another sense it is non-indifference, non-indifference to another, to the other. The very difference between me and the other is non-indifference, is the-one-for-the-other. The-one-for-the-other is the very signifyingness of signification. How can such a research be undertaken without introducing some barbarisms in the language of philosophy? Yet philosophy has, at its highest, exceptional, hours stated the beyond of being and the *one* distinct from being, but mainly remained at home in saying being, that is, inwardness to being, the being at home with oneself, of which European history itself has been the conquest and jealous defense. And we would not here have ventured to recall the *beyond essence* if this history of the West did not bear, in its margins, the trace of events carrying another signification, and if the victims of the triumphs which entitle the eras of history could be separate from its meaning. Here we have the boldness to think that even the Stoic nobility of resignation to the logos already owes its energy to the openness to the *beyond essence*.

But would not the openness to beyond essence, to the "otherwise than being," signify thus the possibility of seeing, knowing, understanding and grasping, which evidently would amount to thematizing, and thus to thinking being, discovering a field for knowledge, taking in hand, displacing, operating and possessing? The openness would thus eventually lead the subject in which these intentions would be recognized to be fundamental or as good to be otherwise but not to "otherwise than be." How can the openness upon the other than being be conceived without the openness as such forthwith signifying an assembling into a conjuncture, into a unity of essence, into which the very subject to which this assembling would be disclosed would at once sink, as the bond with essence at once turns into an inwardness of essence? How can this openness be conceived without assimilating it to a satisfaction of a "need for openness"? Can one avoid the schema of an intentional subject, which is will, inwardness in being, interest? In it the psyche, humanity, would be converted into "experience" and transcendence, into an aim after background worlds of the celestial city gravitating in the skies of the earthly city. Its ecstasy is but the outside-of-oneself of an entity always closed up at home with itself, and concealing itself. Can openness have another sense than that of the accessibility of

entities through open doors or windows? Can openness have another signification than that of disclosure?

If we follow the criticism that is the very foundation of philosophy
understood as comprehension of being, it does not seem so. A "subjective
form of intuition," space for Kant is a mode of representation of entities. It
is neither an attribute of entities nor a relationship between entities; it is a
non-concept. This negative statement, that it is nowise an entity, is something settled.

But for Kant space remains the condition for the representation of an
entity, and thus implies a subjectivity. Not that an entity would be a subjective illusion in the spiderweb of a soul! It is remarkable that the entity
qua entity, *essence*, is not first realized in itself, and then occasionally show
itself afterward. Essence carries on as presence, exhibition, phenomenality
or appearing, and as such requires a subject in the form of consciousness,
and invests it as devoted to representation. This way of requiring the subject and committing it to representation by appearing, in which essence
effectuates its presence, is the objectivity of essence. Space or exteriority is
necessary for objectivity, for it is necessary for appearing as distance filled
with light, the void of transparency.

In referring to the operative and kinesthetic possibilities and the techni-
cal projects of a subject in space, we have not yet ceased to conceive
essence as objectivity. One cannot conceive essence otherwise, one can conceive otherwise only the beyond essence. Kantism is the basis of philosophy, if philosophy is ontology. Objectivity nowise signifies the reification
of essence; it is its very phenomenality, its appearing. In passing from the
consideration of intuition to the philosophy of praxis, one conserves, at the
bottom of acts, the representation that bears them, and, in their finality,
the "bringing to the light," and space as transparency. The whole of the
subjective is, according to Brentano's formula, which was taken up by
Husserl, either representation or founded on representation; every thesis is
convertible into a doxic thesis, a positing or recognition of entities, a welcome of presence. Disclosure remains the event of spatiality and the mission of a subject.

But is the sense of space exhausted in transparency and in ontology? Is it
bound to essence and appearing? Does it not involve other significations?
The trace of a departure, the figure of an irrecuperable past, the equality of
a multiplicity, homogeneous before justice – these human significations
have been evoked in this work. They cannot be interpreted on the basis of
disclosure. And no doubt before them, the openness of space signifies the
outside where nothing covers anything, non-protection, the reverse of a
retreat, homelessness, non-world, non-inhabitation, layout without security. These significations are not only privative; they signify the end, or the

hither side, of the dark designs of inwardness, the demythization of the myths, the enlargement of a closure which the abstract notions of freedom and nonfreedom do not exhaust. For here there is a complex of significations deeper and broader than freedom, which freedom animates. Freedom is animation itself, breath, the breathing of outside air, where inwardness frees itself from itself, and is exposed to all the winds. There is exposure without assumption, which would already be closedness. That the emptiness of space would be filled with invisible air, hidden from perception, save in the caress of the wind or the threat of storms, non-perceived but penetrating me even in the retreats of my inwardness, that this invisibility or this emptiness would be breathable or horrible, that this invisibility is non-indifferent and obsesses me before all thematization, that the simple ambiance is imposed as an atmosphere to which the subject gives himself and exposes himself in his lungs, without intentions and aims, that the subject could be a lung at the bottom of its substance – all this signifies a subjectivity that suffers and offers itself before taking a foothold in being. It is a passivity, wholly a supporting.

It is not a matter of the exposure to views in the transparency of space open to the light, in which the subject would still dissimulate, under the plasticity of a form and the relationships of his volume, his as-for-me of defense and aggression, recommencing the world, in reciprocity. Nor is it a matter of the layout in nocturnal space, exposed indeed to surprise, but in security in insecurity, at rest under the cover of the darkness. The exposure precedes the initiative a voluntary subject would take to expose itself. For the subject does not find itself any place even in its own volume, or in the night. It opens in space but is not in-the-world. The restlessness of respiration, the exile in oneself, the in itself without rest, is not an impossibility of inhabiting that would already become a movement from here to yonder; it is a panting, a trembling of substantiality, a hither side of the here. There is a passivity in the exposure, which does not succeed in taking form. My exposure to another in my responsibility for him takes place without a decision on my part; the least appearance of initiative and subjective act signifies then a more profound emphasis of the passivity of this exposition. It is exposure to the openness of a face, which is the "further still" of the undergoing of the closure of the oneself, the opening up which is not being-in-the-world. A further deep breathing even in the breath cut short by the wind of alterity. The approach of the neighbor is a fission of the subject beyond lungs, in the resistant nucleus of the ego, in the undividedness of its individuality. It is a fission of self, or the self as fissibility, a passivity more passive still than the passivity of matter. To open oneself as space, to free oneself by breathing from closure in oneself already presupposes this beyond: my responsibility for the other and my aspiration by the other, the crushing charge, the beyond, of alterity. That the breathing by which entities seem to affirm themselves triumphantly in their vital space would be a consummation, a coring out of my substantiality, that in breathing I already open myself to my subjection to the whole of the invisible other, that the beyond or the liberation would be the support of a crushing charge, is to be sure surprising. It is this wonder that has been the object of the book proposed here.

To be sure, breathing is said more simply in terms of biology: answering a fundamental need for energy, it brings to the tissues the oxygen necessary for the functioning of the organism, and eliminates the waste. Air and the oxygen it contains are then treated like wood and iron; air can be healthy or unhealthy, conditioned air or liquid air; oxygen is carried in the baggage of astronauts like fresh water on ships. But the relationship to air by which the experiences expressed in these truths are formed and stated is not in its turn an experience, despite the status of objectivity it acquires even in the philosophical language that describes the signification of these experiences by going behind these experiences, or reducing them to the horizon of their thematization. But in reducing the said to the saying, philosophical language reduces the said to breathing opening to the other and signifying to the other its very signifyingness. This reduction is then an incessant unsaying of the said, a reduction to the saying always betrayed by the said, whose words are defined by non-defined words; it is a movement going from said to unsaid in which the meaning shows itself, eclipses and shows itself. In this navigation the element that bears the embarkation is also the element that submerges it and threatens to sink it. Philosophy is perhaps but this exaltation of language in which the words, after the event, find for themselves a condition in which religions, sciences and technologies owe their equilibrium of meaning.

An openness of the self to the other, which is not a conditioning or a foundation of oneself in some principle, a fixity of a sedentary inhabitant or a nomad, but a relation wholly different from the occupation of a site, a building, or a settling oneself, breathing is transcendence in the form of opening up. It reveals all its meaning only in the relationship with the other, in the proximity of a neighbor, which is responsibility for him, substitution for him. This pneumatism is not nonbeing; it is disinterestedness, excluded middle of essence, besides being and non being.

But is not the diachrony of the inspiration and expiration separated by the instant that belongs to an animality? Would animality be the openness upon the beyond essence? But perhaps animality is only the soul's still being too short of breath. In human breathing, in its everyday equality, perhaps we have to already hear the breathlessness of an inspiration that paralyzes essence, that transpierces it with an inspiration by the other, an inspiration that is already expiration, that "rends the soul"![1] It is the longest breath there is, spirit. Is man not the living being capable of the longest breath in inspiration, without a stopping point, and in expiration, without return? To transcend oneself, to leave one's home to the point of leaving oneself, is to substitute oneself for another. It is, in my bearing of myself, not to conduct myself well, but by my unicity as a unique being to expiate for the other. The openness of space as an openness of self without a world, without a place, utopia, the not being walled in, inspiration to the end, even to expiration, is proximity of the other which is possible only as responsibility for the other, as substitution for him. The alterity of the other is not a particular case, a species of alterity, but its original exception. It is not because the other is new, an unheard of quiddity, that he signifies transcendence, or, more exactly, signifies, purely and simply; it is because newness comes from the other that there is in newness transcendence and signification. It is through the other that newness signifies in being the otherwise than being. Without the proximity of the other in his face everything is absorbed, sunken into, walled in being, goes to the same side, forms a whole, absorbing the very subject to which it is disclosed. Essence, the being of entities, weaves between the incomparables, between me and the others, a unity, a community (if only the unity of analogy), and drags us off and assembles us on the same side, chaining us to one another like galley slaves, emptying proximity of its meaning. Every attempt to disjoin the conjunction and the conjuncture would be only clashing of the chains. As disclosed the other enters into the same, and the experience of transcendence immediately becomes suspect of artifice. Are not the solemnity of ceremonies and cults which can transport, the newness of the instants of duration, incomparable springtimes, outside of everyday time, the growth and flowering of nature, the freshness and harmony of the landscapes, the incessant arrival of quality in its immobile presence which Heidegger has been able to catch sight of and speak of as a parousia the effects of some theatre machinery behind the promise of transcendence, of the extraordinary, that they claim to fulfill? In their essence are not these ecstatic moments already degraded into reflections of our own looks, into mirages of our needs, echos of our prayers? Vanity of vanities, all is vanity, nothing is new under the sun. In all the compunction of Heidegger's magical language and the impressionism of his play of lights and shadows, and the mystery of light that comes from behind the curtains, in all this tip-toe or wolf stepping movement of discourse, where the extreme prudence to not frighten the game perhaps dissimulates the impossibility of flushing it out, where each contact is only tangency, does poetry succeed in reducing the rhetoric? Is not essence the very impossibility of anything else, of any revolution that would not be a revolving upon oneself? Everything that claims to come from elsewhere, even the marvels of which essence itself is capable, even the surprising possibilities of renewal by technology and magic, even the perfections of gods peopling the heights of this world, and their immortality and the immortality they promise mortals – all this does not deaden the heartrending bustling of the *there is* recommencing behind every negation. There is not a break in the business carried on by essence, not a distraction. Only the meaning of the other is irrecusable, and forbids the reclusion and reentry into the shell of the self. A voice comes from the other shore. A voice interrupts the saying of the already said.

Our analyses claim to be in the spirit of Husserlian philosophy, whose letter has been the recall in our epoch of the permanent phenomenology, restored to its rank of being a method for all philosophy. Our presentation of notions proceeds neither by their logical decomposition, nor by their dialectical description. It remains faithful to intentional analysis, insofar as it signifies the locating of notions in the horizon of their appearing, a horizon unrecognized, forgotten or displaced in the exhibition of an object, in its notion, in the look absorbed by the notion alone. The said in which everything is thematized, in which everything shows itself in a theme, has to be reduced to its signification as saying, beyond the simple correlation which is set up between the saying and the said. The said has to be reduced to the signification of saying, giving it over to the philosophical said, which also has to be reduced. Truth is in several times, here again like breathing, a diachrony without synthesis which the fate of skepticism refuted and returning, a bastard child of philosophical research, suggests, and which it encourages.

But the appearing of being is not the ultimate legitimation of subjectivity. It is here that the present labors, ventures beyond phenomenology. In the subjective, the notions, and the essence they only articulate, lose the consistency that the theme in which they manifest themselves offers them. Not in finding themselves to be "psychic contents" in a subject opposed to objects. It is on the contrary in the hyperbole, the superlative, the excellence of signification from which they derive, the transcendency that passes in them or surpasses itself in them, and which is not a mode of being showing itself in a theme, that notions and the essence they articulate break up and get woven into a human plot. The emphasis of exteriority is excellency. Height is heaven. The kingdom of heaven is ethical. This hyperbole, this excellence, is but the for-the-other in its interestedness. That is what the strange discussion conducted here about the signification in the-one-for-the-other of the subject sought to say. In extracting signification from the theme in which it presents itself to the comprehension of a subject gifted with reason, it has not reduced it to a lived datum of consciousness. It claimed to describe a third condition or the unconditionality of an excluded middle. Subjectivity is not here aroused by the mysterious house-keeping of being's essence, where, despite all of Heidegger's anti-intellectualism, the gnoseological correlation: man called forth by a manifestation, is found again. Here the human is brought out by tran-scendence, or the hyperbole, that is, the disinterestedness of essence, a hy-perbole in which it breaks up and *falls upward*, into the human. Our philo-sophical discourse does not pass from one term to the other only by searching the "subjective" horizons of what shows itself, but embraces con-junctions of elements in which concepts subtended as presence or a subject break up.

That this signification of saying without the said would be the very signi-fyingness of signification, the-one-for-the-other, is not a poverty of the say-ing received in exchange for the infinite richness of the said, fixed and admirably mobile, in our books and our traditions, our sciences and our poetry, our religions and our conversations; it is not a barter of the duped. The caress of love, always the same, in the last accounting (for him that thinks in counting) is always different and overflows with exorbitance the songs, poems and admissions in which it is said in so many different ways and through so many themes, in which it apparently is forgotten. Accord-ing to the word of Jehuda Halevy, with his eternal word "God speaks to each man in particular."

Signification, the-one-for-the-other, the relationship with alterity, has been analysed in the present work as proximity, proximity as responsibility for the other, and responsibility for the other as substitution. In its subjec-tivity, its very bearing as a separate substance, the subject was shown to be an expiation for another, the condition or unconditionality of being hostage.

This book interprets the subject as a hostage and the subjectivity of the subject as a substitution breaking with being's essence. The thesis is exposed imprudently to the reproach of utopianism in an opinion where modern man takes himself as a being among beings, whereas his modernity breaks up as an impossibility to remain at home. This book escapes the reproach of utopianism – if utopianism is a reproach, if any thought escapes utopianism – by recalling that what took place humanly has never been able to remain closed up in its site. There is no need to refer to an event in which the non-site, becoming a site, would have exceptionally entered into the spaces of history. The modern world is above all an order, or a disorder in which the elites can no longer leave peoples to their cus-toms, their wretchedness and their illusions, nor even to their redemptive systems, which, abandoned to their own logic, are implacably inverted. These elites are sometimes called "intellectuals." We find the agglomera-tions or dispersions of peoples in the deserts without manna of this earth.

But each individual of these peoples is virtually a chosen one, called to leave in his turn, or without awaiting his turn, the concept of the ego, its extension in the people, to respond with responsibility: *me*, that is, *here I am for the others*, to lose his place radically, or his shelter in being, to enter into ubiquity which is also a utopia. Here I am for the others – an enormous response, whose inordinateness is attenuated with hypocrisy as soon as it enters my ears forewarned of being's essence, that is, the way being carries on. The hypocrisy is from the first denounced. But the norms to which the denunciation refers have been understood in the enormity of meaning and in the full resonance of their statement to be true like unrefrained witness. In any case nothing less was needed for the little humanity that adorns the world, if only with simple politeness or the pure polish of manners. A breakdown of essence is needed, so that it not be repelled by violence. This repugnance attests only to the stage of the nascent or savage humanity, ready to forget its disgusts, to be inverted into "essence of breakdown," to surround itself like every essence, inevitably jealous for its perseverance, with military honors and virtues. For the little humanity that adorns the earth, a relaxation of essence to the second degree is needed, in the just war waged against war to tremble or shudder at every instant because of this very justice. This weakness is needed. This relaxation of virility without cowardice is needed for the little cruelty our hands repudiate. That is the meaning that should be suggested by the formulas repeated in this book concerning the passivity more passive still than any passivity, the fission of the ego unto me, its consummation for the other such that from the ashes of this consummation no act could be reborn.

In this work which does not seek to restore any ruined concept, the destitution and the desituating of the subject do not remain without signification: after the death of a certain god inhabiting the world behind the scenes, the substitution of the hostage discovers the trace, the unpronounceable inscription, of what, always already past, always "he," does not enter into any present, to which are suited not the nouns designating beings, or the verbs in which their essence resounds, but that which, as a pronoun, marks with its seal all that a noun can convey.

NOTES

CHAPTER I

1. The term *essence*, which we do not dare spell *essance*, designates the *esse*, the process or event of being, distinguished from the *ens*, the *Sein* differentiated from the *Seiendes*. *Cf. supra*, Note p. xli.
2. For the notion of the *there is* see our book *Existence and Existents*, trans. Alphonso Lingis (The Hague, Nijhoff, 1977) pp. 52-54.
3. "... tout se traduit devant nous – fut-ce au prix d'une trahison." Refers to the saying that every translation (traduction) is a betrayal (trahison).
4. Cf. *infra*, ch. V, 3.
5. The significations that go beyond formal logic show themselves in formal logic, if only by the precise indication of the sense in which they break with formal logic. The indication is the more precise in the measure that this reference is conceived with a more rigorous logic. The myth of the subordination of all thought to the comprehension of being is probably due to this revealing function of coherence, whose lawlike character formal logic sets forth, and in which the divergency between signification and being is *measured*, in which the metaphysical *hither side* itself, contradictorily enough, appears. But logic interrupted by the structures of what is *beyond being* which show themselves in it does not confer a dialectical structure to philosophical propositions. It is the superlative, more than the negation of categories, which interrupts systems, as though the logical order and the being it succeeds in espousing retained the superlative which exceeds them. In subjectivity the superlative is the exorbitance of a null-site, in caresses and in sexuality the "excess" of tangency – as though tangency admitted a gradation – up to contact with the entrails, a skin going under another skin.
6. We will of course have to show that the necessity of thinking is inscribed in the sense of transcendence. Cf. *infra*, pp. 156ff.
7. See "Enigme et phénomène" in the second edition of our *En découvrant l'existence avec Husserl et Heidegger*, (Paris, Vrin, 1967) pp. 207-217.
8. The Good invests freedom – it loves me before I love it. Love is love in this antecedence. The Good could not be the term of a need susceptible of being satisfied, it is not the term of an erotic need, a relationship with the seductive which resembles the Good to the point of being indistinguishable from it, but which is not its other, but its imitator. The Good as the infinite has no other, not because it would be the whole, but because it is Good and nothing escapes its goodness.
9. "... du soi-même, du *se* – accusatif ne dérivant d'aucun nominatif..."
10. *En découvrant l'existence*, 2nd ed., "Enigme et phénomène," p. 203.
11. *Op. cit.*, pp. 187-203.
12. The ego is not the specification of the more general concept of the soul. Kant has seen this in certain passages of the Transcendental Dialectic (B 405a, A 354), when he insists on the fact that to pass from a subject to another subject is the positive act of putting oneself in his place.
13. Concerning the notions invoked in this paragraph; cf. our book *L'humanisme de l'autre homme* (Montpellier, Ed. Fata Morgana, 1972) pp. 83-101.
14. In the sense of dissimulation and suspension of being behind the entities it illuminates.

CHAPTER II

1. In this work the term *essence* designates being as differentiated from entities. Cf. *supra*, p. xli.
2. The prior or preliminary questions are certainly not the first questions that are raised. Men act, speak, and even think, without concerning themselves with principles. And the

188

preliminary, the pre-originary, the hither side, is not even equivalent to a beginning, does not have the status of a principle, but comes from the dimension of the anarchic, which has to be distinguished from the eternal. Starting with the first questions discourse, in an ancillary indiscretion, but which is also the "secret of the angels," divulges and profanes the unsayable, is an abuse of language. It captures in the said the unsayable which philosophy tries to reduce.

3. A discovery of being to itself, truth, which should not take anything from being, also should not add anything. Otherwise, being would show itself only to be already altered by the event of the discovery. Truth would prevent truth, as in the first hypothesis of Plato's *Parmenides*. Then, at the moment being becomes conscious of itself and adds a knowledge of its being or a new knowledge to an old one, it is necessary that the discovery not be an addition to the being that shows itself, but its fulfilment. The exhibition of being, or truth, is the fulfilled essence of being, and time both an exhibition of being to itself and its essence.

4. Inasmuch as an image is both the term and the incompletion of truth, sensibility, which is immediacy itself, becomes an image. This image is thus to be interpreted out of knowing. But our thesis is that sensibility has another signification, in its immediacy (cf. Chapter III). It is not limited to the function of being the image of the true.

5. We will show below (Chapter V) how philosophy, a love of truth which is always to come, is justified in its broader signification of being the wisdom of love.

6. According to what model? The problem has to be dealt with. If time is the horizon of the comprehension of the being of entities, of essence, and if all substantiality can be resolved into duration, what is the principle or the matrix of entities? Does the something of formal logic, Kant's "transcendental object," which the thematization of discourse already presupposes, not deserve our surprise? Does not discourse already refer to the One? Cf. *infra*, note 38.

7. Edmund Husserl, *The Phenomenology of Internal Time Consciousness*, trans. James S. Churchill (Bloomington, Indiana University Press, 1964) p. 142.

8. *Ibid.*, p. 131.

9. *Ibid.*, p. 52.

10. *Ibid.*, end of Appendix V.

11. *Ibid.*, p. 92.

12. *Ibid.*, p. Appendix IX.

13. *Ibid.*, p. 131.

14. *Ibid.*, p. 163. "One may by no means misinterpret this primal consciousness, this primal apprehension, or whatever he wishes to call it, as an apprehending act."

15. Edmund Husserl, *Experience and Judgment*, trans. James S. Churchill and Karl Ameriks (Evanston, Northwestern University Press, 1973) pp. 383-4.

16. Edmund Husserl, *The Phenomenology of Internal Time Consciousness*, end of Appendix IX.

17. Edmund Husserl, *Formal and Transcendental Logic*, trans. Dorion Cairns (The Hague, Martinus Nijhoff) §99.

18. "But is not the flux a succession? Does it not, therefore, have a now, an actual phase, and a continuity of pasts of which we are conscious in retentions? We can only say that this flux is something which we name in conformity with what is constituted, but it is nothing temporally 'Objective.' ... For all this, names are lacking." *The Phenomenology of Internal Time Consciousness*, p. 100. Do we lack names, or is the thing itself beyond the nameable? Do we not in fact find the non-thematizable flow of time by *reduction* from the said?

19. *Experience and Judgment*, p. 73.

20. " ... we cannot represent to ourselves anything as combined in the object which we have not ourselves previously combined ... " Immanuel Kant, *Critique of Pure Reason*, trans. Norman Kemp Smith (London, Macmillan, 1964) p. 151. The reference to spontaneity occurs through the proper sense of objectivity – of synthesis of relation, which here is not the content of an object, but its objectivity. Then the reference to a subject is neither psychological, nor a mere verbal tic ("an object presupposes a subject"), but is in fact tran-

scendental. A phenomenon such as "objective bond" has no meaning without transcendental spontaneity, without a subject structured precisely as spontaneity. This is unlike freedom which in a Hegelian reflection would be inconceivable without institutions or without industrial society.

21. Husserl himself interprets objectification in the sphere of the prepredicative judgment as a doing. There it is prior to language and the social code of signs supplied by it, and one would think it is prior to the said. "Thus, even the purely perceptive contemplation of a pregiven substrate proves to be our achievement, an act, and not a mere suffering of impressions" (*Experience and Judgment*, p. 59.). The failure to recognize this prelinguistic level of words (if we may so name it) leads Husserl astray when he studies prepredicative and presocial judgment. There, despite the absolute silence that should reign in a world without intersubjectivity, to the ineffable ideality of the substrate there responds an echo of the world in which significations are said, "and we have need of an ever-renewed effort to ward off this obtrusive sense that is characteristic of expressions" (*Ibid.*, pp. 57-8).

22. *Experience and Judgment*, for example §12.

23. A word has a "*Meinung*" which is not simply an aim. M. Derrida has felicitously and boldly translated this term by "vouloir dire" (meaning to say), uniting in its reference to the will (which every intention remains) and to the exteriority of a language, the allegedly inward aspect of meaning. Cf. Jacques Derrida, *Speech and Phenomenon*, trans. David Allison (Evanston, Northwestern University Press, 1973).

24. The Mediaeval term intentionality, taken up by Brentano and Husserl, does indeed have in scholasticism and in phenomenology a neutralized meaning with respect to the will. It is the teleological movement animating the thematization that justifies the recourse, however neutralized it may be, to voluntarist language. The *Meinen* in its identifying statement is cancelled when it is translated by aim.

25. How the words, the signs, penetrate into the said of the identifying saying still remains to be understood. But this bears witness to an extreme passivity of saying behind the saying that becomes a simple correlative of the said – the passivity of exposure to suffering and trauma, which the present work aims to thematize.

26. On this point see our analysis in *En découvrant l'existence avec Husserl et Heidegger*, 2nd ed. (Paris, Vrin, 1967) pp. 217ff.

27. Cf. Chapter V. pp. 156ff.

28. These lines, and those that follow, owe much to Heidegger. Deformed and ill-understood? Perhaps. At least this deformation will not have been a way to deny the debt. Nor this debt a reason to forget . . .

29. And that no doubt is what Paul Valéry was thinking of, when he named poetry a hesitation between sound and meaning.

30. The signification of discourse, a condition for the light of intuition, for the brilliance of images, is then here not taken in the Husserlian sense of a correlate of signitive acts, thirsty for images and intuitive plenitude.

31. Cf. *infra*, Chapter V, pp. 156ff.

32. In *La Pensée et le Réel* (Paris, P.U.F., 1966) Jeanne Delhomme showed that the philosophical saying is a modality of saying and not a simple objectification of theses, and thus saying is not only a way to represent being to oneself. In her book the "thought" and the "real" of the title do not announce the problem of knowledge, but two "modalities," where "thought" signifies something like what the present work is calling "otherwise than being." But Mme. Delhomme ascribes this virtue of modalizing saying only to the philosophical saying.

33. The question Who? caught sight of earlier in the Who is looking? will arise out of the original, or pre-original, saying of responsibility. The question Who is looking? has to be reduced to Who is speaking? The Who? of saying is not simply a grammatical necessity (every verb in a proposition involves a subject), nor a withdrawal before the paradox of a language that could not be the saying of anyone, that would be a language that speaks and that would hang in the air. It is not the I of the I think, subject of a cogitation, nor Husserl's pure ego, transcendent in the immanence of intentionality, radiating from this ego (a subject that presupposes the subject-object correlation and refers to the correlation of the saying and the said). The who of saying is inseparable from the plot proper to

speaking, and yet it is not the for-itself of idealism, which designates the movement of consciousness returning to itself, where the self consequently is understood as identical to the return movement, a knowing of knowing. Nor is it the pure form in which the Kantian I think appears. Nor the identity of the Hegelian concept, in which, under the apparent naturalness of expressions such as "for oneself," "for itself," and "by oneself" is cancelled all the singularity of the recurrence to oneself, a recurrence without rest – the genuine problem of the subject.

34. The plot of proximity is not a vicissitude of the plot of cognition. For knowing is justified by communication and by saying in responsibility, which in addition supplies the plane of disinterestedness which preserves science from ideology. The essence of communication is not a modality of the essence of manifestation. The plot of saying in which lies the *who* or the One can be surprised in the trace that the said retains of its reduction is thus possible. The said in absorbing the saying does not become its master, although by an abuse of language it translates it before us in betraying it. The unravelling of the plot of saying does not belong to language qua said, does not belong to the last word. Saying signifies without stopping in the said, does not part from an ego, does not go back to disclosure in a consciousness.

35. The Platonic myth of the last judgment in the *Gorgias* (523 c-e) should be recalled here. The absolute approach of the other required by the "last judgment," which for Plato is a fundamental modality of the approach, is a relation between a dead one and a dead one. The other, a man of quality or a nothing of a man, is here divested of all garments that qualify him, "of every quality," in the nudity of him who passes from life to decease, surprised by an unforeseeable death. The judge, for his part, must approach as someone dead, divested "of eyes and ears," which belong to the body as a whole, and which, far from making the approach by vision and hearing possible, only form a screen before it. The representation of the other would then not be a straightforward relation. Proximity does not belong to any image, to anything that appears. Proximity goes from soul to soul, outside of any manifestation as a phenomenon, outside of any given. The ontological plane then is inessential, though for Plato it is perhaps more real than reality: in it a judgment, that is, an act of cognition, is borne from soul to soul. But one is right to ask what such a judgment consists in, a judgment that is not a priori and is not a judgment put on a datum, is not a judgment of experience, save in the multiplicity of significations in the very contact of the saying, outside of all the "propositions" of the said (cf. *supra*, pp. 5-7). One should then also recall that proximity is not from the first a judgment of a tribunal of justice, but first a responsibility for the other which turns into judgment only with the entry of the third party (Chapter V, 3). Yet we can note that for Plato the approach of the other is beyond experience, beyond consciousness, like a dying.

36. Cf. *infra*, Chapter V, 1: When the subject commits itself in the order it contemplates, the truth of the significations it reads there is compromised. There is lacking the distance which guarantees that the spectacle not be troubled by the look itself. In the signifyingness of saying, the implication of the saying in the spectacle belongs to the signification of this "spectacle." But we are here before the subject-object relation, which such an implication could compromise.

37. The concept of time as a lapse and a loss rejoins the theme of "Temps et l'Autre," a study which was published in *Le Choix, le Monde, l'Existence* (Paris, Artaud, 1948).

38. One cannot say that the noun, by which an entity is as much as it is through being, *is* in its turn. It *is* only in the entity which "participates" in being. This participation, in the form of the time of ageing, is the patience, the passivity, the exposedness to the other, even in the exposure of this very exposedness, of the named. It is summoned or called to responsibility for the other. It escapes the concept of the ego, is me, unique in my genus, an individual fleeing individuality. But the name outside of essence of beyond essence, the individual prior to individuality, is named God. It precedes all divinity, that is, the divine essence which the false gods, individuals sheltered in their concept, lay claim to.

39. Cf. a sketch of the analysis of fatigue in our book *Existence and Existents*, trans. Alphonso Lingis (The Hague, Nijhoff, 1978) pp. 29ff.

40. Cf. *infra*, Chapter V, pp. 142ff.

41. Cf. *Existence and Existents*, pp. 29ff – our efforts at phenomenological analysis of indolence and fatigue.
42. On life as enjoyment, cf. *Totality and Infinity*, trans. Alphonso Lingis (Pittsburgh, Duquesne University Press, 1961) pp. 110-42.
43. Cf. Paul Ricoeur, *The Conflict of Interpretations*, ed. Don Ihde (Evanston, Northwestern University Press, 1974) p. 99.

CHAPTER III

1. Cf. our study "Langage et proximité," in *En découvrant l'existence avec Husserl et Heidegger*, 2nd ed. (Paris, Vrin, 1967) p. 217.
2. It will turn out to be possible to understand the manifestation of being on the basis of justice, to which is led a saying which is not only addressed to the other, but is addressed to the other in the presence of a third party. Justice is this very presence of the third party and this manifestation, for which every secret, every intimacy is a dissimulation. Justice is at the origin of the claims of ontology to be absolute, of the definition of man as an understanding of Being.
3. The soul is the other in me. The psyche, the-one-for-the-other, can be a possession and a psychosis; the soul is already a seed of folly.
4. It is the-one-for-the-other in the incarnation of the same that makes the "transcendence" of intentionality understandable. The for-the-other proper to the psyche is a passivity of exposedness which goes so far as to be an exposure of the exposedness, to be ex-pression or saying. Saying becomes a thematization and a said.
5. Cf. *supra*.
6. Contrary to what is maintained in *Creative Evolution*, all disorder is not another order. The anarchy of the diachronic is not "assembled" into an order, except in the said. Bergson, distrustful as he is of language, is here a victim of the said.
7. Still here too, bread does not belong to the transcendence of the noematic, appearing in the said, offering as a spectacle the infinite peelings of the image. Bread already refers to the incarnate subject who has earned it in the sweat of his brow.
8. In *Totality and Infinity* the sensible was interpreted in the sense of consumption and enjoyment.
9. One can see and hear as one touches: "The forest, ponds and fertile plains have touched my eyes more than looks. I leaned on the beauty of the world and held the odor of the seasons in my hands" (La Comtesse de Noailles).
10. It is as possessed by a neighbor, as relics, and not as clothed with cultural attributes, that things first obsess. Beyond the "mineral" surface of things, contact is an obsession by the trace of a skin, the trace of an invisible face, which the things bear and which only reproduction fixes as an idol. The purely mineral contact is privative. Obsession breaks with the rectitude of consumption and cognition. But caresses are dormant in all contact, and contact in all sensible experience (cf. note 9): the thematized disappears in the caress, in which the thematization becomes a proximity. There is indeed a part of metaphor in that, and the things are taken to be true and illusory before being near. But is not the poetry of the world prior to the truth of things, and inseparable from what is proximity par excellence, that of a neighbor, or of the proximity of the neighbor par excellence.
11. One does have to admire the bold intellectual move in Cartesianism: the body as source of the sensible has no longer anything in common with the knowing of ideas. Even if one does not follow Descartes as to the bond he affirms between sensibility and action and the rank he assigns to the sensible, from now on the union between soul and body is not only an obstacle encountered by thought.
12. Cf. note 11.
13. Cf. *infra*, pp. 81ff.
14. Cf. *infra*, Chapter V, pp. 157ff.
15. Cf. G. W. F. Hegel, *The Phenomenology of Spirit*, trans. A. V. Miller (Oxford, Clarendon Press, 1977) p. 60.

16. This impossibility to slip off even into death is the point where, beyond the insomnia which can still be dissimulated, the subject is a saying, an uncovering oneself to the other, a psyche.

17. And one can deduce from the signifyingness of a subject, from its being one-for-the-other, these possibilities and even these necessities of the theoretical.

18. The implication of subjectivity in proximity, by which proximity is *inevitably* an approach – an implication which conveys the diachrony of signification – nonetheless becomes synchronic in the said, if only in these very pages. Is this simultaneity in the said more or less true than the diachrony affirmed by it? The question presupposes an independence of the true, of manifestation and the openness with respect to signification. With such a supposition there will be no doubt about the answer. The said in which everything shows itself is the origin and the ultimate of philosophy. But one thus forgets the pre-originary in which signification is articulated. One forgets the extraordinary possibility of a skeptical statement, returning as a bastard child of the Spirit after each of the refutations that drive it from the paternal house, contesting truth in a statement alleged to be true, a thought that is one, but at the same time not a thought.

19. Edmund Husserl, *Experience and Judgment*, trans. James S. Churchill (Evanston, Northwestern University Press, 1973) p. 38.

20. A neighbor concerns me outside of any a priori. But perhaps before every a priori, or from an earlier moment than that of the a priori. This is the notion all our inquiry means to bring out, so as to reach the concept of an absolute passivity. Receptivity with regard to the given, a modality of cognition, is not adequate for it, for precisely the a priori that cannot be excluded from it lets all the weight of the given be *welcomed*. This would still be an act.

21. It is perhaps by reference to this irremissibility that the strange place of illusion, intoxication, artificial paradises can be understood. The relaxation in intoxication is a semblance of distance and irresponsibility. It is a suppression of fraternity, or a murder of the brother. The possibility of going off measures the distance between dream and wakefulness. Dream and illusion are the play of a consciousness come out of obsession, touching the other without being assigned by him. A play of consciousness is a semblance.

22. This term translates the Platonic term φρίκη in the *Phaedrus*.

23. Cf. in *Hamlet*, Act II, scene 2: "What's Hecuba to him or he to Hecuba, that he should weep for her?"

24. The obsession is like a relation between monads prior to the opening up of doors or windows, in a counter-direction from intentionality, which is a modality of obsession and nowise a development of this relationship. The expression by each monad of all the others refers to substitution, in which the identity of subjectivity is resolved. The ego obsessed by all the others, supporting all the others, is an inversion of intentional ecstasy. In passivity the ego is a self under a persecuting – accusation of a neighbor. Rabbinical thought states the extent of responsibility: "... to the point of being delivered over to stoning and insults" on the part of the very one for whom the responsible one answers. (Cf. Rachi's *Commentary* on Numbers 12, 12, which here follows the ancient tradition of Siphri.)

25. The passivity of affection is more passive than the radical receptivity Heidegger speaks of in connection with Kant, where the transcendental imagination offers the subject an alcove of nothingness so as to precede the given and assume it.

26. *Canticle of Canticles*, IV, 6.

27. The sense of this alteration must indeed be clarified in its turn. But it was here important to underline the possibility of the libido in the more elementary and more rich signification of proximity, a possibility included in the unity of the face and the skin, even if only in the extreme turnings about of a face. Beneath the erotic alterity there is the alterity of the-one-for-the-other, responsibility before eros.

28. And even with a double alternation. Cf. note 29.

29. In this disparity nothing can be conceived as a correlation, that is, as a synchronization of a temporal succession, whose losses would be recuperated. This equivocation of disparity

is doubled up with an ambiguity in which the contact of proximity takes on a doxic meaning: contact becomes palpation, groping, exploration, search, knowing of a nudity such as that which a doctor examines, or an athlete exhibits in health. This reverting of contact into consciousness and into a discourse that states and that is logical, in which the communicated theme is more important than the contact of communication, is not due to chance or the clumsiness of a behavior. It is due to the relationship between the neighbor and a third party, before whom he may be guilty. It is due to the justice that is nascent in the very abnegation before the neighbor.

30. Even if a caress can reenter the teleological order of the said and become a symbol or word.

31. But obsession is not an intentionality once again, as though there were question in it of an aim at some correlative term, however complex it may be. The obsession by the other in the face is already the plot of infinity which could not materialize as something correlative. and exceeds the scope of intentionality. It is the excession of the here, as locus, and of the now, as an hour, excession from contemporaneousness and consciousness, which leaves a trace. In space as a void which is not nothingness but is a like the night, this trace of infinity shows itself enigmatically, like a blinking light. But this new plot does not remain in a negative theology. Its positive character still leads us to the notion of substitution.

32. *Numbers,* XI, 12.

33. The description of proximity as a hagiography of the-one-for-the-other subtends society, which begins with the entry of the third man. In it my response prior to any problem, that is, my responsibility, poses problems, if one is not to abandon oneself to violence. It then calls for comparison, measure, knowing, laws, institutions – justice. But it is important for the very equity of justice that it contain the signification that had dictated it.

34. Hegel thus formulates the bad infinite: "Something becomes an other: this other is itself somewhat; therefore it likewise becomes an other, and so on *ad infinitum.* This *Infinity* is the wrong or negative infinity: it is only a negation of a finite: but the finite rises again the same as ever, and is never got rid of and absorbed." *The Logic of Hegel,* trans. William Wallace (London, Oxford University Press, 1873) §§ 93, 94. In the situation we have described the other does not become likewise an other: the end is not reborn, but moves off, at each new stage of the approach, with all the alterity of the other.

35. Ethical language, which phenomenology resorts to in order to mark its own interruption, does not come from an ethical intervention laid out over descriptions. It is the very meaning of approach, which contrasts with knowing. No language other than ethics could be equal to the paradox which phenomenological description enters when, starting with the disclosure, the appearing of a neighbor, it reads it in its trace, which orders the face according to a diachrony which cannot be synchronized in representation. A description that at the beginning knows only being and beyond being turns into ethical language. The enigma in which transcendence comes to flush has to be distinguished from arbitrariness and illusions. The exteriority of *illeity,* refractory to disclosure and manifestation, is a having-to-be in the face of another. In it there is announced not a *Sollen,* which is always asymptotic, but glory.

36. Can the question of the divinity of the One God be put as the question of the humanity of man is put? Does the One have a genus? Can the divinity of God be conceived apart from God, as Being is conceived apart from entities? The whole problem consists in asking if God can be conceived as being or as beyond. Even if, by a ruse of language, the divinity of God is enunciated, one will immediately have to add to the being that designates the divinity the adverb *supremely.* But the supremacy of the supreme can be conceived in being only starting with God. This is involved in Malebranche's saying, which has not yet been meditated on enough, "The Infinite is unto itself its own idea."

CHAPTER IV

1. This chapter was the germ of the present work. Its principal elements were presented in a

194

public lecture at the Faculte Universitaire Saint-Louis in Brussels, on November 30, 1967. That talk was a continuation of the lecture entitled "Proximity" given the prior day, and which was substantially the same text as the study entitled "Langage et Proximité" subsequently published in the second edition of our book *En découvrant l'existence avec Husserl et Heidegger* (Paris, Vrin, 1967). The two lectures "La Proximité" and "La Substitution" were given the general title "Au-delà de l'Essence." The text of the second lecture published in the *Revue Philosophique de Louvain* (August, 1968) represented a finished version of the lecture. Certain developments have been formulated in a more severe manner for the reader, who can go further than the listener. Notes were also added. In its present form that text has been further modified.

2. If the anarchical were not signalled in consciousness, it would reign in its own way. The anarchical is possible only when contested by language, which betrays, but conveys, its anarchy, without abolishing it, by an abuse of language.

3. Cf. the pages Bergson has written, in *Creative Evolution*, concerning the notion of disorder, which deserve close attention. Subversion and revolution remain within order. This is to be compared with Hegel: what in the experience of a "new object" appears to consciousness as the "annihilation of a prior object," the philosopher, who can see what is "behind consciousness," sees as the result of a genesis, something coming to birth in the same dialectical order (cf. Hegel, *Phenomenology of Spirit*, p. 120). The movement of genesis traverses the State and issues in absolute knowledge, which fulfills consciousness. The notion of anarchy we are introducing here has a meaning prior to the political (or antipolitical) meaning currently attributed to it. It would be self-contradictory to set it up as a principle (in the sense that anarchists understand it). Anarchy cannot be sovereign, like an *arche*. It can only disturb the State – but in a radical way, making possible moments of negation *without any* affirmation. The State then cannot set itself up as a Whole. But, on the other hand, anarchy can be stated. Yet disorder has an irreducible meaning, as refusal of synthesis. Cf. p. 191, note 6.

4. Yet this is an inability which is *said*. Anarchy does not *reign*, and thus remains in ambiguity, in enigma, and leaves a trace which speech, in the pain of expression, seeks to state. But there is only a trace.

5. It is a relationship without any a priori which arises from a spontaneity, not from that which ontology requires in a finite thought. For, in order to welcome entities finite thought, a pure receptivity, must operate as a transcendental imagination, formative of the imaginary.

6. It is not a question here of descending toward the unconscious, which, defined in a purely negative way with reference to the conscious, preserves the structure of self-knowledge (whatever be the unexpected ramifications that would then complicate this structure), of a quest of self, though it be led astray on obstructed byways. The unconscious remains a play of consciousness, and psychoanalysis means to ensure its outcome, against the troubles that come to it from repressed desires, in the name of the very rules of this game. The play of consciousness does indeed involve rules, but irresponsibility in the game is declared to be a sickness. The play of consciousness is a game par excellence, "transcendental imagination," but as such source of phantasms.

7. We continue to use the term *essence*, underscored, as an abstract noun of action for being as distinguished from entities in the amphibology of being and entities.

8. Cf. *En découvrant l'existence avec Husserl et Heidegger*, 2nd ed., pp. 217-223.

9. The singularity of the subject is not the uniqueness of an *hapax*. For it is not due to some distinctive quality, like fingerprints, that would make of it an incomparable *unicum*, and, as a principle of individuation, make this unity deserve a proper noun, and hence a place in discourse. The identity of the oneself is not the inertia of a quiddity individuated by an ultimate specific difference inherent in the body or in character, or by the uniqueness of a natural or historical conjuncture. It is in the uniqueness of someone summoned.

10. Heidegger's analysis describes anxiety over the limitation of being. Inasmuch as this analysis is not to be read as simply psychological or anthropological, it reaches us that form (which in our philosophical tradition defines a being) is always too small for a being. Definition, which, as form, "formosity," is beauty, lustre and appearing, is also strangula-

tion, that is, anguish. The disproportion between Being and its phenomenality, the fact that Being is cramped in its manifestation, would then be produced in anthropological form in a finite being understood as being-existing-for-death. The measure of a determination would thus be the evil measurement of a Nessus tunic. But anxiety as being-for-death is also the hope to reach the deep of non-being. The possibility of deliverance (and the temptation to suicide) arises in death anxiety: like nothingness, death is an openness into which, along with a being, the anxiety over its definition is engulfed. But, on the other hand, anxiety as the tightness of the "going forth into fullness," is the recurrence of the oneself, but without evasion, without shirking, that is, a responsibility stronger than death – which Plato in the *Phaedo*, affirms in his own way, in condemning suicide (62b).

11. The notion of the hither side is indeed justified by this text from the *Parmenides*. There is question of a withdrawal, a reclusion, which does not go outside of the world in a chimerical effort to set itself up as a force freed from the world and endowed with spiritual powers which may triumph or fail – which would still be to be a presence in the world and in the history of a state or a church. That would amount to a hyperbole of ontological, logical and archic relations, an amplification of order, even though the hyperbole resorts to the superlative of the beyond being. Triumphs and failures presuppose personal freedom, and, consequently, an I endowed with political and religious sovereignty or political principality. On the hither side of that, the I is itself, does not belong to Being or history, is neither an effect at rest nor a cause in movement. The reclusion "in one's own skin," the present essay wishes to suggest, is a movement of the ego into itself, outside of order. The departure from this subterranean digs, from the plenum into the plenum, leads to a region in which all the weight of being is borne and supported in the other.

12. The body is neither an obstacle opposed to the soul, nor a tomb that imprisons it, but that by which the self is susceptibility itself. Incarnation is an extreme passivity; to be exposed to sickness, suffering, death, is to be exposed to compassion, and, as a self, to the gift that costs. The oneself is on this side of the zero of inertia and nothingness, in deficit of being, in itself and not in being, without a place to lay its head, in the no-grounds, and thus without conditions. As such it will be shown to be the bearer of the world, bearing it, suffering it, blocking rest and lacking a fatherland. It is the correlate of a persecution, a substitution for the other.

13. This freedom enveloped in a responsibility which it does not succeed in shouldering is the way of being a creature, the unlimited passivity of a self, the unconditionality of a self.

14. Lamentations, 3, 30.

15. In Otrepiev's dream, thrice repeated, in Pushkin's *Boris Godunov*, the false Dmitri catches sight of his future sovereignty in the equivocal laughter of the people: "... from above Moscow appeared to me like an anthill, below the people were boiling and pointed to me and laughed. I was overcome with shame and fear and in throwing myself down head first, I awoke." Laughter at the bottom of the gesture that points me out, shame and fear of the ego, the "accusative" where everything designates me and assigns me, awakening in a headlong fall – all this is the unconditionality of the subject behind its sovereignty.

16. Every idea of evasion, as every idea of malediction weighing on a destiny, already presupposes the ego constituted on the basis of the self and already free.

17. The passivity of the self in the in itself does not enter into the framework of the distinction between attitude and category. The category, as Eric Weil wishes, is obtained by reflection on an attitude, which is a liberation from the attitude and its particularity. By comparison with the passivity or patience of the Self, the attitude is already freedom and position. The passivity of the self precedes the voluntary act that ventures toward a project, and even the certainty which in truth is a coinciding with itself. The oneself is prior to self-coinciding.

18. Identity not of a soul in general, but of me, for in me alone innocence can be accused without absurdity. To accuse the innocence of the other, to ask of the other more than he owes, is criminal.

19. All the descriptions of the face in the three final studies of the second edition of our book

En découvrant l'existence avec Husserl et Heidegger which describe the very ambiguity or enigma of anarchy – the illeity of infinity in the face as the trace of the withdrawal which the infinite qua infinite effects before coming, and which addresses the other to my responsibility – remain descriptions of the non-thematizable, the anarchical, and, consequently, do not lead to any theological thesis. Language can nonetheless speak of it, if only by an abuse of language, and it thus confirms the fact that it is impossible for the anarchical to be constitued as a sovereignty – which implies the unconditionality of anarchy. But the hold of language on the anarchical is not a mastery, for otherwise anarchy would be subordinate to the *archè* of consciousness. This hold is the struggle and pain of expression. Whence comes discourse and the necessity of the *archè* of sovereignty and of the State; we shall speak of that further (Chapter V, pp. 156ff). It is clear also that in our way of interpreting signifyingness, the practical order (and the religious which is inseparable from the practical) is defined by the anarchical. Theology would be possible only as the contestation of the purely religious, and confirms it only by its failures or its struggles.

20. One could be tempted to take substitution to be the being of the entity that is the ego. And, to be sure, the hither side of the ego lends itself to our speaking only by referring to being, from which it withdraws and which it undoes. The said of language always says being. But in the moment of an enigma language also breaks with its own conditions, as in a skeptical saying, and says a signification before the event, a before-being. Events happen to subjects that undergo or provoke them. The verbs by which the events are said and the nouns by which the subjects are said are ormalized, even the verb being, even the noun being. The homonym is here an extreme amphibology in which the difference rests not on a common genus, but uniquely on the commonness of the word. Language thus shows itself to be something quite different from a doubling up of thoughts. The oneself and substitution do not enter into this framework. The defection or already the defeat of the identity of the ego, which can finally be said to be the event of the oneself, precedes every event undergone or conducted by a subject. On the hither side is expressed precisely in the term anarchy. It is identity undone to the limit, without being remade in the other, prior to a transsubstantiation into another avatar and prior to the putting in place of an other. For it does not rest in the other, but remains in itself without rest. There is a requisition with no escape possible, which, as the irreplaceable one itself, is uniqueness.

21. The vortex – suffering – suffering of the other, my pity for his suffering, his pain over my pity, my pain over his pain, etc. – stops at me. The I is what involves one movement more in this iteration. My suffering is the cynosure of all the sufferings – and of all the faults, even of the fault of my persecutors, which amounts to suffering the ultimate persecution, suffering absolutely. This is not a purifying fire of suffering, which magically would count here. This element of a "pure born," for nothing, in suffering, is the passivity of suffering which prevents its reverting into suffering assumed, in which the for-the-other of sensibility, that is, its very sense, would be annulled. This moment of the "for nothing" in suffering is the surplus of non-sense over sense by which the sense of suffering is possible. The incarnation of the self and its possibilities of gratuitous pain must be understood in function of the absolute accusative characteristic of the self, a passivity prior to all passivity at the bottom of matter becoming flesh. But in the anarchic character of suffering, and prior to all reflection, we have to catch sight of a suffering of suffering, a suffering because of what is pitiful in my suffering, which is a suffering "for God" who suffers from my suffering. There is an anarchic trace of God in passivity.

22. Substitution operates in the entrails of the self, rending its inwardness, putting its identity out of phase and disrupting its recurrence. Yet this occurs in the impossibility for me to evade substitution, which confers uniqueness on this ever failing identity of the oneself. Substitution is a communication from the one to the other and from the other to the one without the two relations having the same sense. It is not like the reversibility of the two way road open to the circulation of information, where the direction is indifferent. We have shown above this dissymmetry of communication in the analysis of proximity. It is the proximity of the third party (cf. *infra*, Chapter V) that introduces, with the necessities of justice, measure, thematization, appearing and justice. It is on the basis of the self and of

substitution that being will have a meaning. Being will be non-indifferent, not because it would be living or anthropomorphic, but because, postulated by justice which is contemporaneousness or copresence, space belongs to the sense of my responsibility for the other. The everywhere of space is the from everywhere of faces that concern me and put me in question, despite the indifference that seems to present itself to justice. Being will have a meaning as a universe, and the unity of the universe will be in me as subject to being. That means that the space of the universe will manifest itself as the dwelling of the others. It is inasmuch as it is inhabited by the others that look at me that the pre-geometrical eidos of space is described. I support the universe. The self does not only form the unity of human society, which is one in my responsibility. The unity of being has to do with the self.
23. Cf. *infra*, Chapter V, 2.
24. Here one has to denounce the suspicion that objectivism casts over all philosophy of subjectivity, and which consists in measuring and controlling the ego by what is objectively observable. Such a position is possible, but arbitrary. Even if the ego were but a reflection forming an illusion and contenting itself with false semblances, it would have a signification of its own precisely as this possibility of quitting the objective and universal order and abiding in itself. Quitting the objective order is possible in the direction of a responsibility beyond freedom as well as toward the freedom without responsibility of play. The ego is at the crossroads. But to quit the objective order, to go in oneself toward the privatissime of sacrifice and death, to enter upon the subjective ground, is not something that happens by caprice, but is possible only under the weight of all the responsibilities.
25. Thus theological language destroys the religious situation of transcendence. The infinite "presents" itself anarchically, but thematization loses the anarchy which alone can accredit it. Language about God rings false or becomes a myth, that is, can never be taken literally.
26. Proximity, obsession and subjectivity as we have expressed them are not reducible to phenomena of consciousness. But their un-consciousness, instead of giving evidence of a preconscious stage or a repression which would oppress them, is one with their exception from totality, that is, their refusal of manifestation. Inasmuch as essence is not separable from exposition, and thus from the ideality of the logos and the kerygmatic principality, this exception is non-being or anarchy, prior to the still ontological alternative of being and nothingness, prior to essence. Non-consciousness is to be sure characteristic of mechanical phenomena or the repression of psychic structures. From this comes the pretension of mechanism or psychologism to universality. But the non-conscious can be read in a different way on the basis of its traces, and undo the categories of mechanism. The non-conscious is understood as the non-voluntary event of persecution, which qua persecution breaks off every justification, every apology, every logos. This reduction to silence is a passivity beneath every material passivity. This absolute passivity beneath the neutrality of things takes on the form of incarnation, corporeity – susceptibility to pain. outrage and unhappiness. It bears in its susceptibility the trace of this *hither side* of things, as the responsibility for that of which there was no will, in the persecuted one, in ipseity, that is, as responsibility for the very persecution it suffers.
27. If obsession is suffering and contrarity, it is that the altruism of subjectivity-hostage is not a tendency, is not a natural benevolence, as in the moral philosophies of feeling. It is against nature, non-voluntary, inseparable from the possible persecution to which no consent is thinkable, anarchic. The persecution reduces the ego to itself, to the absolute accusative in which there is imputed to the ego a fault it has not committed or willed, and which confounds it in its freedom. Egoism and altruism are posterior to responsibility, which makes them possible. Egoism is not a term of the alternative of which altruism would be the other term, freedom choosing in indifference. The terms are not of the same order, but only the ethical qualification here distinguishes the equivalents. But values are valid before freedom: responsibility precedes it. Persecution is a trauma, violence par excellence without warning nor a priori, without possible apology, without logos. Persecution leads back to a resignation not consented to, and consequently crosses a night of unconsciousness. That is the sense of the unconscious, night in which the reverting of the

ego into itself under the trauma of persecution occurs, a passivity more passive still than every passivity on this side of identity, responsibility, substitution.

28. Perhaps the notion of anarchy accounts for the notion of worth, whose dimension is so difficult to distinguish from the being of entities. To be worth is to "weigh" on the subject, but otherwise than the way a cause weighs on an effect, a being on the thought to which it presents itself, an end on the tendency or the will it solicits. What does this "otherwise" mean? We think that to worth there arises a susceptibility incapable of thematizing it, that is, a susceptibility which cannot assume what it receives, but which, in spite of itself, becomes responsible for it. Value in its original radiation renders "pure" or "impure" before any intentional movement, without there being a free attitude toward value that could be taken up. The death of the other makes me impure through its proximity, and explains the "Noli me tangere." That is not a phenomenon of the mystical mentality, but an ineffaceable moment which the notion of value brings us back to.

29. Cf. "Enigme et phénomène" in *En découvrant l'existence avec Husserl et Heidegger*, 2nd ed., pp. 203-216.

30. Cf. *infra*, Chapter V, 3. I cannot detach myself from the self, that is, suspend the responsibility that is incumbent on me and on no one else, independently of the questions and answers of free dialogue, which persecution paralyzes without annulling responsibility, whereas I can pardon others in their alterity inasmuch as they are subsumed under the concept of the ego. Here there is a priority of the self before all freedom (or non-freedom).

CHAPTER V

1. Finitude can be conceived in a more radical way still on the basis of knowing, as the apparition of universality, where the apparition is possible only as a thematization, as objectivity, and where universality, a concept, is possible only on the basis of an abstraction which negates the individual. The individual lends itself to this negation only inasmuch as it is corruptible, or finite.

2. A purely "ethical" impossibility is expressed in expressions such as "impossible without shirking one's obligations," "without fault," "without sin." If there were real impossibility, responsibility would be only an ontological necessity. But a "purely ethical" impossibility is not a simple relaxation of an ontological impossibility. Being wanting, fault, sin, or as it can be put in a way perhaps more acceptable today, "complex" – that is not only a reality "for kids."

3. Simone Weill wrote: Father take from me this body and this soul and make them into your things, and let there subsist of me eternally only this taking itself.

4. Cf. our study "L'ontologie est-elle fondamentale?" *Revue de Métaphysique et de Morale*, 1957, n. 56, pp. 88-98.

5. "I am sick with love." *The Song of Songs*, 6:8.

6. The thematizing logos, the saying stating a said in monologue and dialogue and in the exchange of information, with all the cultural and historical dimensions it bears, proceeds from this pre-original saying. This saying is prior to all civilization and every beginning in the spoken speech that signifies. The unlocking of sincerity makes possible the dimension in which all communication and thematization will flow. The trace of signifyingness in the making of signs and in proximity is not thereby effaced, and marks every use of speech.

7. But, on the other hand, the making of signs in the world in which a language is spoken objectively, in which one is already with a third party, has to break through the wall of meaning said, so as to revert to the hither side of civilization. Thus there is need to unsay all that comes to alter the nakedness of signs, to set aside all that is said in the pure saying proper to proximity. One cannot unambiguously make signs in the night. One has to say something about it, say something, before saying only the saying itself, before making signs, before making oneself a sign.

8. Saying or sincerity is not a hyperbolic giving; otherwise the infinite which it bears witness to would be reached only by extrapolation. But the extrapolation would always presuppose the infinite.

9. The saying could not be interpreted as a sincerity, when one takes a language as a system of signs. One enters into language as a system of signs only out of an already spoken language, which in turn cannot consist in a system of signs. The system in which the significations are thematized has already come out of signification, the-one-for-the-other, approach and sincerity.

10. As a sign given of this signification of signs, proximity also delineates the trope of lyricism: to love by telling one's love to the beloved – long songs, the possibility of poetry, of art.

11. "Here I am! send me." Isaiah, 6:8. "Here I am!" means "send me."

12. Book VI, IIa.

13. This is subjectivity prior to reification. The things we have at our disposal are in their rest as substances indifferent to themselves. The subjectivity prior to this indifference is the passivity of persecution.

14. Cf. *infra*, Chapter V, pp. 156ff.

15. "Producing as the utterance of the lips, 'Peace, peace to the far and the near.'" Isaiah, 57:19.

16. Ezekiel, 8:3.

17. Cf. Samuel I, 17:45 "I come to you in the name of the LORD of hosts." "Here I am! send me." Isaiah, 6:8.

18. Cf. *infra*, pp. 156ff.

19. Job, 4:12.

20. Cf. *En découvrant l'existence avec Husserl et Heidegger*, p. 201.

21. The immemorial past is intolerable for thought. Thus there is an exigency to stop: *anagkè stenai*. The movement beyond being becomes ontology and theology. And thus there is also an idolatry of the beautiful. In its indiscrete exposition and in its stoppage in a statue, in its plasticity, a work of art substitutes itself for God. (Cf. our study "La réalité et son ombre," in *Les Temps modernes*, November 1948). By an irresistible subreption, the incomparable, the diachronic, the non-contemporaneous, through the effect of a deceitful and marvelous schematism, is "imitated" by art, which is iconography. The movement beyond being is fixed in beauty. Theology and art "retain" the immemorial past.

22. Isaiah, 65:24.

23. Cf. *Totality and Infinity*, pp. 212ff.

24. Cf. *supra*, n. 21, "*anagké stenai.*"

25. According to the myth of the *Gorgias* (523 c-d), in the absolute judgment borne on the other (in the direct relationship with him, which judgment is), he is "stripped of all clothing," that is, of every quality expressible by an attribute in a proposition, in the said, and of all that which, like clothing, establishes a "community" between the judge and the judged. In this judgment the judge pushes aside the screen "which is made of eyes, ears and the body as a whole" (that is, of the very ways of thematization). There is thus set aside from the other everything that creates between the judge and the judged – between me and the other – a community or a correlation, which absorbs proximity. This relationship of the judgment, which Plato designates, negatively, as that in which the dead judge the dead, remains judgment. In this suppression of all the conditions for knowledge, in this "contact" without the mediation of skin, a signifyingness remains. What we are calling the infinity of the for-the-other, or saying, is not "poorer" than the said. But, quite remarkably, if the absence of any "community" between the judge and the judged is maintained in Minos, neither Asiatic nor European, and master of arbitration, the necessity of a "certain community" in justice between the judge and the judged is expressed in Aeacus, a European who judges the Europeans, and in Rhadamanthus, an Asiatic who judges the Asiatics.

CHAPTER VI

1. The sages of Israel say, as a parable, that Moses gave up his soul in the kiss of God. To die on the order of God is expressed in Hebrew as dying "on the mouth of God" (Deut., 34:5). The absolute expiration, in the kiss of God, is death on order, in passivity and obedience, in the inspiration by the other for the other.

INDEX

Spectacle, 190
Spinoza, 176
Spirit, 5
Spirituality, 97
Spontaneity, 188–89
State, 159–60, 161, 169–70
Stimmung, 66
Stoicism, 176
Structure, 150
Subject: absorbed by Being, 131–32; not absorbed
    in being, 135–36; service of the system, as, 132–
    33; speaking that is absorbed in said, as, 134–35
Subjectivity, xlvii–xlviii, 8–9, 19, 25–26, 127, 183–
    84, 197: alterity and, xxii–xxvi; essence and,
    17–19; humanity and, 57–59; personal, xvii–
    xviii; proximity and, 83–86; relationship with
    responsibility, xx; temporality and, xxv; theory
    of, xxix–xxxv
Sub-jectum, 116
Substitution, xxviii–xxix, 113–18, 196–97: my,
    126–27; signification and, 13–14, 15
"Substitution, La" xxviii–xxix, xlvii
Succession, 188
Suffering, 196
Suicide, 52
Symbolism, 62

Tale, 36
Temoignage, Le, xlvii
Temporality, 28–31
Temporalization, 9–10, 40, 51–52
"Temps et l'Autre," 190
Thematization, 151–52
Theology, 199
There is, xlii, 3–4, 162–65, 176–78, 183
Third party, xli–xlii, 16: justice as, 191;
    neighbor as other than, 157
Time, 9–10, 28–31: amphibology of Being and
    entities, 38–43; concept of, 190; consciousness,
    32–33; discourse and lived experience, 31–34;
    language and, 34– 37; said and saying, 37–38
To be, 34–35, 41–42
Tolstoi, 129
Totality, 29
Totality and Infinity, xxi, xxii, xxxiv, 191
Toward another, 18
Transcendence, 5, 7, 19, 70, 152, 188–89
Translation, 187
Truth, xlii–xliii, 23–24, 188: exposition of
    being and, 28; progression of, 24; subjectivity
    and humanity, 57–58

Ulysses, 79–80, 81, 132

Unconscious, 194, 197–98
Urdoxa, 36
Ur-impression, 32–33

Valery, Paul, 40, 129, 189
Verb, xxxi–xxxii, 52–53, 54
"Verite comme devoilement et verite comme
    temoignage," xlvii
Vulnerability, contact and, 75–81

Weil, Eric, 195
Weill, Simone, 198
Who? (as question), 189–90
Wisdom, of desire, 153–62
Witness: inspiration and, 142–44; language and,
    145–49; prophecy and, 149–52
Worth, 198

Xenakis, 41

Zeno, 176